LOSING OUR RELIGION

SECULAR STUDIES
General Editor: Phil Zuckerman

Losing Our Religion: How Unaffiliated Parents Are Raising Their Children
Christel Manning

Losing Our Religion

*How Unaffiliated Parents Are
Raising Their Children*

Christel Manning

NEW YORK UNIVERSITY PRESS

New York and London

NEW YORK UNIVERSITY PRESS
New York and London
www.nyupress.org

References to Internet websites (URLs) were accurate at the time of writing. Neither the author nor New York University Press is responsible for URLs that may have expired or changed since the manuscript was prepared.

Library of Congress Cataloging-in-Publication Data
Manning, Christel.
Losing our religion : how unaffiliated parents are raising their children / Christel Manning.
pages cm. — (Secular studies)
Includes bibliographical references and index.
ISBN 978-1-4798-7425-5 (cl : alk. paper) — ISBN 978-1-4798-8320-2 (pb : alk. paper)
1. United States—Religion. 2. Non church-affiliated people—United States. 3. Religious education of children—United States. I. Title.
BL2525.M3565 2015
211'.7085—dc23 2015019843

New York University Press books are printed on acid-free paper, and their binding materials are chosen for strength and durability. We strive to use environmentally responsible suppliers and materials to the greatest extent possible in publishing our books.

Manufactured in the United States of America

10 9 8 7 6 5 4 3 2 1

Also available as an ebook

For Sheila

CONTENTS

Acknowledgments   ix

Introduction   1

1. Who Are the Nones?   10

2. What Do Nones Believe and Practice?   26

3. The Importance of Time   50

4. The Importance of Place   76

5. What Are We, Mom?   104

6. The Meaning of Choice in Religion   138

7. The Risks and Benefits of Raising Children without Religion   162

Conclusion   181

Appendix: Sources and Methods of Research   197

Notes   205

Bibliography   219

Index   233

About the Author   245

ACKNOWLEDGMENTS

I would like to thank Sacred Heart University for several grants that helped support my research. A big thanks to Celia Rumsey, Julie Ingersoll, Nathan Mesnikoff, Julia Graham, Barbara Graham, and Anita Manning for facilitating research outside of my home state, and to the many individuals who opened their homes to share their stories with me. Thanks to Phil Zuckerman for encouraging me to send the manuscript to New York University Press, and to Jennifer Hammer, and all the other folks at NYU who shepherded me through the process (I especially appreciate Michael Koch for his thorough copyediting, and Dorothea Halliday who helped me work through seemingly endless problems with the editing software). I am grateful to my daughter, Sheila, whose questions first inspired this project, and to my husband, Stewart Hutchings, for holding down the fort while I traveled to do research. Finally, I owe a huge debt of gratitude to John Manning for reading and commenting on multiple drafts of this book before it went to press.

Introduction

The idea for this book began ten years ago. It was December, and I had just picked up my then three-year-old daughter, Sheila, from preschool. "Look, look, Christmas lights," she piped up from the back seat of the car, "Mommy, look there's Santa."

"Yes, dear," I replied, "Santa comes every year."

"Why does Santa come?"

"To make people happy."

"Why does he want to make people happy?"

"Because it's Christmas."

"But why?"

I paused. I was not sure what to tell my daughter. Christmas celebrates the day that Jesus Christ was born? But then she would ask, who was Jesus and why be happy about his birth? Why indeed?

My husband and I celebrate Christmas every year. We get a tree, exchange gifts, go visit family and eat holiday foods. But none of our celebration is about religion. I no longer believe in God, much less a personal deity who incarnates in human form, and neither does he. Both of us were raised Christian but left the church as teenagers and have not returned since, except for friends' weddings, baptisms, and funerals. While my husband expresses indifference to anything spiritual, I became a seeker of sorts. Over the years, I experimented with Buddhist meditation and feminist goddess rituals and eventually acquired a doctorate in religious studies. That degree has given me a fulfilling career, but it had not prepared me for my daughter's question about Christmas.

Her questions led to me to ask myself, what do I believe in, and how do I transmit those beliefs to my child? Despite the vagueness of my own spirituality, I began to think that maybe now was the time to introduce religion into Sheila's life. After all, faith had been an important part of my own childhood. I thought of the rich tradition I grew up with in Southern Germany in the 1960s and 1970s: listening to stories of the

Bible, building a crèche with my sisters, lighting Advent candles, singing carols while my grandmother played the piano, our nightly prayers asking God to protect Mama, Daddy, and everyone else. It was all so beautiful and comforting and safe. I wanted Sheila to have what I had. Even if I had rejected it later in my life, why hold a child hostage to my own doubts? Although I could not pretend to convey the faith my mother had, maybe I could have my daughter baptized and enroll her in Sunday school, as my sister did with her children. But when I ran the idea by my husband he was adamant: "I don't want Sheila indoctrinated in all that. Besides it would be hypocritical." He had a point.

I kept thinking about the question, and initially I felt very alone. Although we had secular friends, none of them had children at home. And our religious friends who did have children were raising them either Catholic or Jewish. I did not know anybody else like me. So, as parents often do, I tried reaching out to other moms and dads whom I suspected might be nonreligious. People in Connecticut tend to keep their views on religion to themselves, but when asked directly many were eager to share their experience, and I discovered there were several other parents who shared my concerns. Still, I wondered how representative these parents were of broader trends. After all, we live in New Haven, a college town filled with educated liberals who tend to be more secular than the rest of the population. So, as academics often do, I did some research. An initial review of the relevant work in the social sciences confirmed my growing realization that my struggle is not unusual. Although the majority of Americans are affiliated with organized religion and seek to transmit that tradition to their children, parents with no religion comprise a significant and growing segment of the population.

Recent nationwide surveys show that one-fifth of Americans now list their religious affiliation as "None" or their religious preference as "nothing in particular"—up from only 7 percent twenty years ago. Scholars seeking to compare these individuals to those who do claim a religion, have dubbed them the "Nones," a term that I will explain in the following chapters. In many parts of the country, the number of Nones rivals that of major religious denominations. Significantly, Nones comprise one-third of adults under thirty, those poised to be parents of the next generation.[1] The decisions they make about religion in their families will help shape the future of organized religion in America.

Who are these Nones? Fortunately for my investigation, their sudden growth has increased scholarly interest in the nonreligious. We now know more about the demographic characteristics of the unaffiliated. For instance, although they are more likely to be young and male and live in certain parts of the country, they increasingly resemble the average American in terms of education, income, and race.[2] We also know more about the Nones' religious characteristics, although what those characteristics are depends on who you talk to. While there is considerable debate over how secular the Nones are, they are clearly not monolithic. Their ranks include more atheists and agnostics than those of the general population as well as a wide diversity of religious and spiritual worldviews.[3] Recent studies have closely examined various segments of the unaffiliated population such as unchurched Christians, young people, and atheists.[4] But the segment I was interested in, parents, had received little attention. This book is intended to fill that gap.

How *do* None parents deal with the question of religion in the upbringing of their children? Over the next several years I sought to answer that question by pulling together information from published sources as well as conducting my own qualitative research with parents all over the United States. Much of what we know about Nones is based on quantitative research such as the Gallup polls, the Pew Religious Landscape Survey, and the American Religious Identification Survey, all of which provide a wealth of basic descriptive data. Such data is a powerful tool to identify major cultural changes such as, for example, the dramatic increase in the unaffiliated population. But it tells us little about what this means or about the lived experiences of that population. While surveys show that some None parents seek religious training for their children, they do not tell us why or how. Do they send them to Sunday school or do it themselves? If the parents claim no religion, then why do they want one for their children? And what of those None parents who do not want religion in their child's life? Why not? How, in an intensely religious society like America, do they avoid it? What alternative, nonreligious worldviews do they transmit instead? How do all these parents' decisions impact their children and the parents themselves? To answer these questions it is mandatory to interact directly with parents, to talk in person for extended periods of time, and to observe families in the context of their home or community.

With the help of grant funding from Sacred Heart University, I was able to do this type of research in diverse regions of the United States, including locations where religious disaffiliation is common and others where it is not. The study employed a grounded theory method of qualitative research,[5] drawing on observations of and interviews with parents ranging in age from twenty-three to fifty-five (a detailed description of the research sample, methods, and analysis is included in the appendix). The parents I met do not mirror perfectly the larger unaffiliated population, but they are representative in several important respects. Recent studies suggest that Nones are no longer distinguished from churched Americans by race, education, or income, yet age, gender, religious background and region continue to be significant markers.[6] My respondent pool was more female and a little older than the average None (a single man in his twenties). Then again, my interest was not in the average None but in unaffiliated parents who are most interested in the question of religious upbringing. More importantly, my respondents are representative of two important characteristics of the unaffiliated population. One is religious background: Most Nones do not start out that way but choose to become unaffiliated as adults. Nearly three-quarters of Nones surveyed were raised in a religious home; among my respondents all but three were raised with religion. Another characteristic is regional distribution: The unaffiliated are more numerous in some places than in others. Reflecting recent patterns, two-thirds of the Nones I interviewed reside in the Pacific Northwest, New England, and the Mountain States; one-third are found in the South. These parallels notwithstanding, the results of this qualitative study cannot, of course, be generalized to explain all None parents in America. They do, however, provide a rich source of information to supplement and sometimes problematize and question what we have learned from larger-scale quantitative research.

The parents whose experiences are presented here did not check boxes on a survey but were interviewed in person in various settings. I conducted most interviews at the respondents' homes, but I also spent time with them in public settings such as schools, spiritual centers, or secular community centers. Observing individuals on their own turf gave me insights into aspects of parents' experiences I might otherwise have missed. The ubiquity of religious billboards in one suburb, for example, provided a visible reminder of the strong Evangelical presence in the local culture. Interacting with parents in their own homes also compelled me to ask questions I might otherwise not have asked; for example, while in the home of one atheist family, I inquired about the meaning of a Christmas tree. All interviews followed a semistructured format and typically lasted an hour or more. I would begin by asking my respondents about their own religious upbringings, their reasons for ending their affiliations, and their current worldviews. Next I would inquire about the decisions parents made about their children: what kinds of worldview they wished to pass on, how they went about doing so, and the challenges they encountered. As I recorded and analyzed parents' diverse experiences, and reflected on their meanings in light of broader cultural patterns, a bigger story began to emerge. This book is my attempt to tell that story.

The story of how unaffiliated parents deal with religion in their children's lives is both simpler and more complex than it seems. The media and many academics have tended to frame the discussion of such families in terms of the long-standing conflict between religion and secularism. The rise of Nones may signify secularization, a shift away from America's longstanding reputation as the most religious nation in the developed world. Or it may mean merely a variation of the status quo: a rejection not of religion but of current religious institutions, a temporary pattern that may reverse itself as new institutions arise to better meet Nones' needs.[7] Such a framework assumes a high degree of homogeneity among Nones—they are either religious or secular. It also assumes that unaffiliated parents, like churched parents, would raise their children to be like themselves: either nonreligious or believers in conventional religion (usually Christian). The story I tell here raises important questions about these assumptions.

The book shows that None families exhibit a diverse range of perspectives and behaviors that is not easily categorized as either religious or secular, and that in fact challenges us to rethink the way that we define those terms. Underlying that diversity, however, is a common commitment to what I call *worldview choice*. The word *worldview*, from the German Weltanschauung, refers to a set of beliefs, attitudes, perceptions, and assumptions through which we filter our understanding of the world and our place in it. A more inclusive word than *religion*, the term encompasses both traditional theistic worldviews (such as Christianity, Judaism, or Hinduism) and secular ones (such as humanism or skepticism). Historically, most people have inherited their worldviews, but the last century has seen a steadily growing number of individuals claiming the right to choose their own. Nones represent the cutting edge at this moment in time. While their beliefs and practices vary, they share a perception that all worldviews (religious or secular) are expressions of deeply personal experiences and therefore individuals have the right, and indeed the responsibility, to choose one for themselves. It is that choice they seek to pass on to their children.

To understand how unaffiliated parents deal with religion in the lives of their children, I must first clarify what I mean by the term *None*. Chapter 1 explores this question and discusses how the unaffiliated are similar to and different from churched Americans. Although there is a lot of data about the religiously uncommitted, the terminology used to describe them is confusing and undermines our understanding. Once one sorts through the labels, however, some patterns do emerge. The growth in Nones, I argue, reflects a longer-term movement toward non-commitment in religion. This trend has significant implications for the social status of Nones in America. On the one hand, there is evidence that Nones are becoming "normalized": demographically, the unaffiliated today more closely resemble average Americans than they did a generation ago. On the other hand, having no religion continues to be perceived as deviant from the rest of society, particularly in certain regions, and this perception shapes how None parents think about religion in the lives of their children.

The term *None* defines parents in terms of what they supposedly lack, religion. But this conceptualization ignores the fascinating variety of beliefs and practices that such individuals do have. Chapter 2 explores this variety, presenting a typology of None worldviews illustrated by examples from the parents I studied. Some of these worldviews are secular and some are not, and the lived experience of these individuals raises questions about how scholars traditionally define religiousness and secularity. Indeed, the distinction between religion and secularity may not be the best way to understand what makes Nones distinctive. Rather, what ties this variety of worldviews together is commitment to the sanctity of personal worldview choice.

Our choices are shaped by time. I dropped out of church as a teenager, as many young people do. Not having religion afforded me the freedom to explore spiritual and philosophical alternatives, an adventure that captivated my interests for many years. Having a child changed everything. Being a None was suddenly a problem I had to solve. Although other parents' stories differ, the experience of starting a family always raises the question of religion. Chapter 3 investigates how becoming a parent changes what it means to be a None. First, I will examine why young and single people are far more likely to drop out of church and have no religious preferences. Next, I look at research that shows that many Nones commit to religion when they marry or start a family. Does this life cycle effect mean there is a causal relationship between family and religious commitment? I will evaluate the evidence for and against this theory. Drawing on the stories of parents in this study, I will propose an alternative explanation for the life cycle effect.

Chapter 4 considers how our worldview choices are shaped by place. In the New England city where I live, not having religion goes largely unnoticed. In other parts of the country, however, being a None makes one a cultural outsider. The meaning of being a None is local—it depends on where you are, and how your religious or secular orientation fits into that local cultural context. I begin by examining the differences between what I term *high None zones* (places where the None population is large or culturally significant) and *low None zones* (where this is not the case). I then consider the stories of None parents living in these zones and how that experience shapes their strategies about whether to include religion in the upbringing of their children.

Regardless of where they live, None parents remain a minority in this culture. The majority of American parents do affiliate with religion and raise their children accordingly. Catholic parents send their children to catechism and Jewish parents send theirs to Hebrew school—educational programs that are typically run by the church or synagogue the family belongs to—and what the kids learn is reinforced to varying degrees at home. This strategy is not available to None families. What, then, *are* None parents doing with their children? Chapter 5 presents a typology of the most common strategies they use, illustrated by stories of parents I studied.

Although their experiences are diverse, unaffiliated parents—unlike their churched counterparts who usually transmit the parents' own worldviews to their children—are not necessarily raising another generation of Nones. Rather, these parents frame their strategies as helping children make their own spiritual choices. Chapter 6 reflects more deeply on the meaning and impact of this emphasis on choice. At the personal level, choice means freedom but it can also lead to confusion. I draw on recent research in the psychology of decision-making to explain some of the parents' choices. Choice also has a cultural meaning. I will show that None parents' desire for spiritual choice is embedded in a wider cultural perception that choice is inherently good, not just for individuals but for society. But is it? After all, choosing one's religious or secular beliefs or value system is different from, and arguably more important than, selecting which ice cream flavor to eat or even what kind of house to live in. Various scholars have likened the worldview choice orientation to what they call cafeteria religion, linking it with narcissism, moral relativism, and decreasing civic commitment. Others contest that argument. Chapter 6 engages that debate.

However parents raise their children, their ultimate concern is to do what is best for them. Chapter 7 addresses a common concern among many unaffiliated parents: Is religion good for children? Put differently, even if I personally am not religious, is religion something I *should* be giving to my child? None parents, living in a culture where affiliation with organized religion is the norm, must deal with a barrage of media reporting and research claiming to show that children are better off with religion. The few dissenting voices that exist receive much less attention. I will show how parents hear and respond to those cultural messages. Then I will review what social scientists know about the impact of religion on children and evaluate the evidence.

In the conclusion I reflect on what we—as sociologists of religion or None parents—can learn from this research. For scholars, this book will raise many questions, perhaps most prominently the question of how we define and measure religion and secularity in the populations we study. I will attempt to answer those questions and suggest some avenues for future research. None parents, meanwhile, may be wondering how things turned out for the families whose stories are presented here, including my own, now that several years have passed. I will describe where I fit in the typology of Nones presented and my family's experimentation with some of the strategies described in the book. I reflect on how this journey has shaped both me and my child. Spoiler alert: my husband and I are still Nones, and our now thirteen-year-old daughter is a happy, well-adjusted kid who does not believe in God. But that outcome is less interesting than the process of how we arrived there. Our story is not typical, although it does reflect on many of the larger themes addressed in this book. I am grateful to the many families who shared a slice of their lives with me. It is to their stories that I now turn.

1

Who Are the Nones?

A vast majority of Americans are affiliated with organized religion. Most of them will raise their children to follow in their footsteps. This book is about those who choose a different path. People outside organized religion are a minority, but a significant one that is growing both in absolute numbers and as proportion of the population. That growth has led to much debate, not just among religious leaders seeking to recapture lost sheep but also among academics trying to explain and predict the future of the American religious landscape. Although the debate has stimulated research on people outside religion, we are only just beginning to understand who they are. Consider three examples.

Charlie

Charlie is twenty-eight, tall, and thin with curly brown hair and a ready smile. Recently married, he teaches science at the local high school and his wife is finishing graduate school in nursing. I met Charlie at his home, a modest ranch-style house in Claremont, a Southern California suburb. It was a hot August day, the door was left open but for the screen door. A shaggy brown mutt came running to the door when I rang the bell. "Come on in, he's friendly," a voice called. I did and saw a young man in jeans bending over a laundry machine. He pushed a button, then stepped over to greet me. After some small talk he informed me that his wife had just stepped out to get some groceries. "Let's go sit down," he gestured, "we can talk now and then she'll join us when she gets back." He led me to a small living room with brown wall-to-wall carpeting and a worn beige sofa, a TV set, and a coffee table covered with newspaper. The dog lay down under the table and we started talking.

Charlie grew up in Atlanta and had only recently moved Claremont. His family was part of an Evangelical congregation—as he put it, "a typical conservative Southern church." He attended church every Sunday with his mother and went to Bible camp every summer until at sixteen he realized: "I really wanted to stop going. I really did not like being in the church. I didn't like the people, from the ministers down to the parishioners. . . . I just didn't want to be around them." He made a bargain with his mother that if he agreed to be baptized, she would no longer force him to attend. "I was a holiday Christian after that, Christmas and Easter only." For a while he explored other religions. He read about Islam and Judaism, and "talked to the Mormons who came to [their] door." He even practiced meditation "with a Buddhist nun who made herself available to [his] high school," but found he "was a lot better at falling asleep than . . . at meditating." Eventually, he decided that it was ok to have no religion. "I had this idea in my mind that it was important to find faith. [But after evaluating various options] I came to realize that maybe it's not. I was just used to it." Today he describes himself as neither religious nor spiritual, and he does not attend church, not even on holidays. At the time of my interview, Charlie and his wife were expecting their first child and she had raised the question of religion. Although also a None, she was raised in a very liberal Protestant congregation and feels they should consider that option. Charlie is skeptical. He thinks that religion "for most people is a crutch" and does not want his child to be indoctrinated as he was. He believes that people can derive ethics and meaning from secular sources as well as religious ones—"It doesn't really make a difference."

Rosario

Spirituality does make a difference to Rosario, a thirty-two-year-old single mother of four living in Colorado Springs. She works part-time as a filing clerk for a nonprofit agency and attends night school to finish her associate's degree. I met her at the agency, a low-lying white box of a building next to a gas station and a parking lot. Entering through the gray metal doors, I found a small Mexican American woman stacking papers on a plastic folding table. The room was bare except for several tall filing cabinets in one corner and stacks of folding chairs in the other. "Hi," she said, extending her hand. She was dressed casually, in shorts and a printed T-shirt, her long black hair tied in a ponytail. Two children were lying on the floor, drawing in a coloring book. "These are my two youngest," she informed me; the older two were with their father for the weekend.

Rosario is originally from San Jose, California, but she has lived in Colorado for almost ten years. She was raised Catholic, attending church most Sundays with her grandfather who was very devout. She remembers it as "being very peaceful" but she was "not able to connect with God" there. Drifting and alienated from her parents as a teen, she stopped attending church and did poorly in school. Then, after moving to live with her grandmother, she began talking to God. "I didn't really have any other way of connecting with anything. And so I just started having these conversations." It comforted her to believe that "there was somebody else out there in the universe who was looking out for me." But she continued to drift. By eighteen she was pregnant; she married and had two children. Raising her children and working part-time, she continued to feel spiritually alone. She tried attending various churches but nothing fit until one day she "saw a commercial on TV for the LDS Church" that she found "incredibly spiritual." The next day, she went to their first service and every Sunday after that. Her husband rejected her decision; there were other problems, and eventually they divorced. But she soon married a man within the church and had another two children. She was a stay-at-home mom, raising her children as Mormons, when "several years into our marriage, I found out he was having an affair." Rosario began questioning everything, especially her faith, and, along with her children, left the Mormon Church (although two of them still attend when they visit with their father). Six years later she remains uncommitted. Although she describes herself as "deeply spiritual" and is still looking for a church that feels "comfortable," she is wary of religions and refuses to identify with any of them.

Samantha

Some Nones, such as Charlie and Rosario, make a conscious choice to leave their religion. For others like Samantha, religion was never much part of the picture. Sam, as she calls herself, is thirty-five, blond and stylish, with the kind of sculpted fitness that suggests she likes the gym. She has a master's degree in physical therapy and works part-time, setting her own schedule. She is married to an insurance executive and has two small children. I met her at her home, a handsome grey colonial in a leafy suburb of Hartford, Connecticut. She led me into a bright and modern kitchen and we sat down at a tall granite counter, drinking lemonade. Her husband, James, was at the office. Their children, a four-year-old boy and a seven-year-old girl, ran noisily about the house, occasionally dropping in to grab a cookie from the counter. On the refrigerator across from us was a picture of a smiling older couple. I noticed the woman wearing a crucifix, so I asked Sam who that was. "Those are my in-laws," she said. "My husband's family is Catholic, but mine is not religious at all."

Samantha described her own parents as "culturally Jewish," attending services only for the high holidays. They sent her to Hebrew school for a time, but she soon dropped out "because of gymnastics . . . and when I stopped Hebrew school we stopped going altogether." She was never interested in finding a synagogue or in exploring other religions. "I just didn't feel the need. It's not about rejecting religion, it just doesn't seem relevant." She is not particularly spiritual either. "It's not one of those things I really think about." Until recently, that is, when her in-laws began asking about their plans for religious education. Since her husband is similarly indifferent to religion, their response for now is "we don't have plans." Still, Sam feels that coming from Jewish and Catholic families was "part of our history and background that the kids need to know about," so they have begun to talk about whether and how to incorporate religion into their children's lives.

* * *

Charlie, Rosario, and Samantha meet the main criteria for inclusion in the study that led to this book: they are three religiously unaffiliated parents raising young children. Other than that, they seem to have little in common. They live in different parts of the country—the East Coast, the West Coast, and the Midwest—and in different types of communities; Charlie and Sam live in the suburbs, and Rosario lives in an immigrant urban neighborhood. Rosario is divorced, Charlie is newly wed, and Sam has been married for fifteen years. While Rosario is struggling to make ends meet, Charlie has a modest but steady income, and Sam is rather well off. They come from different religious backgrounds—Protestant, Catholic, and Jewish—and they left those traditions in different ways and for different reasons: Charlie because he lost his faith, Rosario because she has not found one yet that fits, and Samantha because she never really had faith. Perhaps most importantly for my discussion, their current relationship to religion is not the same. Charlie seems the most secular; his worldview resembles atheism, although he declines to call himself an atheist. Rosario is overtly spiritual but also suspicious of organized religion. Samantha is not hostile to religion but simply indifferent to it. As I will show, the differences between Charlie, Samantha, and Rosario reflect broader differences in the None population, and this diversity creates significant challenges for those seeking to understand the Nones.

Definitions

What does it mean to be a None? The definition of *unchurched* or *unaffiliated* may seem obvious at first, as it did to me when I began this research. Just interview other people like me, I know lots of them—people who were raised Christian or Jewish and drifted away from religion when they were teenagers. They might return, briefly, to get married but not to active participation. They often retain some belief in the divine or a higher power and some interest in spiritual matters but it is not clearly defined; they are seekers maybe. Or maybe not.

Once I had put out the word that I was looking for participants in this study, it became clear from the responses I received that the "unaffiliated" category is home to a tremendous variety of people. There are atheists and agnostics, but also fundamentalists who stay out of organized religion because it is not sufficiently orthodox for them. There are Hindus and Muslims who live in small towns that lack institutions to serve their needs, as well as people of various religious persuasions (including Christians) who prefer solitary practice. There are deeply spiritual seekers and those completely indifferent to religion. The kinds of people we find outside of organized religion are arguably as diverse as those who claim an affiliation, which leads one to wonder whether categorizing them by their former affiliation may be more, not less, confusing in the end. The scholarly literature on the unaffiliated reflects some of that confusion—a problem that needs to be addressed at the onset. This chapter, as well as the beginning of chapter 2, offers a guide through the terminology and methods used by researchers who study Nones and aims to disentangle what's helpful and what is not.

People outside organized religion are labeled in different, sometimes contradictory ways. They are called unchurched, seekers, disaffiliates, unaffiliated, defectors, apostates, dropouts, and Nones; and each term has a slightly different meaning. For example, a search for *unchurched Americans* will turn up two Gallup surveys by the same name that define the term as nonmembers of churches and those who attended infrequently.[1] That turns out to be a fairly large number of people—more than 40 percent of the US population. If you try the more inclusive term *unaffiliated*, you may find several recent Pew studies that use that category to designate respondents who decline any ties to organized religion.[2] That number is much smaller—only about 20 percent of Americans. If you look at studies of seekers, you will find the religiously uncommitted portrayed as mostly white, middle-class baby boomers looking for meaning outside the mainline Christian denominations.[3] A search for *defectors* or *apostates* brings up case studies of individuals who break away from small, sect- or cult-like religions.[4] To sort through this multiplicity of labels and figure out what is a valid measure of those outside organized religion, it helps to consider how and why researchers use the terms they do.

One reason for choosing labels is pragmatic. Researchers must develop categories that can be easily measured and compared, and for which data is readily available. For example, it is quite common to talk about those outside organized religion as "spiritual but not religious," but it is very difficult to translate this term into a useful research category.[5] There are many different understandings about what is spiritual and what is religious, and both terms are difficult to quantify. We can count the number of people who self-identify as "spiritual but not religious," but since respondents interpret this phrase in different ways, we do not know what that number means—which is why the application of the phrase is questionable, at least in surveys. By contrast, the phrase *unaffiliated with religion* is among the most widely used labels for those outside organized religion because it lends itself to quantifiable research.

For one thing, religious affiliation or nonaffiliation is easily measured. Most surveys define *religion* in terms of identifiable organization, so respondents asked about religion must select from a list of denominations (e.g., Christian, Protestant, Catholic, Methodist, Muslim, Baptist, or Orthodox Jew) or choose Other or None. This approach is consistent with how most people understand religion (80 percent of Americans do pick a category from the list), although the Other and/or None category becomes kind of a catchall, including not just atheists and agnostics but also anybody who declines to label his or her spirituality.

Defining *affiliation* is also relatively straightforward. The three most commonly used indicators are formal membership in a particular organization (your name is on the roster and they send you a newsletter), attendance (you go to church, at least some of the time), or personal identification with a religious tradition (you consider yourself a Catholic or a Jew). Membership is the easiest to quantify, but it will undercount many individuals who are actively involved but have not formally joined, as well as those who affiliate with smaller religious groups that do not maintain membership rosters. Attendance is arguably the strongest measure of affiliation, but will undercount people who affiliate with a tradition that emphasizes solitary practice (e.g., Buddhism or Neopaganism). Personal identification is least likely to exclude the various ways in which individuals affiliate. But people use religious identification as they use other labels, for symbolic purposes, to identify their membership in a cultural group rather than express their religiosity (e.g., Phil Zuckerman has done some interesting research on Scandinavians who say they are Christian but do not believe in God, Jesus, or the Bible).[6] The best definition of affiliation may be one that combines these measures. If membership or attendance at religious organizations is down, that may just mean that Americans are turning toward more inward forms of religiosity; but if personal identification with religion is also down, the data may indicate a deeper alienation from religion.

The data on religious affiliation and nonaffiliation is easily accessible. Some researchers survey individuals by asking them about their religious affiliation, identification, or preference; the number of unaffiliated is determined by tallying those who identify as such (the Gallup polls, the American Religious Identification Survey and the Pew Religious Landscape Survey all fall in this category[7]). Other researchers solicit reports on membership or attendance from various religious denominations; anyone not claimed by an organization is counted as unaffiliated (the American Religion Data Archive is a good example[8]). It is easier to obtain organizational data than to persuade individuals to participate in a telephone survey about religion. However, many religious people are not part of organizations, and some organizations do not maintain membership or attendance records; hence, studies relying on orga- nizational data report much larger numbers of people as unaffiliated (around 40 percent of all Americans) than studies based on surveys of individuals (around 20 percent). Research also has consistently shown that individuals tend to overstate their religious commitment (as noted above, many people who are only nominally Christian will still identify as such), so the actual number of those outside religion may actually be larger than those who identify as Nones. In short, it is difficult to get an exact count of individuals outside organized religion, no matter what term we use, but some labels get us closer than others.

A second reason researchers choose labels has to do with their in- terests (which are often aligned with those of their research sponsors). For much of the twentieth century, the bulk of research on religion has focused on organized religious bodies and the individuals involved in them. Although there have always been some individuals who turned away from organized religion, the systematic study of this population gained traction only in mid-century when there seemed to be a sudden uptick in its size. Affiliation with organized religion had been relatively constant for most of American history, with church membership and attendance reaching an all-time high in the 1950s. Both surveys of indi- viduals and denominational reports suggest a rise in religious affiliation from the 1930s to the early 1960s, and then a slow and steady decline for the remainder of the century.[9] Something happened in the 1960s that caused significant numbers of Americans to abandon organized reli- gion, and social scientists sought to discover what that was.

Like many cultural changes, this one was spearheaded by the young, or what became known as the baby boom generation, generally under- stood to be those born between 1945 and 1960. Surveys were developed to help estimate how many people were leaving mainline religion and where they were going instead. Some of the dropouts became returnees, but even more of them did not. And although baby boomers were the first generation to leave organized religion in large numbers, they were not the last. Social scientists discovered that religious commitment in America was becoming more transient than it had been in the past.

Researchers were interested in that transience for different reasons, and their use of labels reflects that. For instance, a major study to look at those outside organized religion was the Gallup poll of the "Unchurched American" commissioned by the American Council of Churches and conducted first in 1978 and then repeated a decade later. The studies defined *unchurched* as a person who "is not a member of a church or synagogue or who has not attended church or synagogue in the last six months, apart from weddings, funerals, or special holidays like Christmas, Easter or Yom Kippur."[10] Using this definition, 41 percent (about sixty-one million) of adult Americans (age eighteen and over) were unchurched in 1978 and 44 percent (about seventy-eight million) in 1988. While these numbers must have alarmed the American Council of Churches, the conclusion of the study reassured its readers that few of the survey respondents were truly secular and most still identified as Christian. The numbers reported to support this claim reflect the interests of those who commissioned the study. It tells us that 44 percent of respondents claim a commitment to Christ, but it does not tell us about the commitment of the other 66 percent; it states that 63 percent believed that the Bible is either the literal or inspired word of God, but is silent on the other 37 percent. Perhaps because the goal of the study was finding ways to bring the unchurched back inside the fold, less attention was paid to the varied terrain of the landscape outside.

Other scholars, however, were interested in precisely that varied terrain. They were fascinated by the role that baby boomers played in challenging older religious boundaries and emphasized seekership as a prominent characteristic of the unaffiliated. Wade Clark Roof, for example, reports that two-thirds of baby boomers raised with religion dropped out of their churches or synagogues in their teens or twenties. Although some of these eventually returned (25 percent), even more did not (42 percent), and both dropouts and returnees are characterized by an exploratory attitude toward religion that leads Roof to dub them a "generation of seekers."[11] Robert Fuller distinguishes three types of unaffiliated persons, the largest group of which he calls "Spiritual Seekers." Estimating this group at about 21 percent of the US population, the remainder of his book goes on to further categorize the various types of alternative religion that seekers are drawn to.[12] The goal of these studies was to understand what animates religious seekers, so little attention is paid to secular individuals.

More recently, there has been growing interest in the study of secularism, boosted in part by the work of Barry Kosmin and Ariela Keysar, the principle investigators of the American Religious Identification Survey (ARIS), which reported a major increase in the number of Americans outside organized religion. Defining Nones as those individuals who decline to claim a religious preference, the survey reported their numbers nearly doubled from about 8 percent in 1990 to 15 percent of American adults in 2008. Kosmin and Keysar—who founded the Institute for the Study of Secularism in Society and Culture at Trinity College in Hartford, Connecticut—have produced a profile of Nones that presents them not as seekers or unchurched believers but as "rational skeptics."[13] These researchers' interest in understanding secularism is reflected in their choice of label—Nones—and in the attention paid to the nuances of nonreligious worldviews (which were given short shrift in the Gallup study). Obviously, what we are looking for shapes what we see.

The fact that researchers have a certain slant does not mean we should dismiss their findings; rather, we must consider the studies in combination and look for common themes. If we study the major reports on individuals outside organized religion, we may find that even though they use different labels they sometimes reveal very similar results. For example, the Association of Religion Data Archives (ARDA) estimates the number of unaffiliated based on reports from religious institutions, whereas Gallup calculates the number of unchurched by surveying individuals. In both studies, however, the defining characteristic is lack of formal membership in an organization, and it turns out that the numbers are similar: about 44 percent in the Gallup poll, about 40 percent in the ARDA study. By the same token, Pew's Religious Landscape Study labels individuals who decline to identify with any religion in particular as unaffiliated, while ARIS labels these individuals as having no religious preference. But the defining characteristic for both studies is lack of personal identification with a religious tradition; and again the numbers are similar: by 2008 both the Pew survey and ARIS reported close to 15 percent of Americans as Nones.

We also find a common direction over time. Studies estimate varied growth rates for the population outside religion. For example, Gallup reported a 10 percent increase in the ranks of the unchurched between 1978 and 1988; the General Social Survey reports a 20 percent decline in membership in church-related groups between 1974 and 1996; ARIS and PEW reported a dramatic increase (almost 200 percent) among the Nones between 1990 and 2012. Although we can debate which of these estimates is most accurate, all of them indicate growth in the unaffiliated population. It is clear that regardless of what we call them, the number of Americans who, to varying degrees, are ambivalent about organized religion is increasing and shows no sign of slowing down.

Finally, it appears that the people outside organized religion tend to resemble each other to some extent. Whether they identify as Nones or are just temporarily unchurched, those outside organized religion are more likely to be young (under thirty), male, and politically independent than the rest of the population. More of them tend to live in certain regions (New England and the Pacific Northwest). And, although they hold a variety of worldviews, Nones as a group are more secular than the average American.

Those patterns, however, are stronger for Nones (Pew and ARIS studies) than they are for the unchurched (Gallup and ARDA studies). Thus a typical None is more different from the average American than a typical unchurched person. This should not be surprising. It is one thing not to make formal commitments to organized religion (as the unchurched do when they do not join or rarely attend); it is another to reject even theoretical ties to such organization (as the Nones do when they decline to identify with any religion in particular). We might think of the unchurched (or those unclaimed by religious organizations) as a broader pool of religiously transient people that consists of various subcategories, including but not limited to Nones.[14] While Nones claim no particular religious preference, the unchurched may have stepped away only temporarily from their churches because they moved or went to college; they may be switching denominations; or they may be elderly or sick and watch religious television instead. If we conceptualize all of these categories as degrees of being outside organized religion, then Nones as a group are further outside than the broader unchurched population, and looking at Nones may help us figure out what drives the overall decline in religious commitment.

Demographics

Who are the unaffiliated? For the sake of clarity, I will limit my use of the term *unaffiliated* to refer to those who self-identify as such: the Nones. I will refer to those not claimed as members by organizations (what ARDA calls unaffiliated) as Unchurched or Unclaimed. The typical None is distinctive in several ways. One striking characteristic is their youth. In 2012 the median age of Nones in North America was thirty-one (compared to thirty-seven for the general population), and 35 percent were under thirty compared to only 9 percent of those over sixty-five.[15] The number of Nones in all age groups is growing, but Nones as a group remain younger than the average American.

Another distinctive characteristic is gender: the typical None is male. Pew shows that 23 percent of American men and 17 percent of women were Nones in 2012, up from 18 percent and 13 percent five years earlier. ARIS reports the gender ratio among Nones is sixty males for every forty females—this despite the fact that women outnumber men in the general population. Women are not only less likely to switch out of religion than men but are also less likely to *remain* Nones. The authors of ARIS assert that the gender gap is "the most significant difference" between the religious and nonreligious populations.[16]

Nones are more likely to live in some parts of the country than others, but their geographical distribution is shifting. Surveys have long found regional variation in religious affiliation. In the past, being unchurched was most common in the West and least common in the South.[17] That pattern continued until the end of the last century. Before 2001, the highest percentage of Nones was reported in the Pacific Northwestern states (such as Oregon, Washington, and Idaho) and the lowest in the South (such as Northern Florida or Alabama). By 2008, Vermont (with 34 percent Nones) and New Hampshire (29 percent) reported the highest rates of Nones. Northern New England, historically predominantly Catholic and mainline Protestant, had surpassed the Pacific Northwest as the least religious section of the country. Today, there are three, rather than one geographic areas in the United States that appear particularly nonreligious: the Pacific Northwest, New England, and the Mountain States.[18]

The geographical distribution of Nones coincides to some degree with what some call red and blue states, and much has been made of the fact that President Obama won three quarters of the unaffiliated in 2008 and again in 2012. Yet it would be oversimplifying to characterize Nones as liberal. Their most common party affiliation is independent (in 2008, 42 percent of Nones identified as independent voters, 34 percent as Democrat, and 13 percent as Republican, compared to 29 percent, 34 percent, and 24 percent in the general population). In the last two decades, the proportion of Nones increased from 6 percent to 8 percent among Republicans, 6 percent to 16 percent among Democrats, and 12 percent to 21 percent among independents. It seems that while Nones have an increasing presence in both parties, even more of them eschew any party affiliation. Put differently, those who are religiously uncommitted are also less likely to be politically committed.[19]

For most Nones, becoming unaffiliated is a choice they make as adults. The majority (73 percent) were raised in religious homes, and only 32 percent of current Nones report they had no religion at age twelve. Next to those raised as Nones, Catholics are the single largest contributor to the None population; 24 percent of the overall None population and 35 percent of first-generation or new Nones are former Catholics.[20] Pew reports that more than half of those raised without religion end up affiliating with one as adults. But the number of Americans moving out of religion outnumber those moving out of the None category by a margin of more than three to one.[21] In the constantly shifting American religious marketplace, the unaffiliated today are the biggest gainers.

The religiously uncommitted differ from the average American in several ways, but they are becoming more mainstream in others. Past studies of both the broader unchurched population and the smaller None population found them more likely to be white and unmarried, with higher levels of income and education than the general public.[22] More recent reports show that marital status and class are no longer distinguishing characteristics. Nones are not much different from the general population by education or income, and the difference in marital status nearly disappears once age is accounted for. Although race still matters, it is not a reliable predictor of unaffiliation anymore. Asians and Jews, for example, have long been disproportionately represented among Nones, but today Irish Americans (historically steadfast Catholics) are among the most secularized ethnic groups, and the percentage of Latinos among Nones has tripled (from 4 percent to 12 percent).[23] Being a None, then, is becoming increasingly normal; as the unaffiliated increase their share of the overall population (and current trends suggest that this is likely) they will by default come to resemble it.

That day is still to come, however. As of this writing, the unaffiliated are still a minority. A typical None—say a young, male, Irish American ex-Catholic living in Boston—may not feel himself to be a minority member; yet in a country where 80 percent of the population has a religious affiliation, he is. Not only is he a minority, but he is, in a very real sense, perceived as deviant—not just in the sociological sense of being different from the norm, but in the cultural sense of being abnormal, less trustworthy, perhaps even dangerous. His deviance arises from his label, None, meaning no religion, which to many people is synonymous with atheism. Public prejudice against atheists is well documented.[24] According to a recent Pew survey, 63 percent of Americans would be less likely to vote for a presidential candidate if she or he were atheist—that is a larger percentage than might be influenced if the candidate were Muslim (46 percent) or homosexual (46 percent).[25] It should come as no surprise, then, that divorced parents have had custody rights denied or limited because of atheism and that seven in ten Americans would be troubled if a member of their immediate family married an atheist.[26] Most Nones are not, in fact, atheists but they are often painted with the same brush.

Popular misconceptions about Nones are not helped by current scholarship. Although useful as a quantitative research tool, the term *None* distorts our understanding in several important ways. First, it defines people in terms of what they do not have, implying that they are somehow lacking, when in fact what they have just may not fit the researcher's category. Defining people in terms of lack often leads to prejudicial analysis, especially where the characteristics of the majority population determine the categories by which everybody is measured. We have seen egregious examples of this in the application of racial and gender categories. Only a generation ago, it was common to find medical research that relied on all male samples and then defined female responses as abnormal; or psychological research that based its criteria for moral development on all white samples and then found people of color to be deficient.[27] Similarly, the early history of religious studies was marked by social evolutionary theories (such as those of Edward B. Tylor, James Frazer, or Mircea Eliade) that defined religion in terms of Western, mostly Christian, categories, causing other religions to appear less evolved.[28] Just as we used to refer to Hinduism as prereligious, or to women who stay at home to care for children as not working, the term *Nones* reifies the dominant cultural understanding of what religion is and should be.

By implying that the unaffiliated have no religion, the term *None* suggests that they are more secular than churched individuals. But what respondents are indicating is merely that they decline to choose from the selection of religions presented in the survey. This may mean they are secular or it may not. We know that many Nones hold fairly traditional Christian and Jewish religious beliefs and engage in related practice. Others are drawn to alternative spiritualities and often mix and match elements from various traditions. Even those who reject religion and spirituality and identify as atheist often have philosophically coherent worldviews (and sometimes even organizational affiliations) that are functionally equivalent to religion. In my own research, I found the most secular among the Nones are not atheists but people who are indifferent to the very question of religion, spirituality, or secularism. They often cannot tell you whether they believe in God because they have not given it any thought. They do not attend church because it has not occurred to them; they are too busy doing other things. Unlike atheists and humanists, they do not reject religion; they ignore it. According to recent studies, this indifference is increasingly common among religiously affiliated individuals and suggests that it may ultimately pose a greater threat to religious institutions than disaffiliation.[29]

This diversity of None worldviews hints at another problem with the None label: by lumping all Nones together it implies that they are all the same. A growing body of research demonstrates that so-called None worldviews exhibit as much variation as religious ones.[30] They range from atheists and agnostics to Buddhists to devout Christians and Jews who refuse to align themselves with a particular organization. Ignoring that diversity contrasts sharply with the way scholars treat those who do affiliate—their preferences are differentiated into tens, sometimes hundreds of denominational categories. There may be good practical reasons for the neglect of variations among the Nones. For example, some subcategories are too small to yield statistically significant findings. But that reasoning has too often been used to defend research that overlooks other minorities such as Jews or Muslims. As the None category grows to rival the size of some major religious denominations, the case for devising new, subtler labels becomes more urgent.

For now, at least, we are stuck with the term *None*, and the best we can do is to carefully unpack what it means. The following chapter will explore the worldviews (religious and secular) of Americans outside organized religion, what distinguishes different types of Nones, and what (aside from being unaffiliated) they all have in common.

2

What Do Nones Believe and Practice?

Nones claim no religion but their beliefs and practices are all over the map. Consider a brief sampling of responses from some of my research subjects:

I am neither spiritual nor religious. I do not believe in God or a higher power or energy. We are all particles in the universe when we are alive, our actions speak, and we can never know where on the wave we are on a massive wave of history, and we could be the person that turns the way which should motivate us to be ethical and even kind. (Fran, teacher, environmental activist, mother of three boys and a girl)

I've always been really big into prayer because I think it's so powerful. And it's not necessarily to an entity, but I believe in the ways of the world, and I believe that if you put good energy into the world it returns to you. And so whenever I was in need of strength I always asked for it, but I'd never visualized or, what's the word, anthropomorphized, I've never created like a human figure out of God. In my mind it's more of an energy and just nature that I pray to. (Denise, massage therapist, mother of one girl)

I think that seeing is a religious discipline, or rather a spiritual discipline, and I think that you have to see for yourself. That's I think one of the main reasons why I'm not actively involved in pursuing religion, because I don't believe that it helps me to see, and I do believe that that is a spiritual experience for me, and so I don't believe that religion leads to spirituality in my life . . . I'm not going to church and not participating in anything, it's just my own inner work, so to speak. (Scott, management consultant, father of two boys and a girl)

The problem I have with religion is I have so many different little things that I could take from different ones, that I could never go with just one religion. (Beth, home maker, mother of two boys)

I do not have a religion. I consider myself somebody that has a relationship with Christ. (Lillian, restaurateur, mother of one son)

If we want to understand who Nones are and what they may be passing on to their children, we need to take these differences seriously. Nones are Nones because they refuse either to identify with a particular religious tradition or to affiliate with an organization. But of course religion is about more than just membership in a group; it entails beliefs, practices, moral values, and personal experiences that to varying degrees shape an individual's life. What beliefs, practices, moral values, and personal experiences constitute the worldviews of those who do not claim a religion? The term *None* tells us nothing about this. This chapter explores various kinds of None worldviews and offers a framework for understanding how these may differ from what we call religion.

Previous Frameworks for Understanding None Worldviews

Over the last decade since the dramatic increase in Nones was first reported, various researchers have sought to investigate and explain None worldviews. A good place to start is to distinguish Nones who are religious, but for whatever reason do not want to claim that term, from those who are not.

Religious versus Secular Nones

Lillian, who is quoted at the beginning of this chapter as having a relationship with Christ and who has attended a church twice weekly for the last sixteen years, is a religious None, whereas Fran, a self-professed atheist, is a secular None. More often, however, the distinction is not as clear-cut. Some Nones profess belief in God or a higher power but do not attend religious services or engage in any kind of spiritual practice such as prayer or meditation. Are they religious or secular? Others do practice but reject all supernatural belief. Are they religious or secular? The answer depends on how one defines religion.[1]

Sociologists have developed various indicators of "religiousness" based on conventional understanding of what religion is: belief in God or supernatural beings and practices that give expression to such beliefs such as prayer, attendance at services, or following a particular moral code.[2] The absence of such beliefs or practices is thought to indicate secularism. Applying this framework to the None population yields some surprising results. For example, Rodney Stark and his colleagues analyzed previous survey data asking Nones in the United States and in other nations about beliefs in God or supernatural beings and about practices such as prayer and church attendance.[3] They found that about half of American Nones believe in God and another one-fifth in a higher power. Only 14 percent were atheists. While the vast majority did not attend services at all, about one-third pray regularly (at least once a week). Hout and Fisher report similar findings.[4] They assert that most Nones are unchurched believers: they hold conventional religious beliefs (Jesus is the son of God, the Bible is true) and pray; they just do not attend services much.

Both studies were conducted in the 1990s, and more recent surveys put the proportion of unaffiliated believers at only 23 percent, suggesting Nones have become much more secular.[5] Still, distinguishing between religious and secular Nones helps us see that for at least some Nones that label is a misnomer. People like Lillian, Denise, or Beth clearly have religion, they just do not like to call it that. This framework also offers some clue as to what may be driving the growth of Nones. One reason unchurched believers identify as Nones is because they are alienated by what goes on in religious institutions: leadership scandals, rules that seem out of touch with contemporary morality, or too much emphasis on fundraising. Like Lillian, they believe in God but they find church boring or disingenuous. Another reason Nones claim no religion is that many, the young especially, associate religion with conservative politics and are turned off by that.[6] The anti-institutional, antipolitical stance of younger Nones is vividly illustrated in Jefferson Bethke's video, "Why I Hate Religion, but Love Jesus" which became a YouTube sensation. Bethke, a young white Evangelical Christian, raps about why he claims no religion:

> What if I told you Jesus came to abolish religion?
> What if I told you voting Republican really wasn't his mission?
> What if I told you "Republican" doesn't automatically mean
> "Christian"?

And just because you call some people "blind" doesn't automatically
give you vision?
I mean, if religion is so great, why has it started so many wars?
Why does it build huge churches but fails to feed the poor?
Tells single moms God doesn't love them if they've ever had a
divorce?
But in the Old Testament God actually calls religious people
"whores"
Religion might preach grace, but another thing they practice . . .

Bethke's rhetoric echoes the concerns of many young people who, as I discussed in chapter 1, are disproportionately represented in the None population. He and others like him are clearly not secular, they just do not like what religion has become. The fact that there are more religious than atheist Nones has led several scholars to conclude that what's really driving the None movement is not secularization but privatization of religion, a trend that's been going on for several decades now.[7]

While the religious versus secular None framework is useful, it can also muddy the waters. Although reference is made to practice, religiosity remains primarily defined by creed. Stark, for example, defines religion as "explanations of existence based on supernatural assumptions," including explanations about the nature of the supernatural and the meaning of existence.[8] Secularism is the rejection of such explanations. This is a simple model but one that can also be misleading, especially when applied to Nones. It counts as "religious" those Nones who say they believe in God but are basically indifferent to any kind of religious or spiritual practice: not only do they never attend religious services but they do not pray or meditate, they do not read spiritual or religious books or articles, they are, as one of my respondents put it, "just not interested in that kind of thing." The model counts as "secular" a None who meditates daily and is a strict vegetarian due to his respect for all living beings but rejects the notion of the supernatural. This makes no sense. It appears to be a strange coincidence that the None population includes a disproportionate number of Asian Americans, whose religious cultures place less emphasis on creed. Defining religiosity (and secularism) primarily in terms of beliefs ignores the ways that religious (and secular) values and practices are actually lived out in experience.

Another problem with the religious versus secular framework is that it overlooks a third possibility, the individual who is somewhere in between religion and secularism, or what some call spiritual. Although *spiritual* is a slippery term, those who use it to describe themselves are pushing us to acknowledge that religions versus secularism represents a forced choice that does not adequately define them.[9] Take Scott, quoted at the beginning of this chapter. He lacks the characteristics researchers use to designate individuals as religious (belief in God, prayer). But I would hesitate to call him secular because of the "inner work" that he considers "spiritual." How do we account for this type of None?

Nones as Spiritual Seekers

Various attempts have been made to capture this in-between type. One very useful conceptualization comes from Robert Fuller's widely regarded study, which divides Nones into three categories: Unchurched Believer, secular, and seeker spirituality.[10] Unchurched Believers are conventionally religious, meaning they hold religious beliefs and engage in religious practices that resemble those of mainline Christians and Jews. *Secular* refers to individuals who do not believe or practice in this way. The in-between category is what Fuller calls "seeker spirituality," which he defines as a pluralistic orientation that eclectically combines elements from various spiritual and religious traditions to meet the individual's personal needs. He then goes on to explain the amazing variety of sources that spiritual seeker Nones draw on, which include Swedenborgianism, transcendentalism, mesmerism, astrology, witchcraft, New Thought, and New Age, as well as Eastern and Native American religions. Fuller argues that these ideas and practices may be combined with elements from traditional Christianity or Judaism or scientific theories such as humanistic psychology, resulting in an infinite variety of alternative spiritualities.

Designating some Nones as spiritual seekers gets us beyond the binary, religious versus secular framework and helps us appreciate the diversity of worldviews held by the unaffiliated. It also captures what is distinctive about this type of worldview, its pluralism and individualization. A None who crafts her own personal spirituality from various sources (say Judaism and Buddhism) is very different from someone like Bethke who is practicing a privatized version of a conventional faith.

The downside of applying a category like spiritual seeker is that its use has been plagued by fuzziness and ideology in both popular culture and in academia. The term *spiritual* is amorphous and lacks a clear definition, so it is commonly used to mean different things.[11] A churchgoing Catholic may call herself spiritual because she is more deeply interested in religion than her friends. Beth, quoted at the beginning of this chapter, combines bits and pieces from various traditions into her own personalized religious practice. She calls herself spiritual because her worldview is not tied to any particular tradition or institution. Even atheists use the term to refer to personally moving experiences such as climbing to a mountain summit. Similar problems arise with the term *seeker*: It is commonly used to designate those who drop out of conventional religion to explore alternatives,[12] yet it may also apply to church members interested in questions of philosophical truth. The result, as Nancy Ammerman points out, is that terms like *spiritual* or *seeker* are ultimately political, used to designate a worldview that is somehow more authentic than that of other people.[13]

Although this is a valid critique, I do not think misuse of a term necessarily implies that we must abandon it altogether. Fuller addresses the definitional problem by carefully delimiting *seeker spirituality* to a particular type of worldview: It is distinct from secularism in that it embraces religious beliefs and or practices; and it is distinct from religion, as most Americans understand that term, in the notion that individuals should create their own by combining elements from various sources. Fuller's major contribution was to elucidate the various dimensions of seeker spirituality. He was not interested in nonreligious worldviews, and secularism is still treated merely as the absence of religion. His three-part model does not account for the variations of substantive secular philosophies, practices, and value systems that can give meaning to people's lives as much as religion does.

Varieties of Secularism

Most studies of secular people have focused on why and how these individuals reject religion, rather than what they have come to believe and practice instead.[14] One notable exception is Frank Pasquale's study of secular group affiliates, that is, individuals who claim membership in secular organizations such as the American Humanist Association (AHA) or the American Atheists.[15] Frank surveyed 911 such individuals and found that while there are certain characteristics shared by most seculars there is also a lot of diversity.

Just as Catholics and Protestants share the belief that Jesus was the son of God and the Bible is divinely inspired to guide humankind, most seculars are united by their rejection of a personal deity and look to science and empirical methods to pursue truth and justice. Since there is no deity to worship, the practice of this worldview emphasizes ethical living and social justice, rather than ritual or worship. Many seculars are apostates; that is, they were raised with religion, often a heavy dose of it, and they eventually rejected it in favor of a more rational worldview.

Yet there are important variations. While some are atheist, other seculars believe in a higher power, which they see as an impersonal force of nature that animates the universe. While some eschew any kind of ritual as superstition, others embrace certain religious practices for cultural reasons. Based on the labels most frequently chosen by respondents, Frank identified six distinct types of secular worldview. *Secular humanists* focus on the idea that we can promote good without reference to a deity; it emphasizes the unique responsibility of humanity to use our capacity for reason and the ethical consequences of human decisions. *Jewish humanist* refers to people who reject theism but want to incorporate Jewish culture, practices, and customs (e.g., celebrating a Passover seder as a way to remember Jewish history). There are also *Unitarian humanists* who embrace the ethical principles of the Unitarian Universalist Association (UUA)—a denomination that has provided a home base for many secularists—but who feel uncomfortable with what they see as the association's gradual drift toward theism. Those who call themselves *atheist* emphasize rejection of a deity and generally affirm the search for truth and justice via rational, empiricist methods. Secularists who call themselves *rationalist* or *skeptic* are focused on promoting critical thinking and science; while such thinking will usually result in atheism, it need not. Finally, those who identify as *freethinkers* reject religious, rationalist, and empiricist dogmas. They feel individuals should be able to arrive at a worldview based on their own experience, not some external, religious or secular authority.

Another excellent study of secular worldviews is Phil Zuckerman's book *Faith No More*. Zuckerman, who interviewed more than one hundred secular individuals of different ages and social classes, is less interested in the variations of secular philosophy than in the practical decisions secular people make to deal with the challenges of everyday life, including struggles with sexual orientation, divorce, unemployment, poverty, illness, and death. He asserts that, although religious people may look to God, the scripture, or their priests or rabbis for moral guidance or hope in the face of suffering, secular people rely on themselves: having rejected religion, they feel empowered to reason things out based on their own experience and to take action to solve their own problems. This argument has been made by many writers, most notably the proponents of the New Atheism (Daniel Dennett, Sam Harris, and others). What's different about Zuckerman's study is that he provides data for how this self-reliant secular worldview actually works in the lives of ordinary people.

Zuckerman demonstrates that secular self-reliance can provide hope and moral guidance just as well as, if not better than, religion can. Many Americans see religion as an important source of moral values. They are suspicious of secular individuals, atheists in particular, because the lack of an external moral authority is presumed to leave secular individuals selfish and hedonistic, with nothing to reign in the baser aspects of human nature. By contrast, Zuckerman's study suggests that individuals who hold secular worldviews may actually take ethics and morality more seriously than many religious folk. Because they are motivated by an internal desire to avoid causing pain to others, rather than by the fear of disobeying God, they actually find themselves acting more morally than before. The study also shows how a secular worldview can offer hope and inspiration in the face of despair. A particularly vivid illustration is Zuckerman's profile of two women of lower socioeconomic status whose lives improve after they became secular. These women are interesting precisely because they are atypical seculars: studies have consistently found women and the poor to be more religious, a finding that holds across cultures. Studies also show that secularism is more common in societies with high levels of income and gender equality, suggesting that people in these societies may have less need for the comforts of religion. But causality may also run the other way. In some cases,

Zuckerman provocatively argues, religion may hold people back while the self-reliant worldview of secularism gives them the tools they need to change their lives.

Exploring variations of secularism helps us appreciate it as a substantive worldview rather than just the absence of religion. Once we take the time to study what secular people believe and practice, we see that a secular philosophy such as Jewish humanism or Freethought can function much like religion in providing meaning and moral guidance to an individual's life. A secular worldview can offer comfort in the face of suffering and motivate sacrifice on behalf of others, just as religion does. And like religion, secular philosophies can sometimes become dogmatic, leading to negative prejudice against alternative worldviews (which in this case means religious ones).

* * *

Unchurched believers, spiritual seekers, seculars—these categories capture the majority of the so-called Nones. Depending on which study you consult, you may get somewhat different numbers, but it is fair to estimate that nearly half of American Nones are unchurched believers, about one-third are spiritual seekers, and one-fifth adhere to a secular philosophy.[16]

Some Nones, however, cannot articulate or refuse to follow any particular worldview, be it religious, spiritual, or secular—not because they lack verbal ability or are too shy to discuss their personal lives, but because they are just plain indifferent to the kinds of questions we usually ask about religion. Although they claim to be neither spiritual nor religious, they have no negative opinions about religion as people who claim a secular philosophy often do.[17] Indeed those who are indifferent often see religion as something positive—it just does not suit them.

This category is difficult to account for because their responses are often vague and changing. Ask them if they go to church, the answer is no, as it is for the other three categories of Nones. Ask them if they pray or meditate, the answer is also negative, as it is for seculars. Yet indifferent Nones do not embrace a nontheistic philosophy or even identify as agnostic as many seculars do. If you inquire whether they believe in God or a higher power, the likely response is something like: "Hm . . . I really haven't given much thought to that." Even their identity as None is not definitive: in some contexts, they may opt for the label *Catholic* or *Jewish* or whatever other tradition they were raised with, yet reject those labels in other contexts. A recent study refers to individuals who shift back and forth between None and some denominational identification as "liminal," occupying a sort of borderland between the religious or spiritual category on the one hand and the secular on the other.[18] These findings provide an important reminder of the transience and fluidity of religious identification, but the term *liminal None* does not fully overlap with what I mean by indifferent. While shifting responses may signify indifference to religious or secular labels, it may also indicate quite the opposite: a deep personal struggle over what those terms mean. The term *liminality*, moreover, suggests transition, meaning that these Nones will eventually move to either the religious or the secular side of the fence. Some Nones, however, remain indifferent to religion or secular philosophies for much of their lives. As I will show in the next section, these Indifferents, as I call them, raise important questions for how we understand the None phenomenon.[19]

Toward a Typology of None Worldviews

The Nones who are the focus of this book represent a small subset of the larger US None population—parents. Studying parents offers a unique angle to observe None worldviews because becoming a parent is itself a liminal stage, a time when many individuals reevaluate their worldview as they decide what they want to pass on to their children. As a result, most respondents were eager to talk, plus the small-scale, long-term setup of the study allowed for lengthy (sometimes repeated) interviews about an individual's religious background and current religious identity and behavior. I have drawn on patterns observed among my respondents to construct multidimensional criteria for the four most common types of None worldviews.

Coding qualitative data can be tricky. Different terms mean different things to different people (as shown in my discussion of the meaning of *spiritual* in the previous section), and some criteria may indicate a respondent belongs in one category while other criteria suggest he or she belongs in another (e.g., an atheist who reports a spiritual experience). I have tried to avoid these pitfalls by asking my respondents to clarify

Table 2.1. Parent Worldview

	Unchurched Believer	Seeker Spirituality	Philosophical Secularist	Indifferent
Self-chosen label (if used)	Christian or Jew (reject denominational label)	Pluralist label (e.g., Buddhist Jew)	Humanist, free thinker, skeptic, atheist, etc.	None
Religious or spiritual	Either or both	Spiritual but not religious	Neither	Neither
Beliefs (in God, supernatural powers, or other forces)	Personal god who listens and can intervene in human affairs	Energy or life force that influences nature and human life (reject personal theism)	Our lives are shaped by natural/material forces and by human decisions (not God or supernatural power)	Do not know and do not care
Practices that give expression to those beliefs	Prayer or attendance at services	Prayer, meditation, yoga, reading	Meditation, reading, and social justice work as expression of secular philosophy (no prayer or worship)	None

what they mean by terms like *God* or *spiritual*, by asking them about their practices and experiences, not just beliefs, and by considering observation data rather than just the interview in the coding process. As I reviewed the interviews and observation data, it became clear that many respondents fit into the categories previously described: some were unchurched believers, others adhered to a secular philosophy, and many had created their own unique form of seeker spirituality. However, there were also some who did not fit into these boxes, those whom I call Indifferent.[20] Table 2.1 summarizes all four types, which are capitalized from here on. In the following sections, I take a look at some of their stories.

Unchurched Believers

Some None parents I encountered were conventionally religious, meaning they hold religious beliefs and engage in religious practices that resemble those of mainline Christians and Jews. I coded respondents as Unchurched Believers if they leaned towards a Christian or Jewish label (many were reluctant to self-label, but would say things like "I have a relationship with Christ," or "I am discovering my Jewish roots"). In addition, they were characterized by at least two of the following: (1) they identified as religious (which they understood to mean embracing aspects of a particular tradition) or spiritual (which they usually defined as a personal experience such as a relationship with God), or both; (2) they affirmed traditional theist beliefs (a personal god who listens and can intervene in human affairs); or (3) they engaged in traditional religious practices like prayer or attending services at a church or synagogue.

Three examples of Unchurched Believers are Roxanne, Lillian, and Denise. Roxanne, age forty, is a research scientist and the single mother of two teenage daughters, now living in a college town in Connecticut. Raised a devout Catholic in the Midwest, she dropped out of church at nineteen when she discovered she was pregnant and alone: "There was no one I could talk to about the situation I was in. . . . I really needed support and the church was not there." She ended up marrying her boyfriend (and later divorcing) and spent the next decade "trying on" various religious and spiritual communities including Wicca and Anthroposophy as well as various Protestant denominations. Although none of them really "fit," she said her faith in the God of her childhood never wavered and she continued to pray to him.

Denise, a twenty-three-year-old part-time massage therapist, married with one child, lives in the same city as Roxanne. Raised Jewish, she went to Hebrew school every Sunday and attended temple with her parents on holidays. She and her sister were both bat mitzvahed, and even went on a trip to Israel, but then she moved away for college in New Mexico and stopped her involvement. She learned massage, dabbled in Native American healing and New Age visualization techniques. She recalled celebrating Hanukkah when her mother would visit, but added: "I didn't maintain it very much on my own." She married, had a child, then divorced, and returned to her hometown. Then, she said, "because I live close to my mother, we started celebrating the holidays again, and . . . we have pretty much kept up." Although she came to reject the personal deity of traditional Judaism and instead imagines the divine as an energy or force of nature, she continues to pray. Her disagreement with some Jewish teachings causes her to call herself spiritual rather than religious, but she is now reclaiming her "Jewish identity."

Lillian, forty-one, is a single mother of a teenage boy and the operator of a successful restaurant. She was raised Presbyterian but stopped attending in her teens when her parents no longer pushed her to go. She went to college, lived a bit "on the wild side" and remained unchurched until her early thirties when, she said, "a friend of mine that I used to do crazy, crazy stuff with brought me" to the Evangelical Christian community she belongs to now. The congregation met in an old school building.

> There were maybe about twenty-five people, and there was this Hispanic man up on a pulpit, and he was teaching, and he was really funny. He just brought the word of God down to a level of understanding to me. The fact that he was funny and could incorporate his own craziness, and how God used him, and how we all struggle with the same kind of things. And that he wasn't exempt. That spoke to me and I've been there since, sixteen years. I have gone every Sunday and Wednesday. Bible study and Sunday service. And Friday communion, which is the first Friday of every month.

That was sixteen years go. And yet Lillian continues to deny she has religion because religion to her means "following a set of rules" and what she has is a relationship with God.

Like Lillian, the Unchurched Believer parents I talked to had all been raised with conventional religion. They became Nones because organized religion no longer met their needs—either because of a personal crisis (as in Roxanne's case) or more often because they moved away from home, got busy with other things, and "religion just didn't seem relevant anymore." Now that they are parents, they seem quite comfortable reclaiming the religion of their childhood, perhaps because they never fully left it. Denise claims that she has "always been very spiritual," and whether affiliated or not, she prays every night because she thinks "it is so powerful." And while Roxanne "never went back to the Catholic Church," she continued to believe. "Spirituality is inherent in human nature," she said, "and criticism and doubt just comes with the territory." The Unchurched Believers I interviewed were unaffiliated because they severed ties to particular religious institutions, not because they rejected religion. As I discuss later in this book, having children can provide the incentive to reconnect those ties.

Seeker Spirituality

Other None parents are best characterized as Spiritual Seekers as Fuller defines that term: a pluralistic religious orientation that eclectically combines elements from various spiritual and religious traditions to meet the individual's personal needs. Since Fuller's work was historical in approach (he did not interview any contemporary Nones), I operationalized his definition so that it can be used to categorize respondents. Thus, Spiritual Seekers were those parents who identified with a pluralist label (e.g., Buddhist Jew) or declined a label because of their pluralistic outlook (all religions are true). In addition, they met at least two of the following three criteria: (1) they identified as spiritual but not religious (which they associated with following the dogma and rules of a particular tradition); (2) they rejected theism but believed in a higher power or life force; (3) they engaged in spiritual practices drawn from a variety of sources such as prayer, meditation, or yoga.

Three parents that illustrate this orientation are Rebecca, Susan, and Jay. Jay, an aeronautical engineer in Denver, is married with three teenagers. He was raised Catholic but left the church "at twelve or thirteen, whenever you get confirmed" because he realized he "was an atheist the whole time." At sixteen, he was born again in an Evangelical church where "there were lots of beautiful young women." He discovered, "the more Christian I sounded the better the girls liked me, so somehow it took," and he stayed for nearly a decade. Jay rejected church again, this time more permanently, when he joined the military: "I was on a mountaintop in Turkey in the Air Force, and I met the most profoundly Christian man I had ever met. Unfortunately he was a Muslim. He was very devout, prayed to Mecca five times a day, the whole washing, the whole rhythm, just that sense of devoting himself to God, and reflecting that in his life, devoting himself to his family and the people around him. So I found him a tremendous Christ-like figure who was doomed, doomed, doomed by my Christian God."

Around that time, Jay discovered Rumi, the Sufi poet, and concluded that he could construct his own spirituality from various sources: "yoga, meditation, reading the mystics, and that kind of path; I am probably more Buddhist in my faith, whatever faith is. That's where I am at the moment." Now in his early forties, he feels his worldview will continue to evolve.

Rebecca is an Eastern European immigrant who came to the United States as a child. Now in her early forties, she is a married mother and artist, living in Los Angeles. She was raised Greek Orthodox but developed an interest in Buddhism when her father began experimenting with meditation practice, and she continued studying other religions in college. "I saw how similar people who were called masters or saints are, like there are masters in the Buddhist tradition and there are Christian monks. . . . The Sufi masters, their divine encounters or mystical experiences were so similar. I started thinking about it." She concluded that there is truth in all of them.

Susan, a business consultant in her mid-thirties, lives with her husband and young son in Hartford, Connecticut. Born to a teenage mother, Susan was raised a conservative Jew by her grandparents but abruptly ceased religious participation when she was returned to her mother's care at age thirteen. Instead she began to explore other religions, a search she continued in college and graduate school. Having gone to mosque, attended Christian seminary and participated in Wiccan rituals, Susan concluded, "All religions are valid and true."

All three of these respondents described themselves as spiritual but not religious. They reject theism, especially the personal anthropomorphic deity generally associated with the Abrahamic religions. Instead, many Seeker Spirituality respondents said they believed in a kind of life force or energy. The describe this as "a universal force of nature that works in everything that is," or "a force that connects everyone and that when we would die we become a part of that, and the energy becomes reincarnated, not the person," and they believe that what different religions call "God, Yahweh, Allah are just different names" for the same thing. As Jay jokingly answered my question: "May the force be with you."

Jay pieces together his own spirituality from aspects of Buddhism, Islamic mysticism, and practices rooted in his Catholic childhood like contemplative prayer, with no particular commitment to any of these traditions. Susan and Rebecca, by contrast, feel most at home in one tradition—Rebecca in Hinduism, Susan in Judaism—yet they refuse to identify as such. Rebecca is a devotee of a Hindu guru, and she gathers with friends for potluck and puja about once a month, but she rejects all labels: "I do not feel that any of these traditions is mine, I feel like they all are, but I don't feel like I have to belong to one of them." Susan said that if she had to, she "would choose Judaism, but it's hard to be Jewish. There are a lot of rules and rituals you're supposed to keep," which, at this point in her life she is not going to do; but "I also really love Buddhism, it absolutely makes sense to me. It's about human nature, and meditation practice keeps me grounded and peaceful." Susan does not feel she should have to choose; instead, she selects elements from each tradition based on what meets her subjective needs: "I enjoy Judaism and Buddhism for very different reasons, I like the practice of Buddhism but Judaism has a tradition based on my past and my family and also has God at its center, which I do want in a religious tradition, so I don't think I'll choose one or the other, I'm figuring out how to make the two work for me." These respondents exemplify the highly personal, eclectic style that Robert Bellah and his colleagues once called Sheilaism.[21] They are unaffiliated, not because they reject religion but because they do not want to commit to one tradition.

Philosophical Secularism

About a quarter of the parents I met were secular in the sense that they explicitly reject religion in favor of following a nonreligious philosophy of life. It is important to distinguish these Philosophical Secularists, as I call them, from those who merely ignore religion and have no interest in *either* religious or secular worldviews.[22] None parents were coded as Philosophical Secularists if they self-identified with a label such as humanist, freethinker, skeptic, atheist, or other philosophy that rejects religion. But a worldview is more than just a label; we must also consider what people believe and practice, how they live their lives. Philosophical Secularists typically describe themselves as neither spiritual nor religious, both of which they associate with irrationality. They do not believe in God or other supernatural power that influences the world or human life. Rather, they understand our existence to be shaped by nature, society, and other material forces that we can rationally and empirically explain. They reject widely held perceptions of religion as a source of "good morals" and instead ground ethical decisions in secular philosophies such utilitarianism or the Golden Rule. Philosophical Secularists do not engage in religious practices such as attending services, prayer or meditation, except for nonreligious reasons (e.g., attending church for the wedding of a friend, or meditating to de-stress). Instead, these individuals often engage in self-consciously secular practices such as attending an atheist meeting or celebrating Darwin's birthday. Others are engaged in social justice work (e.g., defending freedom of speech, environmentalism, or gay rights), which they see as an expression of their secular worldviews.

Three examples of Philosophical Secularist parents are Daniel, Robert, and Fran. Daniel, an information technology specialist in a large corporation, is in his forties, a married father of three young children, and a resident of a gated community in Jacksonville, Florida. Daniel grew up in a deeply religious home, "a preacher's kid," but he "became alienated from church teachings from a scientific perspective." Acquiring an undergraduate degree in theoretical mathematics, he came to believe that "the whole notion of any real understanding of something beyond the concrete is doubtful." He now calls himself a humanist.

Robert, in his early fifties, is the divorced father of two teenagers and a tenured professor at a private college in Connecticut. Robert was raised Presbyterian but retained his faith through college, intending to become a minister. It was in seminary that he rejected religion because "the competing truth claims of the religions just negated them" and because "in the face of all the evil and suffering in the world, there's a tsunami, 160,000 people killed, it [Christian theism] doesn't make any sense." Robert, like Daniel, left his church, never to return. He now identifies as an atheist.

Fran, who is quoted at the beginning of this chapter, is married and the mother of four teenagers. She's also a high school science teacher and an environmental activist. She currently lives in Colorado Springs. She too was raised in a religious home and a mainline Protestant congregation. "I sang in the choir and was an active participant. I was born again with Billy Graham before I turned twelve," she said. When she went away for college she explored other religions: "I have read many of the ancient scriptures, the Bhagavad-Gita, and some but not as much as I would like of many other texts. I was very interested in the Gnostics for a long time." But she was eventually disappointed in all of them: "I find that, and no matter how pure the intentions, religion is used to justify what we do, and I reject that entirely." Instead, Fran seeks guidance in the teachings of secular philosophers (her favorites are Stephen Jay Gould and Carl Sagan). Although religion offers "morals which stipulates dogma," she believes secular philosophy provides the basis for "ethics, which benefits the human race; it's much more utilitarian." Fran, who now identifies as a skeptic, understands that worldview as motivating her choice of profession as well as her environmental activism: "I am always questioning."

Fran, Robert, and Daniel do not identify as either religious or spiritual. Yet all of these respondents care about the questions of ultimate meaning and moral discipline that historically have been raised by religion. Robert has made the study of religion his profession. Although the other two have not, they have both devoted significant amounts of their personal time to learning about religious and secular philosophies. Daniel has spent many years seeking for "a way of truth about this existence," including extensive reading on Eastern religions and experimentation with "meditation and self-centering." Fran is an avid reader of the New Atheist philosophers and closely follows news about religion, especially the Christian fundamentalists who, she feels, "dominate this town." Although they all reject religious or spiritual answers to questions of meaning and morality, they do identify with a philosophical worldview—Robert as atheist, Daniel as ethical humanist, Fran as a skeptic—that replaces supernaturalism with materialism, faith with doubt, and a divine moral order with the human responsibility to "rationally determine what is best for everyone." These respondents are unaffiliated because they reject religion. Yet for them secularism is not just the absence of religion but also a substantive philosophy of life.

Indifference

None parents whose most prominent characteristic was complete indifference to either religion or secular worldviews are often grouped with atheists, agnostics, and other types of secularists. In my opinion, however, these individuals deserve a category of their own.

One reason is consistency. If we designate individuals as religious based on their identification with or practice of a particular worldview, then we should do the same for those who are secular. The Philosophical Secularists described earlier rejected religion or spirituality in favor of something else: atheism, humanism, and the like. Indifferents, however, do not so much reject religion as ignore it. Importantly, their indifference also extends to secular worldviews: they do not embrace atheism, or even agnosticism, and are generally unable or unwilling to articulate a worldview other than "none."

A second reason for distinguishing these individuals has to do with practice or the way that people actually incorporate their religion (or their secular philosophies) into their family lives. Unchurched Believers, Spiritual Seekers, and Philosophical Secularists may all be Nones in the sense of lacking religious affiliation, but many are clearly not Nones if you consider how they live their lives, in particular how they raise their children. As I discuss in more detail in chapter 5, Indifferent parents were the only group to consistently *not* incorporate religion, spirituality, or even a secular philosophy that rejects religion into the upbringing of their children, suggesting they may be the only group that deserves to be categorized as None.

I coded parents as Indifferent if they expressed indifference to any worldview, either religious or secular. Like Philosophical Secularists, Indifferent parents identified neither as religious (which they understood to mean following a tradition like Christianity) nor as spiritual (which they understood as a personal interest in the questions of meaning and morality that are addressed by religion and philosophy). Most Indifferents did not believe in God or a higher power, not because they rejected the idea (as Philosophical Secularists do) but rather because they were not interested in it. They were uninvolved in spiritual practices such as prayer or meditation, and (unlike Philosophical Secularists) did not perceive other activities they were engaged in, such as sports, as a substitute for such practices.

Three parents that exemplify the Indifferent orientation are Jared, Peter, and Nancy. Peter, a business consultant in his forties, is married with three children and lives near Boston. He was raised in a mainline Protestant church (he does not remember which denomination), which he attended sporadically with his parents. They stopped going when he was in high school, so he left and never returned. Jared, a computer programmer, is in his thirties and married with two children and lives near

Colorado Springs. He was raised Baptist and regularly attended services and youth group. When he left for college, however, he ceased to affiliate, even though a Baptist church was nearby. Nancy is a mid-level corporate executive who lives near Denver. She is married and has a teenage son. Her family was Methodist and she attended church with her parents "somewhat regularly" until her late teens. She continued participating in religion "off and on" with her first husband, a Pentecostal, until they got a divorce. When her job took her abroad she stopped going to church altogether. Her second husband, an ex-Catholic, suggested they join a church after their son was born, but Nancy declined: "I just didn't see the point."

Unlike the Philosophical Secularists, parents like Peter, Jared, and Nancy did not report experiencing a crisis of faith that led them to reject the religions they were raised in, nor did they explore other religions. Rather, religion just ceased to be relevant. As Nancy put it, "it was just lack of interest." All three decline to identify as either religious or spiritual, and they did not claim any secular label either. Jared sums up the feeling of many Indifferents: "Spiritual to me is more of an inner thing, when someone is *interested in* and *thinking about* it, whereas religious means organized [religion]. I am neither."

That lack of interest is clearly evident in their beliefs. When I asked Peter if he still affirmed any of the religion of his childhood, his answer was vague: "The idea that Jesus was a spiritual being who came to earth and died, I suppose I can believe that, but I do not consciously follow any Christian dogma or ethics, and we don't go to church." Jared's response tended in the other direction but was similarly noncommittal: "Hm, I don't think I believe in God or spiritual beings." And Nancy declined to take any stand: "I don't believe in anything supernatural. But I don't know and nobody really knows, it's impossible, so why spend so much time on it."

Which is, of course, why they do not spend any time on it. While many of the Philosophical Secularists I met regularly engaged in some activity (social justice work, teaching, meditation) that they saw as an expression of their secular worldview, the Indifferent parents saw no need to connect their life styles or interests to some kind of intellectual framework. Jared, Peter, and Nancy all work long hours in professions they enjoy, and they spend what time is left with their children or pursuing their hobbies (skiing, baseball, and computer games, respectively). Why spend time on something you consider irrelevant?

Ignoring religion is quite different from the often passionate rejection of religion among Philosophical Secularists. Nancy, Jared, and Peter have long been unaffiliated, yet none of them has any animus against organized religion. Jared remembers the church he grew up in with fondness. He and his wife have talked about joining a church but they neither have the time nor interest: "We're out of town at the ski condo two to three Sundays per month, and [when] we're here we still don't go." Similarly, Peter's disaffiliation is not rooted in any kind of resentment against the church: "I don't know why I don't [attend church], I don't have that in my life. It's more like, why would I, rather than, why don't I?" Perhaps the most telling moments were when I asked each of these parents if there was some philosophy or worldview, aside from religion, that sustained them. In each case the answer was a long silence, followed by: "I really haven't thought much about that."

What *None* Really Means

The typology of None parents presented here raises important questions about how we define religion and secularity. Americans commonly define religion in terms of beliefs, belonging, and participation. But should we not also consider how much such beliefs or practices *matter* to a person (what sociologists refer to as "salience" of the person's worldview) and how he or she actually lives his or her life (what sociologists call "lived religion")? We generally define secularity as the absence of religion. But should we not consider what a secular person believes and practices *instead?* Might it be fruitful to think of atheists or humanists as another type of religion? Or, given that seculars reject the term *religion,* is it not time to develop a new terminology that includes both religious and secular worldviews? Such questions are not merely theoretical, but have implications for what we can conclude from our research.

For example, many of those we call Nones actually do follow something like religion. This lends support to the arguments made by Stark and others that the growth in nonreligious population has been overstated. On the other hand, researchers acknowledge that some proportion of those who identify with a religion only do so nominally; they may check the Catholic, Jewish, or Presbyterian box on a survey but this may indicate a family heritage rather than what they actually believe or practice. Just as there are Nones who believe the Bible is true and pray regularly, there are people who call themselves Christian but do not believe in God and never go to church.[23] Religious belief and practice is irrelevant to their lives, much as it is for the Indifferents in this study. If we define such Indifference as a form of secularism, then current surveys may actually *understate* the secular population.

If most Nones are actually Unchurched Believers or Spiritual Seekers, and if we consider Philosophical Secularists as having a belief system that is functionally equivalent to religion, then None appears to be a misnomer (except maybe for Indifferents). It would be easy to conclude that the only thing so-called Nones share in common is that they do not belong to organized religion. My research, however, suggests there may be something else.

To the Nones in this study, not affiliating with organized religion was really about making one's own choices: seizing the right to select from among the many religious, spiritual, or secular worldviews that are available to citizens of modern, pluralistic societies the one (or a variation or some combination or none) the individual likes best. For Unchurched Believers this meant choosing to be Christian or Jewish in ways that may lie outside the theology of organized religion: finding God in nature as Denise does, or embracing Jesus outside of church as Roxanne and Evangelical Christians like Jefferson Bethke do. For Spiritual Seekers, making one's own choices usually means combining elements from various religions. This too is not sanctioned by conventional religion, which, in America at least, is exclusive: you are supposed to be either Buddhist or Jewish, not both. But individuals like Susan or Rebecca, *want* to be both. Philosophical Secularists like Robert or Fran are not just rejecting religion but are choosing to embrace a secular philosophy that they see as answering their questions better than religion does. And while Indifferents could be viewed as making no choice at all, we might also see them as making the most unconventional decision: to live without any kind of religious or secular framework.

This "worldview choice" orientation is distinctive in two ways. First, it assumes that most world religions as well as secular philosophies are equivalent. This does not necessarily mean an affirmation that "all religions are equally true," as Spiritual Seekers would have it, but rather an acceptance that there are diverse worldview options and that this diversity is a good thing. Philosophical Secularists like Fran or Robert take pains to point out that religion is not the only source of morality and that atheist or skeptic worldviews are actually a better option. While they reject the truth of religion (especially theistic religion), Philosophical Secularists may celebrate the many ways in which religion informs cultural diversity. Humanistic Jews who gather for a seder to celebrate their family heritage are an obvious example. So are atheist parents who enroll their children in world religion classes (more on that in chapters 5 and 6). Unchurched Believers may personally affirm faith in a particular god or scripture but do not affiliate with organized religion because they associate it with intolerance of other worldviews. Denise, for example, does not like, in her words, "the Zionist ideology" of many synagogues, and disagrees strongly with the view that "Jews are better than other people." Although Indifferents have no use for either religious or secular philosophies, they have no animus against them either, and freely acknowledge that "religion can be a good thing for some people, it just doesn't work for me," as Daniel put it. The whole point of choosing one's worldview is to select one that meets the individual's needs.

Herein lies the other distinctive characteristic of worldview choice: the assertion that the individual should choose the worldview that best suits him or her. That assertion may be most obvious in the case of Spiritual Seekers who mix and match religions according to their own personal preference. It is also obvious in the case of Indifferents who reject both religious and secular options because they are not interested in either. The priority of individual needs is less overt but still evident in the narratives of Unchurched Believers. Denise, who grew up with both Judaism and Catholicism identifies with the Jewish side because, she said, "that's what resonates with me most." Roxanne still believes in the God of her childhood but left church because it failed to support her when she needed it most. Lillian returns to active engagement with a church (though she does not call it religion) when she finds one that "spoke to" her. Ironically, it was Philosophical Secularists who were more likely to assert an absolute standard of truth as the criterion for their worldview selection. Recall Daniel's assertion of the superiority of science over religion, or Robert's questioning of religions competing truth claims. Still, even these parents acknowledged that their worldviews were ultimately about their own preferences. As Charlie put it, "most people need religion; I do not." And, as I discuss in chapters 5 and 6, many Philosophical Secularists do not raise their children to be atheists because they want them to make their own choices.

If there is something that unifies Nones, it is less a rejection of religion than an assertion of one's individual right to choose one's own worldview from a variety of options. Organized religion is rejected in part because it fails to allow individuals that choice. Our choices, however, are made in the context of time. Most Nones are young. Is this because they are expressing their individual identity against that of their parents who typically raised them with religion? Or is it something else? What does it mean to be None as you get older? How does the meaning of being None change when you decide to share your life with a partner who may or may not be a None? How does it change when you have children? I will explore these questions in the next chapter.

3

The Importance of Time

I became a None when I was fifteen, and my decision at that time felt liberating. Leaving religion freed me from tedious weekend obligations. It stimulated me to explore the traditions of other cultures. In my personal life, having no religion meant I could belong, at least temporarily, in any tradition. In my profession, being a None made it easier to be neutral and objective in teaching and researching all religions. Then I got married and had a child. Suddenly, being a None was a problem I had to solve. Now, having no religion was no longer just a personal choice but an orientation that I might or might not transmit to my child. That shift in the meaning of being a None is a common pattern. While the stories vary in detail, most Nones leave religion in their teens, and most report the experience of starting a family causes them to reexamine that decision. This chapter explores that process: why so many young people are Nones, whether marriage and family will bring them back to church, and how becoming a parent changes the meaning of being a None.

Why Young People Are Nones

Much has been made of the fact that so many Nones are young. The decision to become a None is most often made in youth, and the growth in the None population has been most dramatic among adults under thirty. In 2001, Nones comprised 8 percent of the total adult US population but 20 percent of young people. Those numbers had increased to 16 percent and 25 percent respectively by 2008.[1] By 2012, Nones were 19 percent of the total population and 32 percent of those aged eighteen to twenty-nine.[2] By contrast, the proportion of Nones among Americans over sixty-five is around 8 percent and has changed little over the years.[3] In short, age is what most distinguishes Nones from the rest of the population. Why is that?

Various explanations have been offered. One common argument is that as people get older they are more attracted to religion and its promises of an afterlife than younger people are. This "death seems far away" hypothesis is supported by numerous studies that have long shown a strong relationship between age and religiosity: We are more likely to affiliate with a church or synagogue and attend services, pray, or read scripture the older we get.[4] The theory is persuasive because it fits with our experience: we all know people who have become more religious or spiritual in old age; however, the correlation between religious commitment and age does not necessarily prove a causal relationship. And even if their distance from death was a major reason for young people to be Nones, the theory fails to explain the steady *increase* in the number of young Americans who are Nones. After, all there is no evidence that youth today are less concerned with death than previous generations of young people were.

Another explanation that is frequently given, especially by the media, has to do with our conception of youth as a time of questioning what one has been taught by one's elders. Most Nones are raised with organized religion and often attend services with their parents. But the theologies of many religions stand in some degree of tension with the findings of science and modern values of gender equality that students encounter in school and in the media. As they become more independent from their parents, especially if they leave home to attend college, young people may feel freer to question their religion and identify as Nones. A good illustration of this "question theology" theory is found in a broadcast series by David Greene that NPR aired in early 2013, shortly after the publication of a major survey showing yet another jump in the None population. Trying to find out why the young reject religion, Greene asks a twenty-something young man named Kyle: "Do you believe in God?" Kyle answers: "I don't, really. But I really want to. That's the problem with questions like these . . . you don't have anything that clearly states yes, this is fact. So I'm constantly struggling. But looking—like, looking right at the facts; like, looking at evolution and science; you're saying no, there is none. But what about love? What about the ideas of forgiveness? Things like that—I'd like to believe that they're true, and they're meaningful." Greene then tells the audience: "And yet Kyle's uncomfortable with some of the religious doctrine. He doesn't believe in hell. He also doesn't believe homosexuality is a sin." Greene goes on to interview various other individuals, including a thirty-year-old named

Rigoberto, who was abused as a child and whose mother died of cancer. Rigoberto responds: "So at some point, you start to say, why does all this stuff happen to people? And if I pray and nothing good happens, is that supposed to be, I'm being tried? I find that almost—kind of cruel, in some ways. It's like burning ants with a magnifying glass. You know, eventually, that gets just too hard to believe anymore." Greene's message is clear: young people are becoming Nones because they no longer buy into what religion teaches.

There is no doubt some young people leave religion because they reject its theology. A recent survey shows this to be the top reason why people raised with religion become Nones, cited by nearly a quarter of respondents.[5] Still, that leaves a majority of Nones defecting for other reasons. More importantly, it is not clear that theological doubt is higher among young people. Indeed, studies consistently show atheists to be older than the general population. Social scientists who have analyzed the data on age to control for other factors reject the theory that religious skepticism is what motivates most young people.[6] And like the "death is far away" hypothesis, the "question theology" theory fails to explain the sudden increase in young Nones.

If we want to understand why more young adults are rejecting religion than in the past, we need to take the historical context into account. Thus some have proposed that young people become Nones because they are turned off by the politics of religion. Since the 1980s the public face of organized religion has become increasingly conservative as Evangelical Christians have aggressively, and often successfully, sought to influence both local and national elections. Much of their agenda focused on social issues: opposing abortion and gay marriage and, in a few but widely covered cases, anti-Muslim rhetoric. Yet these issues do not resonate with the millennial generation (those coming of age at the turn of the twenty-first century). They have been educated in a school system that promotes multiculturalism and tolerance as American virtues. They have grown up in a media environment that has tended to take a more progressive slant on social issues, especially gay rights. And they are entering adulthood in a society that is more ethnically and religiously pluralistic than it was in the past. Thus many of these young people, including a growing number of Evangelicals, may reject religion because they associate it with a politics of intolerance they reject. The data appears to support the "reject religious politics" theory. The first marked increase in Nones occurred between 1990 and 2000, and the largest increase was found among those with liberal political leanings,[7] and that trend has only accelerated. In the 2012 presidential election, young people and Nones overwhelmingly supported Obama over Romney.[8]

Yet another explanation for the recent growth of young Nones points to the fact that more people are raised without religion. Studies have consistently shown that childhood religious socialization is a strong predictor of adult religious affiliation. Individuals with religiously unaffiliated parents or parents who attend church infrequently are more likely to identify as Nones when they become adults.[9] Given that a large fraction of young people who did have religious parents will drop out as well, the number of young Nones should increase with every generation, and the recent upsurge among the young may simply reflect the cumulative effect of this growth. The available data lends some support to the "raised None" theory. Childhood church attendance has fallen with every generation since 1910, and beginning with those born after 1940, the number of people who claim no religion when they were sixteen years old has increased at a faster rate with every generation.[10] Still, nearly three-quarters of young Nones emerge from religious homes, and only 27 percent of Nones had a nonreligious parental role model.[11] Most Nones in previous generations have eventually affiliated with religion, and even those who remain Nones will not necessarily raise their children as such. The "raised None" theory too provides only a partial answer.

My own hypothesis is that the recent surge in young Nones, especially those raised in religious homes, is also a result of the "no religion" identity gaining legitimacy that it did not have in the past. For much of the last century, American culture, far more than Europe and other developed nations, has embraced church membership and belief in God as symbols for being a moral and patriotic citizen. People who have no religion, therefore, were viewed with suspicion. But this has begun to change. As the turn of the twentieth century approached, several factors converged that challenged the foundation religion rested on. One was the sexual abuse scandal in the Catholic Church that dominated the headlines in the 1990s and beyond and cast serious doubt on the equation of religion and moral trustworthiness. Then, in 2001, in the wake of the 9/11 terrorist attacks, religious terrorism, mostly associated with Islam, took the media spotlight and was met with nasty instances of intolerance from some conservative Christians (efforts to brand Obama as a Muslim come to mind, and more recently the story of Florida Pastor Jones's Koran-burning event). Yet another punch at the religion pedestal was the publishing success of several atheist authors, starting with Sam Harris's bestselling *The End of Faith* in 2004. Harris and others—including Richard Dawkins, Christopher Hitchens, and Daniel Dennett (sometimes referred to as the new atheist movement)—have actively criticized religion in several widely publicized books, on talk shows, and on the Internet, often to popular acclaim. Their arguments are articulate, irreverent and sometimes funny, a style that goes over well with the millennial generation. It is in this cultural context that we began to hear reports of increases in the number of Nones, which continues to grow annually. Suddenly, having no religion is a trend that is widely covered by the media, rather than some deviant exception to the American cultural norm. Whatever reasons may motivate young persons to distance themselves from religion, now that Nones are out of the closet, it is easier for them to *claim* that None identity (rather than, say, check the Catholic box as their relatives have done before them). In short, the growth in the young None population has become self-propelling.

Will Marriage and Family Bring Nones Back to Church?

There are also countervailing processes. The most powerful brake on None growth, based on past research, is marriage and family formation. Surveys conducted in the twentieth century, prior to the recent upsurge in Nones, have consistently shown a life cycle pattern in religious affiliation: young adults disaffiliating with the religion they were raised with and later reaffiliating when they marry and have children. Nones who left often returned to the religion of their childhood; and if they switched denominations, the religion they adopted was almost always that of their spouses.[12] This pattern was particularly characteristic of the baby boom generation, and it appears to continue for the current generation of young people (although the pattern is weaker today). A recent survey reported that Nones are more likely to be single and never married and less likely to be married or widowed than the average

American.[13] Another study argues that low levels of social obligations, including familial ties such as having children, are important factors in claiming to be an atheist.[14] And one analysis of survey data asserts that the recent increase in Nones is partly because people postpone marriage and family to later age.[15]

What is it about marriage and family that causes many Nones to reclaim religion? One reason may be accommodation to a religious spouse. The literature on religious switching (which refers not just to individuals making denominational changes from, say, Catholic to Jewish, but also to those switching from religious to None, or from None to any religion) suggests that people are more likely to switch affiliation for marriage than for other reasons.[16] A recent study finds individuals less likely to claim no religion if they marry someone who attends church.[17] Another study reports that even atheists may attend church if they have religious spouses who want to raise their children in the faith.[18] The religious partner in these mixed None marriages is more likely to be female than male (and the gender gap is even wider for atheists).[19] Add to that the fact that women continue to play a greater role in childrearing, and it is easy to see that spousal accommodation, at least for now, tends to lead None spouses to church, rather religious spouses away from it.

Even when both partners are unaffiliated, some Nones may claim religion for the sake of their children. This pattern is most common among Unchurched Believers, many of whom express a desire to transmit religion to their children which in turn will lead some parents to affiliate with a church or synagogue.[20] While teaching your beliefs and values to your child is something you can do at home, these parents also want their children to participate in life cycle rituals like baptism or bar/bat mitzvahs that are typically provided by institutions.[21] Nones who do not have traditional worldviews—like the Seekers or Philosophical Secularists I discuss in chapter 2—may still have strong emotional ties to their childhood religion that motivate them to stay connected somehow. For example, a parent's own experience of a close relationship with a godparent, or her memory of food and laughter at her older brother's bar mitzvah, may convince her that "I want this for my child." This is particularly true when religion is the carrier of ethnic or cultural identity. Thus, some secular Jews will reaffiliate because they want their children to acquire a Jewish identity.[22]

Nones who start a family may also claim religion because of the community it offers. Having children heightens the importance of the community: the extended family, the neighborhood, and the church. As Hillary Clinton said, it takes a village to raise a child, and this may be especially true in today's society where both parents work and must rely on others to help care for their children. Organized religion in America has historically been an important source of this kind of helping community, although its role may be changing.[23] Regular weekly attendance at religious services is down, but churches, synagogues, and other religious community centers have become the primary providers of day care services in the United States,[24] and many also offer after school programs for older children and summer camps for all ages. A growing number of so-called Evangelical megachurches cater specifically to young None families by offering a host of programs—including daycare, afterschool care, children's athletic teams, social activities for single parents[25]—and some mainline Christian and Jewish congregations are also moving in this direction. For Nones starting a family, enrolling their children in such a program may be the first step in re-engaging with their religious communities. In the city where I live, for example, the day care and summer camps at the Jewish community center have long been a magnet for highly educated, middle-class parents of all faiths including None. As one mom put it, "the facility is beautiful, the programming is excellent, and the religious part is really low key." Five years later, however, she had become more involved in religious activities, placing her daughter in Jewish religious education classes that were not part of the day care program.

As we can see, there are clear life cycle reasons why many Nones may reclaim religion. These patterns have led some observers to explain Nones in terms of a life cycle theory: that claiming no religion is a characteristic of youth, and that marriage and family will bring most Nones back to religion. This theory has become rather popular, especially among journalists, perhaps because it reassures the religious majority that nothing has really changed.[26]

But the life cycle theory does not tell the whole story either. For one thing, many in the current generation of Nones do *not* return to religion, even after they get married and start a family. Although it is true that Nones are more likely to be single and childless than religious Americans, that difference is largely because they are younger. For example, if you break down the numbers for 2008, you find that 39 percent of Nones were never married compared to only 25 percent of the total population. However, if you control for age, the results are 33 percent and 28 percent, respectively—a much smaller difference.[27]

In addition, the societal pressures that may have pushed previous generations of None parents back to religion are less powerful today. The rates of religious intermarriage in the United States have more than doubled over the last century, reducing the expectation that an individual with no religion should convert to that of his or her spouse.[28] The growing number of Nones who are in mixed marriages (28 percent in 2001, 59 in 2008) reflects this change.[29] Many Nones do consider affiliating with religion for the sake of their children or the benefit of being part of a community, but this may or may not change a parent's own worldview. For example, if an atheist parent attended church with his Catholic spouse and children, his *religious affiliation* would be Catholic but his *religious preference* would still be None. Moreover, as I will argue in chapter 5, such parents also have more options than previous generations of Nones did.

Finally, the life cycle theory is problematic in that it reifies the cultural prejudice that religion is normative and therefore good. If being None is a temporary stage that one goes through when one is young and leaves behind once one becomes a responsible adult with children, then what does this imply about those of us who remain Nones as we get older, especially after we have children? Does it mean having no religion is a luxury that goes with being unattached? Or that None parents who do not affiliate are stuck at an adolescent stage of development? Do None parents care less about the morals and values of their children? Surely not. There is no evidence that Nones are morally or psychologically deficient.[30] Yet the patterns that lead to the life cycle effect are real. How then do we explain them?

How Starting a Family Changes What It Means to Be None

My research with None parents suggests that, rather than looking for a causal relationship between parenthood and religious affiliation, it may be more fruitful to consider how parenthood changes the *meaning* of being a None. In my interviews with parents it soon became clear that there is something about having a family that raises questions about religious identity and commitment for people. But those questions did not necessarily lead back to religion; they could just as well lead in the opposite direction. More specifically, I propose that starting a family compels Nones to confront the issue of worldview identity (religious or otherwise) as they interact with others in that family: the child, a co-parent, and extended family members. In the process, Nones begin to articulate the boundaries of their worldviews and to determine how important they are in their lives. The result can be a return to religion. But it can also be a more conscious embrace of a secular worldview.

Research suggests that the formation of self-identity is an interactional process: We define what we are (e.g., Catholic, Muslim, or None) in relation to who *they* are (the Catholics, Muslims, or Nones that we interact with).[31] This is true for individuals who identify with a religion because they were raised that way (what sociologists call "ascribed identity") and for those who switch identifications (or "achieved identity"). So whatever a young person's reason for becoming a None, the process of starting a family creates new or more frequent interactions with others that challenge or confirm that identity, causing the individual to reflect on and reevaluate his or her initial reason.

The Nones in this study (like most of the Nones nationwide) chose to leave religion behind, making theirs an identity they achieved in contrast to their families of origin. Being None was something they chose for themselves, and whatever worldview they held (Unchurched Believer, Spiritual Seeker, Philosophical Secularist, Indifferent) was perceived as a personal choice that does not significantly affect anybody else. To be sure, some Nones had parents and other extended family members who were disappointed when they left church or synagogue. But Nones perceived such reactions to be the parents' problem, not theirs. Starting a family of their own changed this. Suddenly, Nones discovered, your worldview could profoundly shape the life of another human being: the child you are raising.

This raised important questions for parents. If you are secular, should you teach your children not to believe in God? What if the religion you rejected was a rich and wonderful part of your own childhood that made you feel protected and safe? Should you attempt somehow to recreate that feeling, along with transmitting your secular perspective, so that your children can make their own decision? But how can you do that with integrity if you no longer believe what you were taught? If you are an Unchurched Believer, should you have your children baptized or circumcised? Should they attend Sunday school? And if yes, shouldn't you attend services with them? And if you don't, doesn't that send a mixed message? If you are a Spiritual Seeker type, you may be inclined to raise your child in more than one tradition, say Buddhism and Native American spirituality. But not having grown up in either of these, you realize your knowledge base is limited. You may be fascinated by the writings of Thich Nhat Hanh or Black Elk, but since you don't have a family history in these traditions, you lack the "cultural toolkit"—the stories, the rituals, how to cook holiday foods that are the primary means by which children are socialized into religion. Or perhaps your search is still ongoing, you're not sure what you believe, so what exactly do you transmit to your child?

As you reflect on these questions, you must also consider the other parent who may or may not share your worldview. If you're an Unchurched Believer and your husband is Indifferent to religion, chances are you can persuade him to raise the kids Catholic as you were. But this suggestion may also cause him to realize that he's not just Indifferent but Secular and does not want his children indoctrinated. Or perhaps you're divorced, like Rosario. You want to let the children find their own way but your ex insists on taking them to a Mormon church. Should you resist that? Should you tell them you reject your ex's religion? Does that mean you are turning them against him? This can be problematic.

To complicate matters still further, extended family members will also make their claims. You thought your mom made peace with you dropping out of church, but now that your son is born she wants to know when you will have him baptized. And since she babysits for you while you work, you can't avoid the questions. For Nones coming from different religious backgrounds, there may be competing claims, for example, with one set of grandparents insisting on a Jewish upbringing and the other on a Catholic one. Even None parents who share a worldview (e.g., both are Spiritual Seekers) may find themselves reexamining their identity. Whatever the particulars, the process of becoming a parent will challenge your None identity as it intersects with others whom you care about deeply: your children, the co-parent, and your extended family. This process shapes and sometimes changes what it means to be a None.

Nones and Their Partners

Many Nones are married to somebody who does claim a religion. As such, they are part of a growing trend of religious intermarriage in America.[32] The research literature suggests that the increase in such unions has increased conflict over how children should be raised.[33] Parents with competing religious claims resolve the conflict in different ways. Some parents choose to raise children in one of the two religions, most often that of the mother.[34] Other parents try to avoid conflict by exposing kids to both religions and letting them choose for themselves.[35] Still others will raise their children with no religion at all. But this pattern is fairly rare; only 14 percent of interfaith couples choose not to transmit either religion.[36] Most people who have a religion want their children to share it. In some cases couples who were raised in different religions will even make prenuptial agreements about how they will raise their children.[37] Nones are more likely than those affiliated with religion to have a partner who does not share their faith.[38] And if we consider that the term *None* includes a variety of different worldviews, the number of mixed-worldview partnerships is even higher. Yet much of the research on such marriages has focused on partners with different religions, rather than on situations where one partner has none.

How do interactions with a partner parent change the meaning of having no religion? Among the None parents I interviewed, religion was not something they paid much attention to until they decided to have children, or until the children reached the age of traditional religious instruction. When they did finally discuss the religion question, the conversations often created some level of tension, making parents more aware of the differences between them.

Jay and Nancy are one example. Jay, as mentioned earlier, is a Spiritual Seeker whose worldview combines mystical Christianity with Islam and Buddhism. His wife, however, is completely indifferent to religion. In the early years of their marriage the difference seemed irrelevant because Jay's seekership was a solitary pursuit. That changed after their son was born. Nancy recalls: "My husband, he decided we needed to raise Evan in some kind of church, some kind of community, some kind of grounding." Nancy saw little value in this. "I did not think I had gotten that much out of religious training and religious community as a kid, and so it wasn't really that important for me to do it for Evan." However, because it was important to her husband, she decided that she would not stand in the way. After checking out and rejecting various churches, Jay eventually settled on a Unitarian Universalist congregation. Nancy declined to participate.

Meg and Charlie are another example. Both are Nones. But Charlie, raised fundamentalist Christian, is now a Philosophical Secularist, whereas his wife, who grew up in a liberal Protestant home, is now a Spiritual Seeker. Meg recalls, "when we first got married our minister made us talk about it, about future kids and religion, and then of course we continue to do so occasionally." But not frequently. As Charlie put it, "I just kind of put [the question of religion] aside as not being especially important, and really be more of a social concern than an actual spiritual concern." When Meg became pregnant, they started talking about it again—only to realize their differences. In Meg's words, "originally we talked about the fact that we wanted our kids to be in some sort of religious education program, whether that be in the Unitarian church or some liberal Christian church, just to be exposed to some sort of moral framework . . . it's only been recently that Charlie actually has changed his mind on that." Charlie tried to downplay their disagreement:

> Yes, well, I haven't meant to be opposed to a religious education. I just don't really want to involve our child in the kind of organized religion that tends to surround a religious education program. I guess Meg's experience was very good but still, it was a heavy Christian slant. . . . I feel like, I don't know, I just kind of feel like that's dangerous. I am inclined to look at a lot of religions right now, not the religions themselves, but the relationships people have with their faiths seemed to be very dependent, like it's a crutch, something people do under duress rather than something that is coming straight from them. And I don't really want my child growing up with this sense of rightness and wrongness coming from an external force, and coming from almost coercion, and I don't want my

child relying on an external idea of for what is right, what is wrong, what do I do now, where do I go for help.

At the time of my interview, this couple was far from consensus.

In both of these couples we see tension between one parent who wants religion for their child and the other who does not. Yet it is a creative tension in that it pushes each individual to examine more deeply what their worldview is and how much it matters to them. For Charlie this process helped him realize that he is not a Christian anymore. In his words:

> It has actually been a result of the conversation my wife and I have been having about how we would want to raise her child. When we first got married I thought, you know, in the future when a child comes, I definitely want there to be a sort of Christian influence there because that's been an important part of my family. But the more I have been thinking about it and the closer we actually get to the arrival of the child, I kind of feel like I am not comfortable with the idea of raising a child Christian, because I just don't believe in it myself.

In contrast to conventional wisdom that having children would bring Charlie back to church, it seems to push him in the opposite direction.

For Nancy, the tension with Jay's worldview caused her to be more open to religion. "He started going [to religious services] and wouldn't quit," she said, "so I just decided to go and check it out." For many weeks she remained skeptical. "I was like: I work all the time, I don't really want to give up half of my weekend too." But eventually she grew to like it. "We have a lot of friends there now, and it's become an important part of my life." Nancy's behavior would seem to illustrate the life cycle theory—except that she remains secular. Church for her is "about community, not religion." She accommodates her husband's wish because she is indifferent to religion rather than opposed to it. Both couples felt that wrestling with their partners over this topic had given them more clarity about their own worldviews. And, significantly, both felt they probably would not have had this conversation at all if it weren't for the birth of their children. For these and many other Nones, starting a family offers an incentive for parents to discuss their religious or secular worldviews with each other, and that process in turn may either shift or consolidate their identities.

The Encounter with the Extended Family

However Nones resolve differences with spouses or co-parents, they are not the only ones to influence decisions about childrearing. Members of the extended family often stake a claim in the process as well. Even when neither None parent feels particularly committed to either a religious or secular worldview, their own parents, in-laws, and siblings may try to push Nones back to church or synagogue when a child is born. Just as conversations (or arguments) with a spouse may cause a None to shift or affirm his religious or secular identity, so can encounters with other family members.

Starting a family often leads individuals to spend more time with extended family than they did before they had children. Some of this is motivated by practical concerns. For new parents especially, grandparents are a source of advice and instruction on how to care for a child. In most American families today both parents are employed outside the home, and with the rising cost of day care, grandparents have become an important provider of childcare. Reconnecting with extended family is also about maintaining cultural ties. Many parents want their children to connect to family history and tradition that elders can provide, and many grandparents relish the opportunity to transmit their values to another generation.[39] Thus recent research indicates grandparents spend more time with grandchildren than ever before and play an important role in transmitting religion to them.[40]

What role do grandparents (and other extended family members) play when the parents are Nones? For religious parents, taking the kids to spend time with grandma and grandpa usually means interacting with individuals who share your worldview. Not so for None parents, most of whom were raised in families that remain religious. How do Nones negotiate relationships with extended family members who do not share their worldview but who may have strong opinions on how children should be raised? How do these encounters shape the Nones' own religious or secular identities and the decisions they make about their children? My research indicates that such interactions, like those between

None spouses of differing worldviews, may lead to tension, especially when the families of origin are religiously conservative (e.g., Nones who come from a fundamentalist Christian background) or when religion is tied to an ethnic heritage, as is often the case for Jews or Catholics.

Almost half the Nones I spoke to reported their own parents or in-laws pushed them to raise their children with religion. For Nones who are Unchurched Believers this was often perceived as a welcome nudge to reclaim their childhood religious identity (see the example of Denise and Renee in chapter 2). For Nones who are Spiritual Seekers, Philosophical Secularists, or Indifferents, however, such nudges often felt meddlesome and aggressive.

Grandparents, Nones reported, regularly initiated conversations about how they should raise their children. Eric, a Spiritual Seeker, said that after his son, Aden, was born, his mother would call regularly to discuss religion. "Mom wants him to be raised Jewish," he said, "and she tries hard to make me feel guilty about it." Molly, another seeker, said her Baptist dad keeps lecturing her that she isn't "doing right by [her] daughter" if she doesn't take her to church. Linda, a Philosophical Secularist, said that her mother is Catholic and wants her to have her children baptized. Every time the mother calls she reminds her, "don't forget about the Lord." A few grandparents went beyond reminders and lecturing to exert their influence. Ashley, another Philosophical Secularist, said that her fundamentalist Christian parents keep sending Bibles and Christian toys and books to her children, despite her repeated requests not to. Lori, a Spiritual Seeker whose husband is an ex-fundamentalist, complained that when her children were born, religious objects and literature began arriving in the mail: "We got the Nativity scene, the Christian cloth books and characters and things from my mother-in-law. We get *Guideposts* [a Christian journal] monthly because my mother-in-law subscribes to it." Such indirect efforts to influence childrearing were no more welcome than the lecturing.

Religious tensions caused by the parents' extended families are different from tensions with a co-parent in that the latter has a primary claim over the child that the former do not. This may reduce the incentive for the kind of soul searching among parents of different worldviews that I described earlier. Although most Nones whose parents are religious do want to maintain a harmonious relationship with them, it may be easier to avoid tensions rather than confront one's own worldview.

Thus, several Nones I spoke to simply avoided conversations with religious extended family members. Lori and her husband eventually decided to raise their two children in an alternative community of other Spiritual Seekers. But they did not explain that community to either set of grandparents: "My father still thinks my kids are baptized. He was at the dedication service for both of my kids, and he is still saying they were baptized. So I just let it go, and I don't bother explaining or clarifying because . . . I don't want to open up those conversations." Vicky, another seeker, reported "My mother-in-law goes to church every Sunday, and if she doesn't she feels bad. It drives her berserk that our daughter is not baptized. She gives [my husband] a hard time. She knows I refuse to discuss it with her, because I don't fare well with those conversations, because it is not based on reason and you can't argue it." Avoidance, however, does not prevent religious family members from bringing up the issue.

Some Nones resorted to subterfuge. Robert, a Philosophical Secularist, is a good example. He and his now ex-wife raised his children without religion. This decision "had to be kept entirely from my ex-wife's parents," he said, "because they would have gone into some sort of catatonic state to think that their grandchildren were being raised as skeptics or atheists." He explained that they had to coach the children to behavior correctly prior to visits so as not to offend their grandparents:

We would say, OK, now we are going to go visit grandma and grandpa. And of course grandma and grandpa lived clear out in Iowa, which was lucky, we could not have pulled it off if they lived in West Haven. But we would say, you're going to see grandma and grandpa, and we would have to prime them in ways that seem ridiculous because the kids knew nothing about Christianity. It was like, they will want to say a prayer at dinnertime, so just go ahead and say what they say and don't offend them. But we would always be afraid that something would pop out, because of their incredible ignorance of Christianity. . . . You have to go through this elaborate hypocrisy. Though it was in order to be kind. It wasn't that we felt guilty and therefore pretended to the religious, it was more that we didn't want to offend them, and they were too far gone. I could not reason with them, to say something like, well we respect that you are religious but we just don't look at it the same way, different strokes for different folks. No, because it would have been hellfire and damnation as far as they were concerned. God knows they might have kidnapped my children in order to baptize them or something. . . . We even had to go to church out there, Sunday mornings we would go to church with them. There were some funny moments. This was just recently, maybe two years ago, everybody stands up to recite the Lord's Prayer, and my son is looking through the hymnal, saying, where is this? He was no more familiar with the Lord's Prayer than he was with anything else they were saying, and everything else was in the hymnal. It's a Lutheran church . . . and we were thinking like, oh my God, what are grandma and grandpa going to say about this, the kid doesn't know the Lord's prayer, how do you explain that.

This kind of subterfuge is stressful to maintain, and as Robert acknowledges, it may be impossible to pull off when None parents live nearby their religious extended family.

The most common approach among the Nones I interviewed was to seek some kind of symbolic accommodation with religious relatives. Jon admitted giving in to his mother's prodding: "We did have a bris for Aden and I had a naming for my daughter, and [my mother] thinks it means we will raise them Jewish." But, in fact, they are raising their children within their own mystical blend of Eastern and Western religions. Jon believes his mother is in denial: "I think she is hoping we will just grow out of it. I mean I think she's a little hurt, like she pretends it is not there. . . . Like we are going every year to see a guru, and she knows we are, and somehow she still hopes we will raise them Jewish." Jon's accommodation is a token, a nod to his Jewish heritage as he follows his chosen Spiritual Seeker path.

All of these strategies—avoiding conversations, subterfuge, and symbolic accommodation—are ways to avoid tension with extended family. And yet the very act of avoiding tension serves to make individuals more aware of what they believe and how much it matters to them. Like the encounter with a partner, Nones' interactions with their extended families shape their religious or secular identities. And often both types of interactions intermingle in complex ways.

Samantha and James are a good example. Both were mostly indifferent to religion, and like many Nones never bothered to discuss the issue before. Samantha explained: "My husband grew up in a very Catholic household, every Sunday in church, and then he married me, and he did not want to continue to do that. And I wasn't religious so we ended up not doing anything, and same with our kids—until now that they have got to that age were they might go to Sunday school or something." The first impetus to discuss religion for their children came not from her or him but from the extended family. "It was when my husband's side of the family began asking, 'so when are you starting the kids in CCD?' that we began thinking about it."[41] Initially, the couple's response was, "we're not sure we will," but the pressure continued so they began having conversations about it. Those conversations led each of them to reflect more seriously on what they wanted to pass on to their children.

In the process, Samantha came to realize that she wanted "the kids to have a sense of their Jewish heritage." James has remained Indifferent but thinks that if they connect the children to Judaism, they should do the same for Catholicism. After exploring various options, they thought the Unitarian Universalists might be a good option because they offer an inclusive approach to all religions. But this did not go over well with James's parents. According to Samantha: "His family was in tears when they learned of this, because they feel it's not a religion, it's an education, is what they were saying." At his parents' request, they agreed to seek advice from a priest they knew and liked at his parents' church: "So we said, okay, if that's going to make you feel better we will talk to him. So we did, and the priest said, 'I'd rather see you go to a Reformed Synagogue than become UU [Unitarian Universalist].' So he was of the same ilk, he felt we needed a real religion." After having many more "heated discussions about this" with their extended family, Samantha and James made a symbolic accommodation: their children have been baptized. But that, in turn, caused a problem in Samantha's family: "My mother grew up in an observant household, so it was hard for her to see the children baptized. She grew up in a Jewish community, never did consider dating anyone or marrying anyone or even being friends with anyone who wasn't Jewish. So . . . we could not let them know when she was alive about the baptism. Thankfully, my father's side of the family is more open."

Meanwhile, James's parents kept pushing for more than a token baptism, which concerned Samantha: "My husband thinks the only thing that would make [his parents] really happy would be if we raise the children Catholic." When I asked her if she would consider doing that, she admitted: "I'm not ready to do that. . . . My family is not particularly religious, so it would be okay not to choose anything. But there still is that part of me that identifies with being Jewish. . . . Plus I have a lot of disagreements with Catholic social teachings like birth control, gay marriage, all those kinds of things. I just want something less restrictive. I just can't embrace it, and I feel that if I send my kid somewhere, I need to be a part of it."

We can see how the interaction with her partner and extended family pushes Samantha to define the boundaries of her worldview, to articulate more clearly what she rejects (rigid social teachings such as those of the Catholic church) and what she affirms (her Jewish heritage). She also discovers her commitment to religious pluralism and worldview choice: "I would be okay going to the Reformed synagogue, but part of me isn't sure that I want to send my kids to Hebrew school, go through a bar mitzvah; it doesn't feel right to push them in one direction." She also wants her children to honor the "Catholic side of their family," and James is "not sure that the Reformed synagogue would be something that he could really participate in." Samantha thinks the Unitarians would offer something to both of them, but admitted: "My husband still isn't sold on UU. He's not sure what will work for him. So he wants to investigate, he wants to go check out the Reformed synagogue, he wants to explore. . . . I appreciate that he's willing to look into it, I'm just not sure that's where we'll end up." It's clear that this couple is no longer indifferent to religion. The process of interacting with each other and their extended families has led both Nones to realize that the question of religion matters to them after all.

The Encounter with the Child

Starting a family creates a context for Nones to reevaluate what their worldview means to them as they interact with their partners and their extended families. Yet the most powerful relationship to shape a parent's religious or secular identity may be with the child. The literature on religion and child rearing is extensive, and most of it focuses on how parents shape children.[42] For example, research has examined whether religion has a protective impact on low-income children, how religion correlates with authoritarian parenting styles and how this affects children, how parental divorce affects child religiousness, and so on. However, nobody seems to have addressed the question of how interacting with their child changes the parents.[43] According to many of the parents I studied, however, it was precisely this relationship that most profoundly affected them.

Thinking about and interacting with their young children compelled None parents to consciously confront and continuously reevaluate their worldview in ways that are different from those induced by interactions with their partners and extended families. Nones may shift or reconfirm their religious or secular worldviews as they define who they are in relationship to their partners and extended families. But these individuals are adults and thus have (or are perceived as having) religious identities that are fully formed. They help shape None identity by either supporting or resisting it. Young children, by contrast, are unformed. Yet it is through this very openness that they can influence an adult None's worldview by making the parent aware of how much power he or she has over the child. Your three-year-old will not try to draw you back to church, as your mother might, nor will she affirm your decision to stay out, as your secularist spouse might. Instead she looks to you to tell her a story, celebrate the coming of a new year, explain where grandpa went when he died. Because a None's worldview can be transmitted to another, it suddenly matters.

Children ask questions and they imitate adult behavior. But, as the old saying goes, they learn more from what we do than from what we say. In doing so, they can help move our worldview from the theoretical to the concrete, from the mere assertion that "I have no religion" to a realization that my values have real life consequences. Children, as one of my respondents put it, offer a "mirror that reflects back what you actually believe rather than what you think you believe."

Children ask simple but powerful questions about life and death and meaning and belonging. My daughter, Sheila, has asked me: "What if I was born to a different family, would I still be me?" "Why did Snowflake [her pet chicken] have to die?" "My friend Carlin goes to church on Sundays. Why don't we?" " Do you believe in God, mommy?" We tend to think of parent answers in terms how they influence children. But these kinds of questions, say None parents, push them to articulate, clearly and honestly, what they believe. As Brenda, a Philosophical Secularist, told me, "I think it kept the questions alive, so I had to face them. I might have just drifted into a certain way of thinking, I might not even have gone back to church; having them certainly was the impetus to get back to church." An Indifferent mom admitted: "My daughter's questions made me think more about it, to take a new look at where I stand on the topic. And what role I need to play. I don't think it changed my perspective, but *clarified* would be a good word."

For some parents, children's questions led them to affirm the God of their childhood. For Renee, mother of two young children, it was their questions about why grandma died. She had to explain that to them, which led her to fall back on her faith. "It helped us to deal with the loss, and it helped them," she said. For Denise, her daughter's questions about God after her Jewish grandmother began taking her to synagogue, made her realize, "I do believe in God, even though I imagine him differently now." Other parents found that their desire to be honest with their children led them to finally affirm their own atheism. Robert recalls when he had this conversation with his son: "When a child asks you, 'who is God?' I just had to tell him, well, people believe that God created the world but I don't happen to believe that."

Sometimes None parents come to realize they are no longer sure what their worldviews are and interacting with their children may actually help them figure it out. When I asked Lori if she believes in God or higher power, she laughed.

> I have been struggling with that one. I am kind of at one end of the ex-treme of being agnostic. I don't think I need to believe in God right now. In previous times of my life I did need to believe in God. It's hard for me to get past the cosmic Santa Claus or peeping Tom or whatever it is taught in mainline Christian churches. So the broader concept of a higher power I struggle with, especially now because my kids ask that question. My son in particular has picked that up, and so he and I talk about it.

Rebecca told me: "There are times when my son asked me a question about God and I get to a point where I do not know the answer. So I tell him, this is what I believe, it's hard to demonstrate that you have a clear proof of this, certain things you just have to accept. So I'm trying to share my thoughts, like to talk out loud. Since having children, I have had to articulate more what I believe." For Nicole, a Spiritual Seeker, it took some time to get comfortable with not knowing: "I feel this self-imposed pressure to figure things out, because I wanted to have answers for my kids. I wanted to say, 'Here it is, here is what I believe and you can take it or leave it,' rather than, 'Here is my path and I don't know where it is going to end,' which is more the model I present now." It seems the process of answering their children's questions leads Nones to more fully own their worldview.

Children imitate adults. They imitate both good and bad behavior in ways that are often amusing but can also be sobering. I will never forget the time I was driving on Interstate 95 and somebody cut me off and my daughter loudly hollered the F-word from the back seat. Although I had taught her early on that four letter words are not polite, I had evidently not sufficiently monitored my own behavior in the car. As with children's questions, we tend to analyze their imitation of adults in terms of what the child is learning. But parents are learning too. Religious or secular worldviews are not just a set of beliefs but also entail values, customs, and behaviors that can be imitated by children. And what is reflected back to us may lead us to affirm or question our worldview identities.

None parents told many stories of their children's behavior's putting them on the spot. Denise's daughter loves to go to services with her grandmother, pushing Denise to think about why she herself does not. Lori found her son "playing monk," dressing up in brown blankets and pretending to meditate with his friend from kindergarten who was visiting their home. Lori wondered if the other child's parents, conservative Christians, might prohibit future playdates if they found out. Then she caught herself: "What does this say about how I feel about my worldview?" Lori realized she wanted her son "to fit in" but she also wanted him to be proud of "who we are." Roxanne, an Unchurched Believer, ended up reaffiliating after one of her children asked if they could go to church: "The intensity with which Jillian felt this need to be part of a church, I think that that made me rethink church a lot." Susan, a Spiritual Seeker, eventually decided to raise her son Jewish. His learning about the holidays and playing with a stuffed Torah made her more aware of her outsider identity: "It's forced me to think about how I'm going to be a role model for him. Currently, I'm a drop-in practitioner, at synagogue or the Buddhist meditation center. . . . The identity I put forth, how I want others to see me, has been to be anomalous, to not fit into a particular tradition. So in raising him in a particular way, I'm almost declaring one, like, yes we're Jewish." This is a change, and she's not sure how she feels about it yet.

The desire to be a positive role model made parents pay more attention to their own behavior. This often entails translating what was previously more of an intellectual interest into how they actually live their lives. Linda admitted: "Before I had kids, I kept thinking about how I should buy organic food, but often I didn't, too expensive, not available at local supermarket. . . . But then when I got pregnant, I really started paying attention to what I eat. It's the same with religion." Prior to starting a family, Molly's identity—"I'm a seeker"—was expressed mostly in her choice of reading. "But having kids," she said, "made me look for ways to put it into action . . . not just reading but joining a community, and to think about how I act, what values I model to my children." Isabel, an Unchurched Believer, told me her "kids have made [her] more conscientious of making rituals and atmosphere in the home, and they've opened [her] up to seeing them as blessings and spiritual beings." Lori summed it up nicely: "Every kind of upbringing is walking the talk, is living what you say you believe. Because we all have our biases, and our prejudices. As much as we try to get beyond them, they are still there. And having kids is just like having this mirror that you keep looking into." She laughed. "And everything you see in your child that you don't like, you eventually figure out that it came from you." Lori feels that mirror is "probably the hardest part of being a parent." But it also holds the potential for growth and change.

The growth and change in a parent's worldview that comes with raising children may lead Nones back to church. Rachel, a Spiritual Seeker who recently joined a Unitarian congregation, is a good example:

> Our daughter, she is what brought us to the church, but she's not what keeps us there. I mean she's part of what keeps us there, but she's actually given us a gift by being the catalyst that brought us to this church.

Because what we didn't actually realize, we kind of needed that. And I've never been a joiner, but it's nice to have a place to go where you can feel like you can believe what you want to believe. And I'm really, really glad that there is a place for my daughter for her to develop her spiritual path.

But the worldview reexamination that comes with parenting can also push Nones further away from organized religion. Eileen, a single mother, told me that when her twin sons were about three years old, she felt she should find a church to raise them in because "that's how [she] grew up." So she did some shopping around. They attended a liberal Protestant church, a Quaker service, a Unitarian meeting. In the process Eileen found herself critically examining the role of religion, wondering: "Exactly what function religion serves that I would want to retain for my children, that would be worth the problems inherent in it that I have encountered. Because they are more vulnerable to it because they have no father around. And what I have decided is very valuable is just that human connection with people who feel about the world the same way you do. It nurtures you." The churches she visited did not give her that, and her sons, as she put it, "hated it, they found it boring." In the end she found that having children, she said, "has actually, surprisingly for me, led me away from wanting to be part of organized religion because I figure I have enough to deal with." Contrary to life cycle theory's prediction that parenthood brings people back to church, the soul searching precipitated by starting a family can actually strengthen the conviction to stay out.

Among the parents I studied, Charlie's experience offers the most dramatic illustration of this process, and I will end my discussion of the life cycle by reconsidering his example. Charlie told me that becoming a parent was pivotal to affirming his atheist identity:

A lot of my belief structure just kind of came crashing down because we're having a child. I went into our marriage sort of a pseudo-Christian, feeling very comfortable with that tradition, that faith. But as I came around to the idea of, okay, now I am going to pass this on to another person and have someone else think this way, I realized that I can't stand by this. I don't want to lie to my child. This is just some stuff that I've cobbled together out of a family tradition or what feels nice and comforting, and none of it is actually something that I would say, oh yes that is true.

Charlie came to realize that he does "not believe in much of anything out there." Perhaps even more important, he realized, "that's okay." Arriving at that point was a struggle for Charlie, who is in a sense "coming out" in a culture that still sees being an atheist, especially an atheist parent, as not okay. Americans expect young people to explore and even rebel against the religious traditions they were raised with, but we also expect them to settle down and appreciate those traditions when they become more mature and start a family of their own. Maturing into a parent who is Secular, Indifferent, or even one who continues to be a Spiritual Seeker clashes with those expectations, raising questions about what went wrong. Why are Americans turning to Eastern religion? Why are church attendance and giving declining? How have traditional churches failed the young? Such questions were widely raised when large portions of the baby boom generation dropped out of church, and generated a huge volume of commentary from academics and the popular press. The debate quieted down somewhat when many boomers returned to church after they started their own families, but it has been reignited by the renewed increase in the numbers of Nones in the current generation.

Underlying the questions about what went "wrong" is the assumption that Nones *should* eventually come back to church—an assumption that, I hope, has been challenged by the examples and reflections presented here. Explanations for the None phenomenon have used a simplistic application of the life cycle theory, which treats being a None as a developmental stage of youth that will eventually be reversed when individuals start a family. Instead, my research suggests that starting a family is life changing indeed, because it motivates None parents to reexamine their worldview identities as they interact with their partners, extended families, and children. That reexamination leads some individuals to church; for others, however, it may lead to a more conscious affirmation of a secular identity.

This chapter has explored how parenthood changes what it means to be a None. But families do not live in isolation. We interact with schools, neighbors, and people at work. We watch TV, listen to talk radio, surf the Internet, or stare at billboards while we are stuck in traffic. And while we like to think of ourselves as independent from media influences or above what others think, these interactions also shape our identities and the parenting decisions we make. The meaning of being a None, then, is shaped not just by the passage of time but by social context and the places where we live.

America has long been a highly churched nation, and continues to be so even as the Nones' fraction of the population grows. But that growth has been highly uneven. Nones are far more numerous in some places, like the urban Northeast or the Pacific Northwest, than they are in the rural or suburban South, or what we commonly identify as the Bible Belt. Because there is strength in numbers, the degree to which Nones will feel like (and be treated like) a minority may vary from place to place. What is it like to raise children in New England, where the number of Nones rivals that of Catholics, the region's largest denomination? How is it different from raising children in Northern Florida or in Alabama where 60 percent of the population belong to a Protestant church? Is it harder or easier? Do numbers even matter? And if so, how? I explore these questions in next chapter.

4

The Importance of Place

In a recent survey Americans were asked whether they think the growth in numbers of Nones is good for this country. A majority thought it was not.[1] I was not surprised, but as someone who is herself a None, it made me wonder when such attitudes might change. This perception that lack of religion is somehow a problem is a peculiar characteristic of Americans. In Europe, where secularism is widespread, it is news when churches are growing.[2] By contrast, American media and scholars are fascinated by Nones because they, or at least their large numbers, are a novelty, a dramatic departure from the American cultural norm. This is particularly true of Nones who are parents, at least those who resist family and cultural pressure to return to organized religion when they have children.

Although Nones, as I have shown, are a diverse lot, they do share something: their rejection of organized religion. That refusal puts them at odds with two powerful narratives about what it means to be an American (citizen of the most religious country in the developed world) and a parent (who should want religion for their children because it is good for them).

For many people in the United States, being a moral and upstanding citizen is synonymous with having religion. American civic discourse has deep roots in what Robert Bellah called the "biblical ethic," and political leaders have made liberal use of biblical metaphors to cast the history of this country as right and good.[3] Thus we frequently hear that our founders were not conquerors but pilgrims who escaped religious persecution and sought to establish an ideal society in a promised land. America's continued expansion westward, pushing natives off their lands, was not imperialism but manifest destiny, carrying out God's plan. Our foreign wars were not just about protecting American commercial interests but also about fighting godless communists or empires of evil. Although the United States prides itself on its religious diversity, the vast majority of people in this nation belong to only one religion, Christianity, and tolerance of others varies from place to place. In places like Texas there have been efforts to officially declare America as a Christian nation.[4] But the confluence of religiosity with patriotism is not just a red-state Republican obsession. It is evident in every nationwide election where candidates of both parties feel compelled to trot out their church-going credentials. Surveys show Americans would sooner vote for a Mormon or Muslim than someone who has no religion at all, apparently because many equate being religious with being a moral human being.[5]

The idea of a good American as church-going American is related to popular notions of good parenting. With very few exceptions, the popular parenting literature tells us that religion is good for children (a claim I will examine more closely in chapter 7). Conservative Christian books and magazines, of course, admonish parents to teach their children to love Jesus. The message imparted by other authors is more inclusive, often substituting the term *spirituality* for *religion* and encouraging respect for all religions, but nonetheless pro-religion. Parents learn from news magazines and television news shows that report on studies showing religious children do better than those raised without it.[6] Best-selling psychologists describe children as "naturally spiritual" and see religion as not only imparting moral values but encouraging self-esteem and kindness to others.[7] Some of the most popular rites of passage for children (e.g., baptisms, bar/bat mitzvahs, or quinceañeras) are rooted in religious traditions, creating occasions for family celebrations that people have enjoyed for generations. Thus it may not be surprising that a nationwide public opinion poll found that 74 percent agreed, "it is a bad idea for families to raise children without any religion."[8] Parents who have no religion, then, especially those who might consider raising their children with no religion, are in a real sense cultural outsiders.

If we consider the history of this country, many cultural and religious outsiders were eventually integrated. America has shifted from being a predominantly Protestant nation in the nineteenth century to accepting as "mainstream" three religions—Protestantism, Catholicism, and Judaism—in the twentieth century, and, more recently, to conceding that all religions are good.[9] Although prejudice persists, there are signs that even Muslims and Mormons are included in this acceptance as long as they are moderate. Consider, for example, Imam Warith Deen Mohammed, a prominent spokesperson for American Islam, who in 1993 and 1997 was invited to deliver an Islamic prayer as part of an interfaith prayer in Congress. The 2012 presidential bid of a Mormon candidate, Mitt Romney, is another example. Those with no religion, by contrast, appear to be the last outpost for legitimate suspicion and prejudice—despite the fact that they vastly outnumber other worldview minorities.[10] How big does the None population have to get in order to be accepted? A recent speech by President Obama at the National Prayer Breakfast that pointedly included those with "no faith" suggests change might be afoot, at least in some quarters. But there are other parts of the country where such inclusiveness is taken as yet another sign that this president is suspect.[11] If Nones become part of the mainstream, how does it change what it means to be a None, especially a None parent? If Nones remain outsiders, how do None parents deal with cultural prejudice and how does this affect the decisions they make about their children?

One way to explore these questions is to look at None parents in different parts of the country. Studies consistently find significant regional differences in distribution of Nones. While the Pacific Northwest has long been known as a high None zone, the states with the highest proportion of Nones are now found in New England (with Vermont topping out at 34 percent Nones in 2008). The lowest concentration of Nones is found in Southern states (e.g., Florida with 13 percent, Alabama with 11 percent).[12] The direction of these trends appears to continue. While the number of Nones are increasing in all regions, they have increased less in the Midwest and in the South.[13] It appears that, for now at least, the American South retains its reputation as the Bible Belt, with higher rates of church attendance and people more likely to say religion influences how they vote, while the urban Northeast and the Pacific Northwest live up to their reputation as secular havens.

I was curious whether the experience of None parents would reflect such differences. So I designed my study to allow me to do some comparison, conducting the bulk of my interviews in four regions that differed significantly in terms of the relative size of their None populations. Two states, Massachusetts and Colorado, are what I call *high None zones* (nones constitute close to 25 percent of the total population of the region) and two, Florida and Connecticut, were *low None zones* (Nones constitute less than 15 percent of the total population).[14] My interview guide included questions about insider or outsider status (e.g., does having no religion ever make you feel different from other people in your community?), but there were also many unsolicited comments that could be coded as measures of insider or outsider identity (e.g., one respondent said, "I am concerned that other children will not play with my son if they find out that we don't go to church"). My expectation was that parents in high None zones would feel less like cultural outsiders than parents in low None zones. I was wrong. The differences I found were compelling—but more complex and interesting than I had expected.

Outsider Narratives

About a year or so into this project, when friends and colleagues would ask me what I was learning, I would always hedge, telling them I did not have enough data yet, or that it is too soon to see any clear patterns except for one: I had noticed that some parents were telling *outsider narratives*. By this I mean stories in which individuals define their own worldview and how they are raising their children as *different* from other Americans, and they perceive this difference as both a source of discomfort and a point of pride. As my research progressed, I realized that these kinds of narratives, expressed mostly by Seekers and Secularists, were much, much more common in some parts of the country than in others.

The cities where None parents felt most like outsiders were Jacksonville, Florida, and Colorado Springs, Colorado. We might expect this of Jacksonville, a port city of more than 830,000, located in the low None zone. But Colorado Springs, a city of about 430,000 way up in the Rocky Mountains, is in the high None zone. What both cities share is the strong and vocal presence of Evangelical Christians who make up the largest portion of the local population.

Parents in both cities perceived the public culture of their communities as dominated by conservative religion where being a None is frowned upon. For example, Teresa, a Jacksonville resident, is thirty-four, married with two preschool age children, and works part-time as a sales associate in a department store. Her own worldview is that of a Spiritual Seeker, a position that she feels is not accepted here. When I asked why, she told me that Jacksonville is part of the Bible Belt: "There's like this line that cuts through Florida around Daytona Beach, it gets more liberal as you go South toward Miami, but here it's like in South Carolina when I was growing up. It is clearly not okay to be unchurched." Olivia in Colorado Springs shared a similar story. She is forty-seven, a married stay-at-home mother of two teenage boys. She is an Unchurched Believer with very liberal Christian leanings, and she too finds her city dominated by what she calls "fundamentalism" and less than welcoming of Nones. Her view of Colorado Springs is telling: "You have Focus on the Family headquarters, they publish Sunday school material. Young Life is here, Mission International . . . there is probably a dozen major mission groups headquartered in here. They run the city, they run the politics, they run the schools because they are the majority, so this is an extremely religious and political conservative place." Olivia clearly did not see herself as one of "them," and she is angry because her voice is left out.

Parents in these cities frequently complained that they felt pressured to join a church. Olivia told me: "There is pressure on both adults and children to join a church. You meet a new person and within fifteen minutes, they may not ask you flat out where you went to church, but in fifteen minutes something about church will enter the conversation." She is careful not to share her own worldview with neighbors or co-workers: "I am not going to get into that discussion with people, they will dismiss you as not quite right because you don't believe in the whole Jesus as God thing." I heard similar complaints from parents in Jacksonville. Gino, a fortyish truck driver and divorced father of two boys, is a Philosophical Secularist but he usually keeps that to himself, as he put it: "Down here you need to belong to a church, otherwise people think you're strange." Daniel, another Secularist also feels pressure to belong where he lives: "People here will notice [that you're a None] because everybody is affiliated with the church, and the phrase *what church do you belong to?* leaps out of the mouth. You meet your neighbors and the first thing they ask: have you found a congregation yet? They all want to recruit you." Daniel is clearly annoyed by this. It makes him yearn for Chicago where, he claims, "nobody would even notice that we were unchurched."

It is striking how parents in both cities believe that the majority of people in their communities disapprove of having no religion. Their perception that they need to hide their worldviews in order to fit in is reminiscent of other minorities who have sought to "pass" (e.g., Jews as Christians or blacks as whites) in an oppressive majority culture. Of course, the comparison only goes so far. I found no evidence of Nones being persecuted or discriminated against, so these narratives must stand as expressions of subjective parent experience. But we should not dismiss that experience either because it reveals what being None means to these parents. Nones in these cities expressed a sense of being embattled, of needing to defend their decision to be unaffiliated. They also see themselves as bucking the trend: they are nonconformists in an oppressively religious culture, in other words, "true individuals." These perceived outsider identities shaped how they raised their children.

Fighting Back versus Fitting In

One big concern parents had was that their children would not fit in among their peers. Because church-sponsored activities are such a large part of youngsters' social lives, what church you belong to is an important part of children's identities. Parents told me that "school children actually discuss religion amongst themselves," and so Nones were worried that their sons or daughters would not be able to participate in such conversations, or, worse yet, be ostracized by other children. Beth, a Spiritual Seeker in Jacksonville, said that after her daughter's friends at preschool talked about church, she came home clamoring, "Mommy, I want to go to church, I want to go to church." Beth explained, "We don't believe what those people believe" but she also is afraid her daughter will not be able to answer the kind of "questions her friends have about this." Lori in Colorado Springs told me that her son Michael "is definitely a minority" among his friends at school, and she worries about that:

> I have a much greater sense of what it feels like to be a minority now. I have the sense to not let everybody know about it, but my son doesn't have the filters yet, he doesn't have those screens to know that you don't share with everybody. So sometimes I am afraid that he will get hurt, that he will be ostracized or something. One time, my son was playing with this little boy . . . and they had invented a new religion, and they had a book of readings. Michael had written something and he was dressed in

some elaborate get-up because he likes to do that, and they said that is how Dotist monks dressed, because that was the new religion, Dotism.

As she told me this story, Lori laughed nervously: "So the other little boy was really into it. But I am really afraid he's going to go home and tell his mom and they'll never let him play with Michael again. . . . So I do worry, I do not want my kids to get hurt emotionally or any other way, and I worry that he will do something else that will not go over well socially in Colorado Springs." Lori and Beth's primary fear seems to be that their children will be hurt. They may not make new friends, they may be teased or bullied, or their self-esteem may suffer because they are different from other children.

A second common concern among these None parents was that their children would go over to "the other side." Parents in Colorado Springs and Jacksonville talked a lot about their child experiencing peer pressure—not pressure to do drugs or have sex, but pressure to conform to the local conservative religious values. Beth, whose daughter is in pre-school, worries that "there is going to be peer pressure on her, in school, because this is an extremely conservative, right-wing, fundamentalist Christian [place], everything to the right to the right to the right. You have to really find your niche here when you're not that." Andrea, a Philosophical Secularist, told me the greatest challenge of raising two teenagers in Colorado Springs was peer pressure to become a Christian: "The kids would come home from school in a very conservative community, and we've raise them to be very liberal, and so it would be hard for them oftentimes in school, because—how do they answer kids who were challenging them?" Andrea's children are agnostics, but that's hard to maintain, she said, "because some of these kids who come from a fundamentalist background, they are so strong in their beliefs, that it was often difficult for our kids to counter them." She is relieved that her kids are almost done with high school because "college is usually a more open-minded" environment.

Olivia's children are in middle school, and she is afraid that her son will be brainwashed. She recalled that one day, when her son was in second grade, she asked him, "What did you learn in school today that you didn't know before?" He told her, "I learned that dinosaurs lived at the same time as people." She thought maybe this came from his classmates, but he insisted that was what his teacher had said. So Olivia confronted the teacher, saying jokingly: "You are not going to believe what James told me; he told me that you told him dinosaurs and humans lived at the same time. And she looked at me absolutely straight faced and said: 'but I do believe that.'" Olivia ended up going to the principal who did nothing, although the teacher was later transferred to another school. But the incident taught her that she needed to be vigilant to counteract the religious proselytizing her son was being exposed to.

These parent narratives may sound like so much paranoia. Although, I met at least one parent who told me her children succumbed to the pressure. Brenda, another Colorado Springs mom, is a Philosophical Secularist. She said she took pains to refrain from imposing her own worldview on her children. Her two teenaged daughters took a course on world religions at a local Unitarian church, and she told them that they "could select from any number of different beliefs and come up with their own, it wasn't necessarily that I wanted them to stay within my belief system." The public high school they attended, however, was dominated by Evangelical Christians. "This is a very religious community, the high school they went to, Young Life, was very strong. . . . The cool kids went to Young Life, it was very well done." Eventually, she said, "both of them in high school went strongly Christian." Both girls would often go to Bible studies and to church with their friends. Brenda recalled that one of her daughters "had Bible verses taped to the mirror in her bathroom." She admitted, "that was difficult for both my husband and I." But they tried to be supportive, even allowing Young Life to run a meeting out of their house. Both girls are now in college, and Brenda is relieved that, in her words, "they seem to have come back around" to a more liberal kind of belief system.

Whether it is the threat of fundamentalist brainwashing, or the risk of social exclusion at school, many None parents feel they need to protect their children from harm. A common way to do that is to seek out a community of like-minded people and educate children about religion and other worldviews reasonably so that they can choose for themselves. In Jacksonville, Daniel told me he searched online to locate a chapter of the AHA, which turned out to be a forty-five-minute drive away. "That was something that I very much wanted for my kids . . . to be part of a community like that without having to compromise [my intellect]." At the AHA his children learned about all the different religions as well as secular humanism. Such knowledge will protect them in times when they are vulnerable, he told me, "so that they don't magically discover something that *seems* to have all the answers; they're not going to discover anything because they will have already been exposed to Judaism, the Catholic Church, Islam." The community also provides social support, a place where one can "celebrate things with others," a "spiritual home . . . that they have a place they can go, like the police thing, you call 911."

Another Jacksonville mom expressed similar motives. She told me: "My daughter is actually a catalyst for why we joined [a Unitarian Universalist congregation]. . . . We live across the street from an Evangelical church, it's huge, you see hundreds of cars there on a Sunday morning, and she would say, 'Mom I want to go to church too,' so then I said: 'That church doesn't really fit what Mommy and Daddy believe in, but if you want to go to church, I will find one we can take you to.'" Thus began a period of church shopping that eventually ended in the local Unitarian Universalist community. As I will explain in chapter 5, the Unitarian Universalist Church, which often hosts the local affiliate of the AHA, appeals to all kinds of Nones. Beth likes them because they are open to all worldviews but, she said, "the biggest reason [she] joined was so Emily [her daughter] can tell her friends that she has a church."

I heard similar stories in Colorado Springs where many None parents seem to drift toward one of two Unitarian Universalist communities in order to protect their children from what they saw as an intolerant religious culture. One father decided to homeschool his son in part because of, as he put it, "my fear that he would easily be swept up in the prevailing youth culture in Montgomery or in Colorado Springs, which I find stultifying and denigrating to humanity." But he and his wife also wanted community so their son can "find open-minded kids who are also exploring and interested, a group of adults who don't have an expectation that you will be born again, who are supportive of him as he is, however he turns out to be." After exploring several liberal Christian congregations they ended up at a Unitarian Universalist congregation. This is eventually what happened to Lori as well. The Unitarian Universalist Church provides her and her children a clear identity. The meaning of being a Spiritual Seeker is difficult to articulate; in Lori's words, "It's easier for me to say what I do not believe." But she *can* affirm the ethical principles of Unitarian Universalism, and this allows Michael to say, I belong to something. Lori feels this new identity helps her fight back against religious peer pressure: "I volunteer in his [her son's] classroom regularly, and one time this little girl came up to me and said: why don't you go to church? And I said, we go to church every week, I'm glad you asked. And she said: Michael said you don't believe in God. Why do you go to church if you don't believe in God? So I said: to live good lives and be better people and help others. And then she proceeded to tell me about her church." Lori was clearly pleased with this outcome. Becoming Unitarian Universalist allowed her and her son to fit in without compromising her secular worldview.

For other parents, finding community was more about fighting back. Olivia joined a Unitarian Universalist congregation because of the children's program where she found many other parents like herself. "It is a younger congregation; there are 130 active members, we have over a hundred children enrolled in religious education each year, so obviously a lot of us have young kids." She asserts: "A lot of parents want their children to have, I call it ammunition, they want their kids to be able to articulate what they believe so that they don't feel attacked by their right-wing religious classmates who say, you are going to fry in hell for all eternity because you don't belong to my obscure religious sect that meets in my father's living room and my father is the minister." Olivia's language is clearly angry, and there is more than a touch of self-righteousness here. But her underlying concern is similar to that of other None parents—they want to protect their children in what they perceive as a hostile environment.

Religion Is a Private Matter

The outsider narrative—so ubiquitous in Colorado Springs and Jacksonville—was virtually absent from my interviews in other cities. This might not be surprising in Boston, a major metropolis on the East Coast, which is in the high None zone. But this is also true in the case of Hartford and New Haven, two much smaller cities (population around 130,000) in a state with a low proportion of Nones. As in Colorado and Florida, these New England cities are dominated by one religion: in this case, Roman Catholicism. Yet not one of the None parents I interviewed in these cities expressed concern with being an outsider.

Whereas parents in Florida and Colorado would often bring up the issue of social tension early in the interview without my prompting them, my respondents in Massachusetts or Connecticut never did. Here, when I asked parents, does having no religion ever make you feel different from other parents in your neighborhood or at your children's school, the response was markedly restrained. Many would say no, or "it doesn't come up," or "I think most of them are Catholic but we don't really talk about it." Sometimes the question of feeling different prompted a discussion about family interactions (such as those discussed in chapter 3)—but never about neighbors or co-workers.

Several parents described visiting religious communities as part of their worldview exploration. But Nones here never reported being evangelized even when they mingled with religious folk. Barry, a programmer in his early forties, is a Spiritual Seeker who lives in Cambridge with his wife and teenage stepson. He occasionally attends religious services with friends. "I went to Catholic churches, Protestant, Buddhist," he said, "I am curious about it." But he has never felt any pressure to join. Eileen, a paralegal and divorced mother of two boys, lives in New Haven. "I have some friends who go to church, and sometimes I envy them, they seem to have a sense of certainty that I lack," she said. Yet her friends never tried to recruit her. Eileen once joined them, but she did not like it, and they respected her decision. Being unaffiliated (because one is a Seeker or a Secularist) for these parents is not an identity they must hide or defend—although it is not something they broadcast either.

Nones in these New England cities perceived religion as something you do not discuss with people other than your family (or other church members if you belong to one)—unless you are invited to. Unlike respondents in Colorado Springs and Jacksonville, most New England parents claimed to know nothing about the religious affiliation of families at their children's schools (although, as I will discuss in the next chapter, the children often do know), or even about the religion of their neighbors. While parents everywhere wrestled with the kinds of family and personal identity questions described in the previous chapter, I did not meet any None parents in New England who were concerned that their children might be evangelized at school or ostracized from a play group for religious reasons. What emerges from these narratives is a sense that religion (or a secular worldview) in this region is a very private matter.

The presumed privacy of religion had a clear impact on how parents think about its role in the lives of their children. Even Seeker or Secular parents did not describe organized religion as a threat from which they needed to protect their children. Rather, they tended to see local churches and synagogues as benign, a kind of useful resource that you can draw on when you need it—which many of them did. There were Philosophical Secularist parents who sent their children to the Jewish day care center because of its reputation for high-quality care. There were Seeker parents who considered a Catholic high school because it is a less expensive private school alternative to weak inner-city schools, or because it has a fabulous hockey team. There were Indifferent parents who decided to have their child baptized to "keep the parents happy." Barry's stepson went through a "seeker phase" in his early teens, so he reached out to the boy, sharing some of his own spiritual interests. Barry gave him some books to read on Buddhism, they meditated together a couple of times, and they went to hear a famous rabbi give a lecture. But then the phase ended, they boy developed other interests and Barry decided it was not appropriate for him to "push [his] worldview on this kid." Eileen took her two boys to Quaker service for a while; they also tried the Unitarians, and even attended a Reform synagogue for a while. But the boys found it boring, so they stopped going, and Eileen is not raising them in any particular tradition or philosophy, religious or secular.

Eileen's decision was much more common among New England Nones than it was in my Florida or Colorado locations. There, many Seeker and Secularist parents I spoke with eventually affiliated with a community of other Seekers and Secularists to protect their children. Where such protection was deemed unnecessary, parents with similarly unorthodox worldviews were disinclined to do the legwork for church shopping or to make a commitment to community. Religion or secularity for New England parents was not a source of cultural embattlement and social tension—but they also seemed less concerned with establishing boundaries that defined their own or their children's worldview identity.

Place clearly does make a difference when it comes to the mainstreaming of None parents, but in ways more complex than one would expect. As I have discussed, None parents in some places feel less as outsiders but that is not necessarily because of the numbers of Nones in the region. In other words, the mere growth of the None population is not sufficient to bring the nonreligious into the mainstream. This problem echoes that of other worldview minorities like Mormons or Muslims for whom periods of rapid growth initially did not translate into social acceptance.[15] However, outsidership seems to make None parents more motivated to seek out and join forces with others like themselves, helping them to feel stronger and bolder about their Seeker or Secular identity. In this respect, too, Nones' experiences reflect that of other worldview minorities whose tension with the wider culture increases cohesiveness of the group.[16] Nones, of course, are *not* a cohesive group. But the point is that living in a place where Seekers and Secularists perceive themselves to be in tension with the larger culture may move them in that direction.[17]

Places That Put Nones Outside

If not their numbers, then what is it that makes None outsiders? And what role could None families play in changing that status? Part of the reason why Nones remain outsiders in some places has to do with the culture of those places, or more specifically the role that religion plays in the local public culture. By culture I mean the system of symbols and language that a society uses to communicate and perpetuate commonly held values.[18] By public I mean those aspects of culture that are accessible to—that is, can be used by and therefore have impact on—everyone in that particular society, as opposed to the more private symbols and language that make up a family culture or an organizational culture (although there can be overlap). Clothing habits provide apt illustrations of this. The fact that American men but not women can go topless in the summer is an expression of our public culture, symbolizing common (albeit not uncontested) values pertaining to male and female sexuality. If Mom, Dad, and the kids regularly wear pajamas for a late breakfast on weekends, it may symbolize the value placed on relaxation in this particular family culture. The organizational culture of many tech companies allows employees to wear jeans and hoodies, reflecting the value placed on informality, nonconformity, and creativity; by contrast, most law firms still require suits and ties, symbolizing the value placed on professionalism and authority. And both families and organizations share in the public culture's taboo against female nudity.

The symbols and language pertaining to public culture are everywhere. They include civic rituals such as voting, reciting the Pledge of Allegiance, raising the flag, or singing a national anthem before a football or basketball game. Public culture includes the games themselves, as well as the office betting pools that go along with them. It includes the speeches given by presidential candidates, the articles written about those speeches, the commentary on those speeches given by ordinary readers as well as by talk show hosts like Glen Beck or Jon Stewart. It includes our schools and what children learn there and how they learn it. It includes the arts and literature, music, films, television series, and books people read and talk about. It includes fashion and food and speaking styles. Together all this conveys a powerful, sometimes confusing, and often changing message about what is right or wrong, cool or not cool, including what it means to be an American and what it means to be a good parent.

The values underlying a public culture are not uncontested—but you challenge them at your peril. Once again, clothing offers a good point of illustration. Just remember the furor over the brief exposure of Janet Jackson's naked breast during the Super Bowl. Or, to offer a more personal example, I remember taking my three-year-old daughter to a public beach and allowing her to run around wearing only her shorts. Her long hair and her name, Sheila (which I called frequently), identified her as a girl, but her chest was physically indistinguishable from that of a boy. Yet several people gave me disapproving looks, and after about ten minutes one woman came over and suggested I put a shirt on my child. I ignored her. But the following summer I bought Sheila a one-piece suit. In doing so, of course, I helped to perpetuate the value system of the public culture even though I do not share that particular aspect of it.

Religion has long served as a source of social values and a producer of symbols and language to communicate and perpetuate those values. Although the secular media seems to be the most powerful influence in shaping our common symbols and discourse nowadays, organized religion remains an important producer of American public culture. The influence, however, varies from place to place. In their ground-breaking series on religion and region, Mark Silk and colleagues have explored how religion shapes the public culture in different parts of the United States, raising interesting questions about what makes one an insider or outsider in our culture.[19]

There is no doubt that numbers play a role, that is, major religions tend to have a bigger impact on shaping public culture than minor religions. For example, the popularity of pork in America or the fact that so many people (even some Jews, Muslims, and atheists) buy Christmas trees in December reflects the cultural influence of Christianity rather than Islam. The relative size of religions can help explain regional cultural differences as well. The stereotypes of New England Catholics, the Southern Bible Belt, or California as a haven for religious seekers reflect hard numbers: New England has more Catholics and fewer Evangelical Christians than the rest of the United States (37 percent compared to 13 percent), while in the South the reverse is true; and in California no particular religion dominates.[20] Those numbers send a symbolic message about a place and its values. The ubiquity of fundamentalist Christian radio talk shows when I drove across the Southern states searching in vain for an alternative rock station or NPR was a powerful reminder that many people there did not share my values. And while I love visiting my mother in Cape Ann, the colorful pageantry of the week-long St. Peter's festival seems exotically similar to the religious pageants I encountered on my recent sabbatical trip to Hindu India. It is entertaining, to be sure, but I am still the outsider looking in. When a single religion dominates a culture, nonmembers may well feel excluded.[21]

Silk and his colleagues show that other factors can be equally, if not more, important. Whether members of minority worldviews are outsiders or part of the cultural mainstream depends not just on their numbers relative to the majority religion, but also on the particular characteristics of the local community where they live. I will consider several of these influences and how they may or may not apply to Nones.

Local concentration of a worldview minority can mitigate the experience of outsidership. Jews are a minority (less than 4 percent of the population) everywhere in the United States but in some parts of New York City or Chicago the Jewish population is sufficiently concentrated to be a local majority. The same can be said of Muslims in Detroit, or Buddhists in parts of greater Los Angeles. Unlike Jews, Muslims, or Buddhists, however, Nones are not defined by shared beliefs or practices. A scholar like me may categorize them as Unchurched Believers, Spiritual Seekers, or Philosophical Secularists but they do not necessarily use these labels to describe themselves. Even if they did, I am unaware of any particular city or town where Nones are locally concentrated (the Pacific Northwest has been dubbed the None zone, but that is a very big geographical area). The locations of my research were not characterized by a local concentration of Nones, at least not in in any visible way that is analogous to, say, a Jewish neighborhood in New York or the Muslim quarter in Paris.

The experiences of religious minorities as outsiders can also be shaped by ethnic and class divisions within their communities. For some religious minorities (e.g., Arab Muslims), racial prejudice may aggravate the experience of outsidership.[22] Most Jews and Catholics in early twentieth-century America were white, but they did not become part of the mainstream until they entered the middle class.[23] Such divisions, however, do not adequately explain the differences in Nones' experiences. National surveys suggest Nones are predominantly middle class, white, or Asian, and the composition of my respondent pool reflected this.

A more promising explanation for the insider/outsider status of Nones in different regions lies in the degree of religious diversity of the communities in which they live. Silk argues that in regions without majority religion like California or New York, celebration of diversity may become a core value of the public culture. He points out that diversity functions in different ways. In New York religion acts as a carrier of ethnic identity, whereas in California "the dominant ethos emphasizes the individual shaping his or her own spiritual existence" so religious tradition has less cultural significance.[24] Even when a dominant religion exists, the presence of multiple outsiders changes that religion's influence over public culture. Nones may not be concentrated in a neighborhood or connected by race or class; however, if they live in highly pluralistic communities, they may feel more integrated into the mainstream than those who live in a more homogenous place.

Diversity does seem to play a role in the experiences of None parents in my study. Cities like Boston and New Haven—home to elite universities like Harvard, MTI, and Yale—have attracted a cosmopolitan population that results in more religious diversity (Catholics, Jews, Muslims, Buddhists, Hindus, and so on) than Jacksonville or Colorado Springs, for example. These differences shape the public culture in visible ways. Recall Olivia's complaint described earlier that the public school in Colorado Springs failed to sanction a teacher's reference to creationism. By contrast, in one New Haven public school, the music teacher rewrites the lyrics of popular Christmas songs she teaches so as to excise any reference to Jesus or God; and the annual fourth-grade holiday pageant has children present songs and poems from Judaism, Hinduism, Kwanza, Christianity, Islam, and Chinese culture as celebrations of universal rejoicing over the "return of the light" after the dark part of the year. While Olivia felt that Colorado Springs public schools were imposing religion on her child, the message of New Haven schools, that religion is a just an expression of cultural diversity, is fully inclusive of children with no religion. The battles already won by other religious minorities for tolerance of diversity create a climate that is more hospitable to Nones than in less diverse cities.

Another way that religion shapes the public culture has to do with institutional power. Institutions produce visible symbols of a religion's presence in the culture: the Crystal Cathedral in California or Central Synagogue in New York, the St. Patrick's Day parade in Boston, television images of Billy Graham leading a revival, or the bishop speaking out against abortion or the death penalty remind us of the importance of America's dominant religions. Strong institutions can also help minority worldviews gain access to the cultural mainstream by offering human capital and financial resources. If members of the minority can access the media or academia to disseminate positive information about their worldview or support a political candidate who represents their interests, this can counter their outsider status. The strong presence of Jews in the academic and media establishment is an oft-cited example. Less well known is the impact of Muslim organizations such as the Islamic Society of North America or Warith Deen Mohammed's American Society of Muslims in shaping cultural perceptions of Islam (especially in the aftermath of 9/11, they have played an important role in helping Americans distinguish mainstream Islam from more fundamentalist varieties). Nones, by definition, lack the institutions to legitimate and promote their value system in the public culture, so their status as insiders or outsiders is dependent on the relative power of religious institutions. Silk writes that the Pacific Northwest has long been known as "America's secular frontier," with a greater proportion of Nones than any other place in the country.[25] This is driven in part by the lack of religious institutions there, whereas the institutional power of the Catholic Church in New England has helped it maintain more influence over the public culture even as large numbers of members are defecting to the ranks of the Nones.

Organized religion has institutional presence in all locations in this study, but that presence is arguably stronger and more visible in some places than in others. In Colorado Springs and in Jacksonville, organized Evangelical Christianity shapes the culture in ways that the Catholic Church, the dominant religion in New England, does not or perhaps no longer can. Jacksonville is home to at least seven Evangelical megachurches (churches with weekly attendance of two thousand or more), including some of the largest in the nation such as Bethel Baptist (weekly attendance twelve thousand). Colorado Springs, like Salt Lake City (the home of Mormonism), has been described as a "religious oasis" in the otherwise widely unchurched Mountain West.[26] In some sections of Colorado Springs, for example, there are big, gleaming churches on nearly every street corner and they are packed on Sundays. Christian preaching permeates television and radio. The national headquarters of conservative Christian organizations like Focus on the Family are a source of local pride, and they stimulate the local economy. By contrast, while the little stone church on the green is a picturesque symbol of New England, the building is often empty or rented out to Zen meditation groups or Alcoholics Anonymous. The institutional image of the Catholic Church remains tarnished, particularly in Boston, which was the epicenter of the church scandal. Catholic churches in the area are being closed, budgets of the survivors cut. The powerful and largely positive image of conservative Protestant institutions in the public culture of the South and in pockets of the West creates a climate less hospitable to Nones than in New England where the institutions of the dominant religion have become weaker.

A third and perhaps the most important way that religion's cultural role shapes the experiences of Nones in this study is rooted in what sociologists call *religious privatization*. Privatization is the removal or with-drawal of religion from effective roles in the public sphere (e.g., political and legal institutions) and its relegation to the private sphere (e.g., the family or personal identity).[27] Some degree of religious privatization is an inevitable result of the process by which modern democratic societies have separated church and state, and it is found to varying degrees in all Western societies, including the United States. Privatization clearly benefits minority religions and other groups who oppose the dominant religion; yet, it may also reduce the ability of any religious institution to effect positive influence on society. When the government enforces particular religious values this legitimates discrimination against those who reject those values. When religion is considered strictly private, dissenters will probably be left in peace, but it may also be more difficult for them make their voices matter.[28]

The privatization of religion has proceeded to varying degrees in different parts of the world and within different regions of the United States. Silk and colleagues show that in some regions of the United States, people embrace religion in a very public way: talk of one's faith is an accepted part of discourse even with strangers at the mall or city hall. In other places, public discussion of religion is considered rude and boorish. As Silk remarks humorously about his move from Connecticut to Georgia:

> The first day I went to work, the woman who lived across the street cor-ralled my wife at the mailbox and asked what church we all belonged to. With visions of a cross burning on the front lawn, my wife allowed as how, actually, we were Jewish and did not belong to any church. Within half an hour Mrs. Jones was at the door, a list of Atlanta-area synagogues in her hand. Back in Milton, a housewife would no more have opened a first conversation with a new neighbor by inquiring into her religious identity than she would have opened the day by running naked down the block. And during the time I spent as a journalist in Atlanta, I never had reason to doubt my original impression that religion occupied a different place in the civic culture of the South than it did in New England.[29]

Silk and his colleagues offer several reasons for this. They argue that the very private religious culture of New England derives in part from

Protestant-Catholic tensions of the past, but also from higher education, Yankee reserve, and liberal politics (both Connecticut and Massachusetts are considered blue states).[30] By contrast, in places like Colorado Springs or Jacksonville, Evangelicalism functions as a kind of civil religion.[31] It is understood here that we are one nation under God, not just under any god but the God of the Bible, and publically professing one's commitment to that God is a sign of one's trustworthiness and morality.[32]

Silk's experience moving from Milton to Atlanta is echoed in the differences among None parents discussed here. The reports of parents in Colorado Springs and Jacksonville about neighbors asking what church you attend and children evangelizing each other at school reflect a public culture that enthusiastically embraces religion, as is true in Atlanta. The stories of parents in New England, where religious identity and affiliation scarcely seemed to matter, show a culture where religion is privatized. It is important to note, however, that Nones are different from Silk in that he and his wife do claim a religious affiliation. That fact prompted his neighbor to produce the list of synagogues, an act that symbolically says, you are one of us, you share my values. Mrs. Jones might have had a different reaction had Silk said, "I don't have a religion," or even, "I am an atheist." If you had asked the parents I interviewed, they would have predicted Mrs. Jones coming back with a Bible tract, seeking to bring her new neighbors some good news.

The opposite may be true in Silk's former home in Milton. Nones are no more numerous in Connecticut than in Florida or Atlanta, but in a place where nobody talks about religion in public it is being too public about one's religion that can make one an outsider. One Connecticut mother told me how, after many years of no religion she had joined an Evangelical church, and decided to raise her son there. She felt that her son's Christian identity made him an outsider at his school:

> I think right now he is definitely struggling with it. Because he had to come up with two questions for homework, questions to debate. I asked him well why don't you bring up: does Jesus really exist? And in his mind he thinks not everyone knows about Jesus, because everyone is not a Christian. So I think he is uncomfortable of bringing up the topic right now. I think he is afraid that he will get ridiculed and picked on, because no one else in his class that he knows of goes to church.

The language used by this mother strangely resembles that of the None parents in Colorado Springs and Jacksonville. Whereas they complained of outsidership in what they saw as oppressively Christian public cultures, this mother feels oppressed by a culture that she believes excludes religion from public discourse.

Putting all this together, one can conclude that variations in religious diversity, the relative strength of religious institutions, and the extent of privatization of religion all combine to make Nones feel either more or less welcome in their communities. Moreover, greater privatization of religion intensifies the effect of other cultural factors. When religion is a private matter, we can tolerate a great diversity of worldviews since none of them impinges on us. As people come to see religion as a personal, private matter they are less committed to institutions, which tends to further weaken organized religion. In short, there is a kind of feedback loop that seems to benefit Nones.

However, there is a downside to privatization as well. Privatization may protect None parents from harassment by fundamentalist Christians, but it also keeps their worldview hidden from view. It does not promote the value of or legitimize a secular philosophy, spiritual seekership, or a personal unchurched faith. As Peter Berger commented more than half a century ago, privatization of religion may actually undermine the power of all worldviews to claim truth.[33] As I will discuss later in this chapter, the tension generated from public interaction and engagement of diverse worldviews (including secular ones) can actually strengthen a minority perspective and its potential impact.

Nones Who Put Themselves Outside

In his classic monograph, *Religious Outsiders and the Making of Americans,* R. Laurence Moore shows how religious minorities often chose to define themselves as outsiders and thereby increase their cultural influence. "Religious outsidership," Moore writes, "has been a "characteristic way of inventing one's Americanness," and religious movements often employ a "language of dissent" to define themselves against what they see as the established culture.[34] In their narratives, the establishment has corrupted America's ideals (freedom, equality, hard work, and tolerance of diversity) and it is the religious minority who is trying to preserve and defend them. This story goes all the way back to the foundational myth of America. Like the Puritans who fled King George and eventually came to rule the colonies, the righteous outsiders acquire identity and eventually even power.

The Mormons are a good example. A Christian sect that began with the visions of Joseph Smith in the 1820s, Mormons were, and to some extent still are, perceived as deviant. They were lampooned by the media and persecuted by the state, and their founder was eventually killed by an angry mob. Fast forward to 2012: more than fifteen Mormons have been elected to Congress, and the 2012 Republican candidate for president was a Mormon, who lost the election not because of his faith but because he was widely viewed as insensitive to the plight of poor and working-class Americans. How did the Mormons accomplish this transformation? Much of Mormon outsidership has been blamed on polygamy, a powerful symbol of cultural deviance, but Moore argues it is far less significant to Mormonism than it is made out to be. The majority of nineteenth-century Mormons never practiced polygamy and the church dropped the practice in 1875. Yet as Washington leaders worked to pass increasingly restrictive legislation to suppress it, Mormon leaders described it as a "precious and distinctive feature of their church" and sought to protect it under the First Amendment. The Mormons, Moore argues, were perceived as deviant in large part because their leaders, Joseph Smith and Brigham Young, emphasized how they were different from, rather than what they might have in common with, other Americans, "which was a great deal." For example, the principles of economic cooperation that helped the Mormon sect succeed in the nineteenth century are based on "an emphasis on self-help and self-reliance, a deference to authority, a strong preference for local control, an insistence of privately administered charity based on traditional group ties, and an aversion to any sort of social legislation engineered in Washington."[35] Under Joseph Smith, Mormons described these principles as distinguishing them from the heartless capitalism of the wider culture. These very same values are used by today's Mormons, including a recent presidential candidate, to assert themselves as quintessentially American.

Moore also examines the cases of Catholics, Jews, Christian Science, Adventists and Jehovah's Witnesses, Fundamentalists, and Black churches, all of whom were to varying degrees excluded from so-called mainstream American culture. He shows how each created distinct identities through a "rhetoric of deviance" from a culture that excluded them, a rhetoric that ultimately helped many of them organize to influence that culture. In some cases, they even became part of the mainstream. A more recent example is Evangelical Christianity in the late twentieth century, a movement that was only beginning its ascent to power when Moore published his book.

Evangelicals (a.k.a. conservative Protestants or fundamentalist Christians) in the 1950s and 1960s found themselves in many ways at odds with the rapidly shifting values of the public culture: the growing cultural acceptance of premarital sex, the call for women's equality and accompanying critique of male authority; the ideology of multiculturalism and its implication that all religions are equally valid. A group whose worldview that had once been mainstream felt itself pushed outside. And they fought back—by embracing the outsider narrative and recasting it, as so many other minority groups have, as representing core American values. Their leaders (who eventually became known as the Religious Right) claimed America had been corrupted, this time by secular humanism and feminism against which they railed in countless speeches, in books, on the radio, and on television shows. Their movement, they claimed, sought to restore "true" American values, which they saw as rooted in the Bible and Christianity. Jerry Falwell's Moral Majority (a group who claimed the fundamentalist majority had been silenced by the cultural elite of the Washington Beltway) is probably the best-known example of Evangelical outsider narratives, and it was surprisingly powerful. The Religious Right was instrumental in electing President Reagan and the younger President Bush, as well as many conservative Christian members of Congress. In the long run, the conservative revolution was successful in shifting cultural values to the right, resulting not only in rollbacks of progressive legislation (e.g., chipping away at abortion rights in many states, or presenting intelligent design as a scientific theory that could be taught in public schools) but also in redefining the language and symbols of public culture (e.g., feminism and liberalism have become dirty words even among those who support women's rights and strong social services).

Moore's model does not deny the very real ways in which various minority groups may be excluded, but it draws our attention to how such groups may use their exclusion to their advantage. As an outsider, you can blame the failings of society on those who are in power. You can promise that if everyone followed the values of your worldview, society would be better, more just, more loving. And you cannot be held accountable for those promises because, after all, you are not in power and most people do not share your values. Once an outsider group arrives at mainstream status, however, it may actually lose some of that moral high ground as new groups claim the outsider narrative.

Nones, especially those living in regions where Evangelicals dominate the culture, seem to be doing exactly that. The election of President George W. Bush, a self-identified born-again Christian, in 2000 symbolized the ultimate victory in the Religious Right's quest to shape American culture (Jimmy Carter was also a born-again Christian but he was a liberal). Bush was active in promoting the conservative Christian agenda, including the restriction of abortion rights, opposition to gay marriage, promotion of government funding for Christian schools and charity organizations, and the understanding that God had chosen America to promote freedom in the world. But he also initiated a long and unpopular war in Iraq and presided over a deep economic recession at home. By the end of his presidency, his promises that Christian leadership would usher in a kinder, gentler conservatism rang hollow, even to many of those who elected him. Especially for young people, who came of age facing bleak job prospects and hearing steady reports of their peers dying in Iraq, Bush became the ultimate symbol of what was *wrong* with the establishment. Conservative Christianity, at least when allied with powerful institutions like government or church, was now associated with rising intolerance and income inequality. So young people voted against Bush in record numbers, and they disassociated themselves from organized religion as well. Claiming to have no religion (even for many who were Unchurched Believers) was a way of saying, "I am not part of the establishment, I am an outsider"—and in the long run this narrative may once again turn out to be an effective strategy for gaining cultural influence.

Using Moore's framework suggests that None parents living in places where Evangelical Christianity dominates the public culture, like Jacksonville or Colorado Springs, may be *choosing* to identify as outsiders. As discussed, Nones hold very diverse worldviews and are unified only by their rejection of organized religion. By claiming the outsider narrative, Nones here gain a clear sense of identity, of boundaries, which are otherwise absent. In the context of a strong Evangelical public culture, which they perceive as irrational and intolerant, being a None comes to mean not just the absence of affiliation but the presence of important values like free thinking and tolerance of others. For a group that is not unified by creed or custom, living in tension with public culture pushes them to seek out or create community among other people with no religion. Being an outsider justifies affiliation with an organization because it helps them in transmitting to their children the language and symbols of their nonreligious identity, be it seeker or secularist. This trend is supported by a recent national study that showed more atheist and secularist organizations in regions with strong Evangelical presence, and fewer such organizations in regions with more Nones.[36] Tension with mainstream culture, it turns out, may actually strengthen a dissident movement.

To assert that Nones are choosing outsidership is not to dismiss the real ways those cultures may be excluding them. Indeed, it may seem as if some None parents are caving in to the cultural pressure of the Evangelical Christian majority. Parents like Daniel or Olivia may join a Unitarian Universalist congregation or the AHA as a "cover" that makes their children's lack of religion less visible among their friends. Although most elementary school children do not know that in the eyes of Evangelical Christians, Unitarianism and humanism are not legitimate worldviews, they can now say, "I go to Sunday school" or even "I go to church." They can "pass" in a church-going society, and their parents, strictly speaking, should no longer be counted as Nones because they have shifted to the ranks of the affiliated. It may seem that way—but it is not. After all, their worldviews (Spiritual Seeker or Philosophical Secularists) have not changed. And their religious preference may still be None. Perhaps most importantly, searching out fellow outsiders can actually help these parents strengthen their commitment to an unconventional worldview. This is certainly what they want for their children—to learn that being a Philosophical Secularist or a Spiritual Seeker is a legitimate worldview that is shared by others; to learn to articulate, this is what we believe, this is what we celebrate, rather than feeling they lack something all other children have (religion). Most of all, parents want their children to learn to resist the cultural pressure of the majority and to feel confident in their own, nonreligious, identity.

By contrast, parents living in cities in New England, where their None identity creates no such tension, stand little to gain from identifying as outsiders, even in locations where their paucity of numbers would justify doing so. Without cultural pressure from religious folk, None parents may be less inclined to spend the time looking for a community of fellow seekers or secularists. While the privatization of religion makes it easier to raise your children as Seekers or Secularists, it also seems to make whatever worldview you hold less important or urgent. Many families are severely overscheduled; with both parents working and kids involved in school and various extracurricular activities, it is easy to put off the transmission of a particular worldview. Plus Secularism and Seekership do not have ceremonies (such as First Communion or bar/bat mitzvah) that would mark a deadline for educating one's child on the duties or responsibilities of an adult.

As a result, parents often end up doing nothing, as I can attest to from personal experience. I started this project when Sheila was three, spurred in part by my desire to explore whether and how to incorporate spirituality into her life. As I conducted interviews in Colorado and Florida I was intrigued by the various worldview education programs parents told me about, programs that do not indoctrinate kids but teach them about various religions and humanism. I kept thinking: I need to find something like this for Sheila. But living in a city where there is little opposition to our being Nones, this impulse did not feel urgent. My husband and I both work; he hunts and fishes, I am active in the neighborhood association. Our daughter, besides school and homework, plays two musical instruments and is a member of an ice hockey travel team. Without cultural pressure, adding yet another item to our schedule is not something that is going to happen anytime soon. Like Eileen and Barry described earlier, we considered it, and I even took Sheila briefly to two different kinds of educational programs, but we did not commit to either of them. In short, parents who do not feel as outsiders may be less inclined to take active steps to transmit a nonreligious worldview to their children.

Nones like me who are doing little to transmit any particular worldview to their children find it easy to rationalize our choices. We are free thinkers, we do not want to conform to the ideology of some organiza-tion; we do not even want to impose our own worldview on our child. We are giving our kids the freedom to make their own decisions. But without community to reaffirm the plausibility and salience of their nonreligious worldview, Nones and especially their children may not retain their current worldview. The existing literature seems to supports this prediction. We know that individual commitment to a particular worldview will be stronger if he or she is part of a community that shares that worldview (this is why young people who go away for college so often "lose" their religion).[37] And numerous studies support Moore's ar-gument that communities that are in tension with the larger society are stronger and more effective at constructing a distinct worldview iden-tity.[38] While much of both bodies of literature focus on people who be-long to conservative religion, it is reasonable to suppose these findings would also apply to Nones. Although more research is necessary, the stories presented in this chapter bear this out as well.

* * *

America is still a long ways from becoming a place where having no reli-gion is considered mainstream. Nones remain outsiders in part because they choose to be, and in part because organized religion's continued influence on public culture renders some regions inhospitable to those who opt out. Moving from outside to inside the mainstream may be a mixed blessing as well. For those of us who like having no religion and who believe (in contrast to the majority of Americans surveyed) that children are fine without it, all this raises some interesting questions about what is best for our kids.

If we do nothing to formally incorporate religion or some other worldview into our children's lives, we run the risk that they will turn to an ideology we reject. In the case of Brenda, the Colorado mother cited earlier whose two daughters joined Young Life was relieved to find that both eventually dropped out of Evangelical Christianity. But research shows that many Nones eventually do join a church, and conservative Christian churches especially are actively engaged in reaching out to them.[39] If we look to join a community of like-minded parents, as some of the parents presented here have done, the question is which one. Can we even find an alternative nonreligious organization to support our

Seeker or Secular outlooks? Or should we just tread the path of least resistance, reaffiliating with a congregation we were raised in while making clear to our children that there are many parts we disagree with? Or perhaps there are other options? I will explore these questions in the next chapter.

5

What Are We, Mom?

A couple of years ago my daughter, Sheila, came home from school and initiated a conversation about religion. Her best friend, Abby, is Jewish, and that day she said she had learned, "Carlin is Christian and Gargi's family is Buddhist. So what are we, Mom? Are we Christians?"

"No," I responded.

"Why not?" she insisted. "We celebrate Christmas."

"Yes," I acknowledged. "But we don't believe or do the kinds of things that Christians believe in or do. Christians celebrate Christmas because it commemorates the birth of Jesus Christ. They believe he was the son of God. They think he rose from the dead and somehow that makes up for the sins of humanity, especially if you go to church and pray to him. We don't believe that. We don't pray; we don't go to church. We have Christmas because it's fun, we like decorating the tree and giving presents to each other."

"That's true," she said thoughtfully. And, after a pause, "what *are* we then?"

Good question. Religion is not just about holding certain theological beliefs or attending organized services. It is also about identity and values—and perhaps most importantly about community. For the majority of Americans who do affiliate with organized religion, their community provides the intellectual framework and social support system to transmit that religion to their children. Parents take their children to religious services, especially on holidays, where they hear priests, ministers, and rabbis convey a specific message. They also see other families, often friends, participate in ritual actions (singing, praying, taking communion, touching or kissing the Torah scroll) that indicate their acceptance of that message. Christian parents send their children to catechism classes or Sunday school and Jewish parents to Hebrew school—educational programs that are typically run by the church or synagogue the family belongs to—where they are taught in more detail what their

religion entails. Finally, what the kids learn is reinforced to varying degrees at home. Families may say grace before meals or at bedtime; they
may have dietary rules; they may celebrate holidays like Passover or Lent
with special foods; and they may put religious imagery such as a mezuzah in their doorways or a picture of the Virgin Mary on their walls to
remind children of their religious beliefs and give them a sense of who
they are: Jewish, Christian, Buddhist, or whatever.

But what if you are a None? The families I studied in this book were
not lacking in values. Many could articulate systems of belief or practice
that, even if not religious, are just as effective in offering them meaning
and ethical guidance for how to live their lives. But without organized
tradition or community, there is no ready-made path for transmitting
None worldviews. What, then, *are* None parents doing with their children? Why are they making the choices they do? And how are those
choices similar to or different from those of churched parents? In this
chapter, I will try to answer these questions.

Most religious parents raise their children within the tradition they
themselves follow. Our Catholic friends are raising their kids Catholic,
our Jewish friends are raising theirs as Jews, and so on. It would make
sense to assume, as many researchers have, that None parents would
raise their children to have no religion. For example, one major study
of Nones did not even bother to ask respondents how they are raising
their children unless one of the parents is religious (e.g., if a None is
married to a Baptist, the researcher wants to know if the kids will be
raised Baptist).[1] Another study did ask the question and found, unsurprisingly, that "religious Nones" were more likely than "secular Nones"
to send their children to Sunday school. The study defined respondents
as secular if they said, "religion is not important to me." Researchers did
not ask what *is* important to these parents. And they did not ask why
or how parents made the decision about Sunday school or what kind
of school it was (there are Christian, Jewish, and even atheist varieties).
However, there are good reasons to question the assumption that most
None parents will raise another generation of Nones. As I discussed in
the previous chapters, even secular Nones may hold a worldview that
gives meaning and moral order to their lives and which they may wish
to bequeath to their children. Moreover, Sunday school is certainly not
the only way that parents transmit their worldviews to children. What

goes on in the home is more significant in shaping children's worldviews than religious education programs. Several studies have shown
that children raised without religion are more likely to become Nones
themselves.[2] But it does not follow that None parents intentionally try
to raise their children as Nones. Quite the contrary: my own research
suggests that most do not.

To fully understand how and why None parents are actually dealing
with the religion question in the lives of their children, we need to approach the problem from different angles. One has to do with defining
religiousness and secularity. None parents hold a range of worldviews,
and the binary framework that labels these as either religious or secular
limits our understanding of these individuals. Why do some so-called
religious Nones choose to do little or nothing to incorporate religion
into the lives of their children? Why do some so-called secular Nones
send their children to Sunday school? And if parents choose not to incorporate religion into their children's lives, what other worldview might
they be transmitting instead?

A second angle looks at when such transmission takes place and how
it might change over time. As described in chapter 4, parent decision-
making about how to raise children is a process that develops over several years. Parents may experiment with various strategies before settling
on one. And the parents' own religious or secular worldviews and commitments may alter in the process. For example, the desire to transmit
religion to children has been shown to lead some unaffiliated parents to
reaffiliate with institutional religion.[3] Other None parents find that raising children moves them further away from religion, but this pattern has
received much less attention.

A third angle has to do with where children learn about a worldview.
The transmission of religion or other worldviews to the next generation
typically occurs in at least one of two contexts: via institutional education such as a parochial school or Sunday school, and/or via the presence of that worldview in the home through symbols, rituals, dietary
rules, and the like.[4] But the two contexts of transmission may or may not
overlap. Parents who send their children to Sunday school may not be
reinforcing those lessons at home. Parents who avoid institutional settings may take actions to incorporate their spiritual, secular, or religious
worldviews into their home life. And some parents may do neither.

Table 5.1. Strategies for Transmitting Parental Worldview to Children

	Intentionally incorporate worldview in home life	Enroll child in institution that transmits worldview	Change in parent affiliation
Conventional	Yes	Yes	Yes
	Judaism or Christianity	Sunday school, CCD, or Hebrew school	From None to Christian or Jewish denomination
Alternative	Yes	Yes	Yes
	Secular Philosophy or Seeker Spirituality	Plural worldview education	From None to UU or AHA
Self-provider	Yes	No	No
	Judaism, Christianity, Seeker Spirituality, or Secular Philosophy		
Outsourcing	No	Yes	No
		Sunday school, CCD, or Hebrew school	
Nonprovider	No	No	No

In order to give justice to all three of these angles, parents in this study were interviewed extensively and in person about their children's upbringing and how their strategies may have changed over time. Parents were also observed interacting with their children, both at home and in institutional settings. The data derived from these sources were analyzed along three dimensions: (1) the parents' incorporation of religion or spirituality into their home life; (2) the provision of religious or alternative worldview education outside the home; and (3) the impact over time of this process on the parent's own institutional affiliations. From this analysis, five distinct combinations were observed (see table 5.1), each of which represents a unique way that None parents deal with the religion question.[5]

Going Back to Church

Much of the literature on None parents emphasizes how starting a family leads them to return to the fold. Some parents in this study fit that pattern: they decided to come back and raise their children within the same tradition the parents themselves grew up with. Typically, this goes with enrolling their children in a formal religious education program and making some effort to incorporate aspects of religion into the home. I refer to this as the *conventional strategy*.

In my own research, the conventional strategy was most common among Unchurched Believers who saw parenthood as the time to go back to church or synagogue. For those who had been too busy for church, recommitment was simply a matter of reaffiliation. For those who left because of a personal crisis, recommitment often meant switching to another denomination. But other researchers report seeing this strategy among secular parents as well, particularly those who are married to a religious spouse.[6]

Here are two parents I met who illustrate the conventional strategy particularly well. Renee, age thirty-six, is a stay-at-home mom with two children. Raised Catholic, she lost interest in church as a teen and remained a None throughout her twenties. She moved away from her hometown north of Boston and married a Jewish man whom she later divorced. Her second husband, who is Catholic, briefly brought her back to church to get married, but they continued to stay away because, she said "church just wasn't relevant." After the children were born, "[the couple] started thinking about it again," but they did not reaffiliate. The priest scandal only increased their ambivalence about religion: "With what happened in the church with the priests and all, we wondered, can we still consider ourselves a part of this, because we really questioned how things were dealt with, how the archdiocese didn't do anything." As the children grew older, however, she changed her mind. After moving back to the town where she grew up, she reaffiliated with her church; they attend mass regularly as a family, and both girls are enrolled in Catholic school.

Denise, age twenty-three, is a massage therapist with a four-year-old daughter, Lisa. She was raised Jewish but ceased involvement when she left for New Mexico to attend college. Although Denise considers herself "very spiritual," she does not connect with religion. Judaism to her always has been about family: "I don't think it was ever important to me as an actual religion." She attended services and went to Hebrew school "because it was important to [her] mother." Later "[she] stepped away from it because [she] wasn't with [her] family anymore." She married and had a child, then divorced less than a year later. When she moved back to New England her mother urged her to attend services with her but Denise was ambivalent: "Judaism has become so foreign to me." Three years later, however, she is attending services at the same synagogue she attended when she was growing up, and is urging her new husband (a nonreligious man) to convert. And she raises her daughter in the tradition; "she is so proud to be Jewish."

What changed? Not that much, actually. Most of the parents who took the conventional route are Unchurched Believers: Although they claim to have no religion, they continue to hold conventional religious beliefs and engage in traditional religious practices. They drift away from church or synagogue because, as so many of them put it, "religion was no longer relevant to my life." Once they have children of their own, religion becomes relevant again, and they gradually reconnect. Renee, for example, had her children baptized as infants but did not reaffiliate with the Catholic Church until several years later.

> What changed us, was my husband lost his sister to cancer, and I think when you lose people in life, that's what brings your faith back. . . . And then after my kids were born, my mother [died]. Having to explain that to them. My natural reaction, and my husband's, was to go back to our faith. It helped us to deal with the loss, and it helped them. It's like, okay they are in a better place, with God, with the angels, and that's comforting for them to hear and for us to share that with them. So that brought us to going back to church every Sunday. We had them baptized but we hadn't been going to church, and we started to talk to the kids about church.

Denise did not fully reconnect with Judaism until her daughter was about four. When I asked whose decision it was to raise Lisa Jewish, she answered: "My mom. She told her she was Jewish before I told her she was Jewish. I said, 'Mom!' I was just shocked that she did something like that before I did. And she said, 'Well, I'm a Jewish woman which makes you a Jewish woman which makes your daughter or Jewish woman.'" She laughed, then continued, "And I'm like, okay I guess I have no say here." She said she had been considering teaching her daughter about Judaism. "But I was planning to expose her to it later." At her mother's prodding, she is doing it now, and, like Renee, she has come to shed her None identity for a religious one.

For None parents who reaffiliate, the process often begins with enrolling their child in traditional religious education program such as the Confraternity of Christian Doctrine (CCD), Sunday school, or Hebrew School. Formal religious education offers regular, usually weekly sessions in which children are taught the history, official teachings, moral rules, and ritual practices of their religion. This goes on for several years and culminates in the child's participation in a rite of passage such as First Communion or a bar/bat mitzvah. Older kids may participate in youth programs that encourage them to share their faith with others, participate in social services, or just engage in fun and games making friends with other teenagers who share their religion. Protestant churches have long offered summer Bible camps, and many Catholic and Jewish congregations offer summer enrichment programs. Staffed by volunteers and financially subsidized by the donations, such programs provide a wholesome and affordable option for keeping kids occupied in summer which further reaffirms religious socialization.

Denise is still on the fence about Hebrew school, but she has enrolled her child in a Jewish day care center. Renee's children are first and second graders in a local Catholic school.

> We put both kids into parochial school, for religious reasons but also because the public school is very large—combined with middle school, it's a thousand kids—and Alex is a very sensitive kid. So combined with the moral values being provided, it seemed like Catholic school was a better place. And she loves it. . . . Religious education is provided once a week by the school. They use workbooks where they learn about Jesus, the Bible, being kind to others, how to make choices. Alex received first communion last week and there was lots of preparation for that.

Renee plans on having her children continue Catholic education through high school, provided they can afford it.

When None parents go back to church or synagogue, their children's formal religious education is reaffirmed to varying degrees in the home, depending on how fully the parents have embraced their religious identities. Some parents say grace before meals or pray or read Bible stories at bedtime; some do not. Religious symbolism was often on display in the home: I saw Bibles, a crucifix on the wall, a mezuzah on the door. All parents made use of the holidays to convey religion to children. Setting up a menorah or a tree, eating special foods like fish on Good Friday or unleavened bread during Passover, learning traditional songs or rhymes—all these are opportunities to explain religion to children in ways that are concrete and engaging. As Denise put it: "I think in Judaism there is no way of escaping the religious aspect because each celebration requires us like . . . for each celebration we would have a book to read, like for Passover we would read my mother's Haggadah and we would have a seder and my mother would light the candles and we would talk about what it meant, and we would have the matzoh hiding." She now tries to replicate these traditions with her daughter. Renee also uses the holidays to teach her children about religion. "Christmas and Easter are big ones," she said. "When [the children] were really young it was Santa and Easter bunny, but as they get older religious meaning becomes more important. We attend mass, Santa brings two or three gifts, the rest goes to families in need. We go there together, so they understand it's about love and helping others. We also read the Bible and stories. We do an Advent calendar. Easter is different, harder to explain, right now it's still mostly bunny." Renee, like Denise, is raising her children with religion much as her own parents did.

All this religious activity does not mean either Renee or Denise have morphed from Nones into devout Catholics or Jews. Indeed, as some of the comments below illustrate, some residual ambivalence about organized religion remains. Moreover, as other researchers have noted, even some atheist parents go the conventional route of reaffiliating with organized religion, especially if they are married to a religious spouse. What is it that draws them back? As parents explained why they chose the conventional route, four themes stood out in their narratives.

One is the perception, based on their own experience growing up with a particular tradition, that religion is a good way to teach morality and values. Religion teaches children right from wrong, how to be good person, within the framework of a tradition that has withstood the test of time. As Renee put it: "Religion instills good morals and values, encourages being kind to others, realizing we're not alone in world, not being selfish. If I raised them in another Christian religion it would probably be okay too, and I've always felt that way. My sister raised her kids Jewish and that's fine too. But I never explored other religions." So it made sense to go back to church. Denise too values the moral aspect of religion. She admitteds that she did not agree with everything Judaism taught, like the concept of a chosen people: "I do not think Jews are superior to other people. . . . [However,] I talked to Lisa about my own beliefs, like why people are equal and that kind of thing, and sometimes it coincides with the Jewish belief. So I think that a sense of spirituality and all the morals that Judaism teaches . . . even if I did not claim myself as a Jew, there is a lot of influence that Judaism has on how I think and feel." Denise's admission that her own worldview does not always coincide with Judaism as well as Renee's assertion that it does not matter much which religion the children are raised in illustrate a kind of pragmatic attitude I found among many former None parents: religion is a useful tool to instill good values.

A second reason commonly cited for returning to church was that religion connects children to a family history. Renee explains that both she and her husband come from big Italian Catholic families. The town they live in is a historic fishing community that has always been predominantly Italian and Portuguese, and Catholicism is a big part of the local culture. Fishing families traditionally belong to the St. Peter's Club, and in summer huge crowds gather for a week-long fiesta to celebrate his feast day. The cardinal comes from Boston and blesses the fleet, and there is a big parade where the statue of St. Peter is carried through town. Families still expect children to marry within the religion, and everybody knows everybody else's business. Renee left town in part to get away from that. But now that she is raising children she wants to pass on the tradition. "I moved a lot as a child, so it was important to me to keep my kids grounded. That's why I like being here and why I want them to be Catholic. I want them to have something they can go back to. I had that." For Denise too, returning to Judaism is about passing on a family tradition: "I really enjoyed Judaism and I enjoy its teachings and now that I have a daughter I want to create that sense of like a family gathering and a holiday ritual, all of the smells I enjoyed. Like we just had Rosh Hashanah here and we made brisket, and all the smells I remember from years ago, and it's more that ritual that I enjoy than the religion. And so I think I want to give the same thing to my daughter and I want to cel-

ebrate those same holidays with her." In my research, this desire to connect children to a family tradition was particularly pronounced among
parents who came from Catholic or Jewish families, that is, where religion was embedded in a particular culture and so passing on religion
was partly about passing on that culture.

A third reason None parents gave for going back to church was the
desire that their children experience rituals like First Communion or
bar/bat mitzvah. Renee's daughter Alex just had her first communion,
a festive affair where the little girl gets to wear a special white dress and
the entire family comes together to celebrate; "It was a beautiful experience for everyone." Denise fondly remembers her own experience with
such rites of passage: "When we turned fourteen, my sister and I were
both bat mitzvahed, and I went to Israel for that and it was very special,
and then we had like a tour of Israel, and it was just a neat experience."
She wants to give the same to her daughter.

Finally, None parents cite the supportive structure and community
offered by organized religion. This includes a community of other parents who share your values, plus inexpensive or free afternoon and summer programs that help keep your kids out of trouble and encourage
them to do good in the world. Many churches and synagogues offer
programs to help teens navigate the common challenges of adolescence
(such as becoming sexually active or exposure to alcohol and drugs)
and programs where teens help the less fortunate (e.g., working in soup
kitchens or volunteering for Habitat for Humanity). In Denise's words:

> [The Jewish community] gives families something to do that is very
> wholesome, something you can do all together. . . . Like being in the
> temple with other people and saying prayers, there is a very powerful
> feeling behind it, and I always enjoy that, that's something I felt really
> good about. Or saying prayers for people that have passed away, that have
> touched our lives in some way, and I remember there was a lot of emo-
> tion, and it's a time to release, to be with other people, feeling the same
> thing. I really think Lisa had a sense of that, even though she's only four,
> when we went on Friday she had a sense of that togetherness and prayer.
> Yes, it is going back to a sense of structure, that's exactly what it is, it
> creates a sense of commonality between each member of the household,
> where people are going in ten different directions every day, and then you

come together at night and it's nice to have a nice dinner together, but it's also nice to be tied together by something deeper, like a religion, to create a unity and household.

Denise's experience of the synagogue creating a supportive community within which to raise children is echoed in other studies of unchurched individuals who reaffiliate with religion when they start families. Considering the wealth of resources that organized religion offers to families, the appeal of the conventional strategy is obvious.[7]

Finding an Alternative Community

Not all None parents are comfortable with going back to church. This is particularly true for those Nones who have adopted nonconventional worldviews such as the Philosophical Secularists and Spiritual Seekers described earlier. Many of these parents reported that having children led them to search for and eventually affiliate with an organization that welcomes doubters and the nonreligious. I call this the *alternative strategy*.

The alternative strategy resembles the conventional one in that parents go looking for community but it differs significantly in the type of community chosen: one that is supportive of being nonreligious. Several organizations in the United States explicitly embrace nonreligion and are becoming a home for Nones. One is the American Humanist Association (AHA), which was established in 1941 to advance the ideas of humanism and other nontheistic philosophies such as atheism, agnosticism, rationalism, naturalism, secularism. The AHA is best known for its political and legal efforts to promote public awareness of humanism and to defend the rights of humanists against what they see as religious encroachment on their lives by the government or other institutions (e.g., filing law suits on behalf of parents who do not want their children to say the Pledge of Allegiance because it makes reference to one nation under God). However, the AHA also articulates a comprehensive worldview and set of ethical values to guide human behavior, much as religions do.[8] More recently, AHA chapters in various parts of the country have begun to organize themselves more like churches, offering a Sunday morning lecture and discussion of humanist ideas and encouraging members to become involved in social justice issues such as women's rights and the rights of gays and lesbians.[9]

Another alternative to conventional religion is the Unitarian Universalist Association (UUA). Although the UUA originated as a Christian denomination, it has since evolved into perhaps the most inclusive spiritual alternative in the United States, offering a home base to groups as diverse as atheists, agnostics, pagans, and others. Unlike liberal denominations that may welcome people from other faiths to participate in a Christian or Jewish service, the UUA does not identify with any particular tradition. The UUA tries to incorporate aspects of all of them. Thus a Sunday morning service is as likely to include the lighting of a menorah as a children's Maypole dance or a sermon on humanist ideas. Instead of a creed, the UUA is guided by seven ethical principles including one that encourages the individual's freedom to pursue his or her own truth and meaning.[10] The UUA is actively engaged in social justice work promoting peace, helping the poor, protecting the natural environment, and championing the rights of various oppressed groups.

While some UUA members would categorize the association as a religious denomination, the respondents in this study understood it as an alternative to conventional religion. They were either Secularists (who embrace a nontheistic philosophy such as atheism or humanism or skepticism) or Seekers (who combine elements from various different traditions), and having children motivated them to find a community that shared their worldviews. They would shop around, and find that numerous churches claim to welcome doubters only because they hope to convert them to Christianity. Parents settled on the Unitarians because of their tolerance; as one parent put it, "you really can believe whatever you want." Several parents said they did not think of the UUA as a religion but as a "community of seekers." Others joined because the congregation sponsored an active chapter of the AHA. They were looking for and found what they saw as an alternative to religion.

Among the parents who illustrate this strategy are Daniel, Teresa, and Beth in Jacksonville, Florida, and Lori in Colorado Springs. Daniel, an avowed atheist, was introduced earlier in this book. He and his wife Teresa, age thirty-four, began looking for a community after the death of their first child. He resented his family's efforts to draw him back to church. But, recognizing the need for a supportive community—

for themselves and their remaining child—he went on the Internet and found a local chapter of the AHA close to their former home in a suburb of Chicago. They joined the society and enrolled their child in Sunday school. The AHA did not have a meeting place near their new home in Jacksonville, so after several years of commuting for nearly an hour they joined the UUA instead. "You don't have to believe anything in this church," he said—and that's just the way he likes it.

Beth, age twenty-seven, is a married homemaker with a boy and a girl ages seven and three. A Spiritual Seeker type, she is "turned off by religion" but considers herself "extremely spiritual" and has dabbled in Buddhism and Wicca. "[Before having children,] we weren't really doing anything. She [their daughter] was the catalyst that got us to [look for a community], because she would say stuff to us like: 'Who was the first person on earth? What happens when you die?' And we were just like, 'Um, I don't know,' I really have no clue how to answer this question." She had visited a Unitarian Universalist church around that time, "just to see a show [someone had rented their hall]," she told me, "so I thought, 'Oh this place is nice,' and we checked it out, and we ended up really liking it, because we learned they have a program for children's education, so it ended up being a really good fit for us." Like Daniel, she likes it because, "there's no set rules about what [she has] to believe." She said they were planning to join later that Spring.

Lori was raised Episcopalian but she left church in college because, she said, "I started feeling like a hypocrite . . . because I was pretty sure I didn't believe any of it." For the next decade she was pretty much indifferent to anything spiritual: "NPR was my religion." Her then boyfriend, now husband, is an ex-Evangelical turned Seeker. At his initiative they started looking for an alternative community the year before their first child was born. They attended various informal group meetings of other Seekers who held discussions about various spiritual topics in people's homes. At one of these gatherings they learned of the Unitarian Universalist Church where they have been members for several years now.

Like parents who return to conventional religious communities, None parents who take the alternative route also seek formal education for their children. But the type of education is not the same. Rather than teaching the history, beliefs, and practices of a particular tradition like Judaism or Christianity and socializing the child into a particular religious identity, the programs offered by alternative organizations typically teach kids about many different worldviews, including secular ones, and encourage them to chart their own path.

The UUA has a comprehensive worldview education curriculum for both children and adults that is available in most of their congregations. The children's program has several age-appropriate levels. For example, it includes a curriculum entitled "Love Will Guide Us" for elementary school children that draws on stories about Jesus and the Buddha, stories by neopagan authors like Starhawk, and a story about evolutionary biology. Programs for older children are oriented more toward ethics and applying one's values in the world. The UUA offers afterschool and weekend programs to involve youth in social justice work. It also runs its own scouting organizations (which grew out of their opposition to the Boy Scouts of America's anti-gay policies) and summer camps.

More recently, humanist organizations such as the AHA have moved in the same direction. The AHA has published a resource guide for local chapters to create programs for children,[11] an initiative that seems to be driven by a desire to attract and keep young families in the community.[12] I interviewed a member of the society in the San Francisco Bay Area who said they were in the process of establishing such a program in response to several requests from parents. There are two AHA chapters that already have Humanist Children's Programs up and running: the Humanists of Greater Portland, Oregon, and the Humanist Society of New Mexico. Both programs are described in the manual, and leaders of the programs are available to help answer questions. In addition, several AHA chapters and affiliates have children's programs through the American Ethical Union—the Ethical Humanist Society of Great Chicago (the Golden Rule Sunday School) and the Ethical Humanist Society of Long Island have run successful programs for children for many years. Humanists have also begun offering other youth programs. For example, Camp Quest, founded in 1996, is the first residential summer camp created specifically for the children of atheists and other nontheists as an alternative to the many religious-based summer camps. Open to campers age eight to seventeen, Camp Quest now offers programs in sixteen different states as well as in the United Kingdom. The camps offer traditional activities such as campfires, games and crafts, swimming, and canoeing, but they also introduce the history and ideas of Freethought, as well as a variety of science topics, critical thinking, philosophy, world religions, and mythology.[13]

These kinds of programs are often the draw that motivates the Seeker or Secular parent to affiliate with an alternative community. Beth told me: "What was really the jumping point for me was what my daughter learns at Sunday school. She was about four when the questions started, and then when she was five was when I felt, I don't know what to say anymore. Before that, I could say anything and she would just run off and play, get distracted, but at five she became more persistent, she wanted real answers, so that's when we started thinking, we really should start looking into providing religious education." She recalled how they had searched around but admitted, "There really wasn't anything, there really wasn't anything that provided the option of *options*." At Unitarian Universalist congregations they do provide options. "The first year they talk about different religions," Beth explained, "so [my daughter] would come home and talk about Muslim prayer rugs, and she would talk about Hanukkah and the candles at the light, so it was just a broad presentation of religion, and so for this half of the year, they have touched upon different celebrations, not just religious celebrations either." The children also learn "the way people can be humane to each other and kindness, so ethics and such, not just religion." Lori's kids also go to a Unitarian Universalist religious education service: "My five-year-old is telling me about Buddhist monks and what their life is like, so I appreciate them getting the knowledge of the different religions." Meanwhile Daniel's children are learning about secular philosophies: "This semester, January through June, they teach holidays and traditions . . . Susan B. Anthony's birthday, Darwin's birthday, and other humanist kinds of things [as well as celebrate] a Passover seder, Chinese new year, and Mardi Gras."

The alternative education programs are typically supplemented by what goes on at home. Like those who choose conventional religious upbringing, None parents who go alternative reported taking intentional steps to incorporate religion or spirituality in their homes, but they do so in consciously pluralistic way. For some parents this means remaking traditional holidays, for example, by combining imagery from both Buddhism or Judaism, celebrating the holidays of various religions, or reinventing the meaning of a holiday. Beth explains:

We celebrate holidays but I can't say that we celebrate them as *holy* days. We celebrate Christmas, but we don't celebrate it as Jesus's birthday; we celebrated as the day that Santa Claus comes to share love and peace. Easter, we celebrate Easter as in they decorate eggs, but without the Christian aspect. We take a more traditional pagan approach where it's about fertility, the groundhog may come back up, the plants coming back up, rather than Jesus coming back up. So it's a celebration of life, new beginnings, starting the cycle again. We celebrate Halloween too, in more of the pagan, Wiccan way, a day to remember our ancestors.

Daniel and Teresa also impart their own, more pluralistic meaning to the holidays. I visited their home in early January and noticed a tall Christmas tree in their living room with a plastic Minnie Mouse perched on top. The mouse was a way to show the tree was not a Christian symbol—as Teresa put it, "it was very anti-angel." Instead of elements from one tradition, they incorporated elements from various traditions: "We do Hanukkah at the same time, we also do the pagan Winter solstice celebration." She has put quite a bit of time and research into how to engage her children: "There is a good animated story, Little Bear, about the Winter solstice celebration, and there was another ritual, an Indian light ceremony that we did. All of the major religions celebrate light at that time of the year because it's the darkest part of the year." Rather than being raised in one tradition, these children are raised with various traditions, so that "they can make a choice for themselves when they are ready."

Daniel, Teresa, and Beth are very comfortable appropriating and remaking religious holidays. For other parents, these occasions were the source of some psychological conflict. Lori and her husband were not sure if they wanted to do Christmas. Lori told me, "I had always worried about hypocrisy." But over time she decided: "it's not . . . we can celebrate Christmas without getting into the religious piece of it. . . . I came to the conclusion, probably four years ago, that I can celebrate the life of an exemplary human being. We have Martin Luther King Day, we have Christmas, and so that's how I reconcile celebrating that particular holiday." For the sake of his and her parents, who are Christian, they often take the children to be with grandma and grandpa for the holidays. "We do a family thing," she added. "We do those family celebrations, Easter and Christmas." But Lori and her husband remain uneasy about celebrating these holidays at home.

> Those [Christmas and Easter] I can also justify in terms of celebrating the original traditions of the seasons, light returning, so we have an annual solstice party, and we call it a solstice party, in December. And we have books about other religious holidays, we talk about Hanukkah and different things, but we don't celebrate them. I am slightly uncomfortable, and Ben [her husband] is even more uncomfortable. . . . I would like to be more comfortable with rituals like lighting candles and be mindful and contemplative, but I have a slight sense of embarrassment around it, and so we don't do it very much.

Parents who adopted the alternative strategy had a different take on raising children with religion than those who went the conventional route. Although many saw value in religion—saying it *can* be a source of moral guidance, a link to family history, and a way to participate in important rites of passage—they felt uncomfortable committing themselves to a particular religion, either because they are Seekers (who combine elements of various religions) or because they are Secular (do not believe in God). They like the communal aspect offered by churches and synagogues but they did not like the message, especially the idea that each religion claims unique truth or that religion is the only source of meaning and value in life. So they were drawn to communities that offered an alternative message. Two themes stood out in their narratives. One was the value of pluralism; the other was the need for support.

A pluralistic religious upbringing fosters tolerance for diversity. Alternative worldview communities like the UUA or AHA offer a context where children can learn, as Beth puts it, "the different ways that people are religious, and whichever way you choose is fine." The key benefit of a pluralistic religious upbringing is that it creates tolerance of diversity. It helps children gain, in Lori's words, "an understanding of the value of all human beings, regardless of what their religion is, and to be accepting of people of other religious beliefs, that we don't have to believe the same things, but we can still get along with one another and be respectful of one another." To these parents religion fosters morality only if it remains tolerant of others. Lori told me that she wants her children to have strong moral values, but, she added, "there is an element of our society here that says in order to be a good person you must be a Christian, and I reject that." She wants them "to have moral values that are not the exclusive domain of Christians" which is what the UUA principles provide.

A pluralistic religious upbringing is also beneficial because it expands the pool of wisdom from which children can draw. Beth told me: "It helps give them not just the knowledge of these other things but it's still a little bit of the morals and ethics from each of those religious traditions, instead of just taking one path. Like in Earth-based religions they learned to respect the earth, and of course I want my children to respect the earth, but in other religions they learn other values that are important too." Similarly, Daniel said: "The real thing I want [my children] to do is to have the values to be a right-thinking person in the community so that they don't have to rely on anybody . . . and part of that means that they have to have the tools to make good decisions. You can't get it from any one religion, you can't get it from science exclusively, you need to have a broad understanding of a lot of different things." Another benefit of this approach is that it fosters cultural literacy. Thus Beth admitted, "in a world where religion is referred to nonstop . . . I do feel lost from time to time in conversations." Because she has not read much of the Bible, she told me, "people will talk about something and I won't know what that means, and I don't know that much about the rest of the world religions . . . because we in America, we are not it, there's plenty of other religions, I love it that my daughter is exposed to all different types of thought." Teresa wants her children "to get an understanding of other religions so that you are familiar with what is out there, so that when you are talking to other people outside of your community . . . they know a little bit about what else is going on; [so they are] familiar with, not shocked by [different views]."

As beneficial as a pluralistic religious upbringing may be, it is not the norm. None parents who adopted the alternative strategy also emphasize the need for a supportive community. Lori worries that her children will feel like outsiders in the conservative Christian town they live in:

Living in Colorado Springs, kids actually discuss religion amongst themselves . . . at school, and [my son] is definitely a minority. . . . I worry that

he will do something else that will not go over well socially in Colorado
Springs. . . . I'd like to live in a community where we are not as different
but that's not really a possibility for us for a number of reasons, and we
really do like Colorado Springs for many things, and at UU we have definitely found a community of like-minded people."

Daniel feels similarly about both the UUA and AHA: "To my mind,
the spiritual home community, that's very important. . . . [We] can come
to this community."

Doing It Yourself

Not all parents searched for or found community to raise their children, conventional or otherwise. Some parents tried to transmit their
worldviews without institutional support. While these parents remain
unaffiliated and do not enroll their children in formal religious education programs, they do take active steps to incorporate religion,
spirituality, or a secular philosophy into their homes. I refer to this as
self-providing.

In recent years, several advice books have been published to help
guide parents with nontheistic or other unconventional worldviews at
doing it yourself. One of the best known is Dale McGowen's, *Parenting
beyond Belief*, a collection of essays compiled by an atheist parent helping other parents to raise their kids to be "good without God." Other
books have a more religious or spiritual focus such as *Planting Seeds:
Practicing Mindfulness with Children* by Thich Nhat Hanh or *Circle
Round: Raising Children in Goddess Traditions* by Starhawk.[14] Some of
the parents I talked to reported buying such books and finding them
helpful. Others chose to muddle through on their own.

Doing it yourself will take a variety of forms, depending on the parents' worldview and various personal factors such as the personality of
the parent and child or how much the parent knows about religion or
other worldviews. Reading to and with children was a popular option.
Some parents went online to search for appropriate children's books.
There are lots of Christian and Jewish books for children, far fewer if
your worldview is nontheistic or a more pluralistic spirituality (at the
time of writing, a search on Amazon returned more that 47,000 titles

for Christian children's books, and only a little over 5,000 for Jewish, 260 for Buddhism, 161 for Pagan, and 37 for humanist books), and several parents complained about this.[15] Some parents reported talking to children about the existence or nonexistence of God or other supernatural beings. Some prayed or meditated with their children. For all self-providers the holidays were an opportunity to convey religious or spiritual meaning in their home.

None parents who decide to raise their children Christian or Jewish typically have their own childhood experiences to draw on. When the kids are small, parents may tell stories or teach prayers that they themselves learned as children. They remember how to make hamantaschen or build a crèche out of Play-Doh. They can call grandma to help organize a Hanukkah party or a seder.

Isabel is a good example. Married with three kids and teaching public school in the Boston area, she is an Unchurched Believer and a deeply spiritual person. "There has never been a time when I did not believe in God," she told me. Yet, she does not identify or affiliate with religion: "I don't particularly feel drawn to any church." She had her children baptized in an independent church but it was almost an hour away from where they live now. They considered some other churches but none of them appealed to them. So she tries to do it alone: "I pray with my youngest two children [at bed time], and sometimes we talk about angels or spiritual beings when it comes up or when there's a death or when we're praying for somebody. . . . I don't pray with [my oldest son]; he's thirteen." At Christmas they read stories and "sing songs [Isabel] grew up with as a child." They also celebrate with her mother who lives nearby.

Doing it for themselves can be harder for None parents who are Seekers or Secularists wanting to raise children in a pluralistic or nontheistic worldview but without an alternative community. Advice books are wonderful but only a pale substitute for drawing on your own experience or the participation of extended family members. Jon and Rebecca, whom I introduced earlier in this book, are both Spiritual Seekers living in Los Angeles. She was raised Christian and he Jewish, and they have explored various spiritualities. Currently they are into transcendental meditation; they follow a guru and meditate daily. They want to raise their children pluralistically drawing on the three traditions to which they have an affinity. "We do celebrate most of the Christian holidays because I like them," said Rebecca. "And why not? I find Christmas in America is really not about Jesus, it's about presents; it's a national holiday." They also do Jewish holidays, "Rosh Hashanah, Passover, and we do Hanukkah." For Passover they often fly to New York to have a seder with Jon's mother, and they also "participate in a lot of Hindu holidays." Although both have practiced other religions, Rebecca told me, "we don't do Buddhist and others because it's too much." Indeed, it would seem they have their hands full with three.

Jon admitted that it was easier to pass on the traditions they grew up with:

> I think we do more observance of Jewish and Christian holidays than we do Hindu holidays, because they seem very culturally strange. Like if its Holi (a popular Hindu festival) am I going to run around and pour colored water over a statue? It may be fun for little kids but it feels weird. So I don't teach that but it's not because it's wrong but it's just strange. When I think of a spiritual path, it's like real, like taking medicine or doing exercises, not like masquerading pretending to be an Indian. It has to feel genuine.

He and Rebecca try to involve their son in the parents' own spiritual discipline. "Children kind of learn what you are rather than what you say," Jon told me, "so I don't sit down and say, 'I want you to memorize this story or that,' because then all he'll get is the feeling that he's being forced to memorize the stories." Instead, Jon encourages Aden to "do" spirituality with his dad: "He sees me meditate and sometimes he'll copy, and he'll see a sitting [a group of Jon and Rebecca's friends meditating in their living room] and he'll copy that." This is, of course, what religious parents have done for generations.

But None parents also create their own unique ways to help transmit their worldviews to children. Jon is a screenwriter and he wrote a play in which his son plays the Hindu god Rama, and, as John put it, "[Aden]'s into that because he's into being in a play." Other parents were creative in less formal ways. Fran, a secularist, recalls how she dealt with Christmas when her two children were still small. She and her husband, also a secularist, celebrated the holiday as an occasion to focus on joy and hope. But Fran got a new job that required her to work over Christmas.

> I couldn't run home and be Momma and cook all day and get up at the crack of dawn and walk [home]. So because I knew that I was not going to be getting up with my young kids, I had made a lasagna a week before and froze it. We had gotten some major project for the kids and us to just sit around and build stuff all day, and no cooking other than throwing something in the microwave. And I would talk about looking for hope in the darkest nights of the year.

This became their annual tradition. "Christmas Day became a no hassle, wonderful time," she asserts, "where we all, probably for five years, every year . . . would build something huge together and just sit around, and we would graze all day long and there was no plan to [cook a] meal, and it was marvelous." " For Nones like Jon and Fran, who hold unconventional worldviews that they adopted as adults and do not have childhood tradition from which they can draw, it can be more challenging to engage their children; yet, it also offers them the freedom to create rituals and practices that genuinely reflect their values.

Creating rituals is one way None parents who choose to do it themselves make up for the lack of structure provided by an existing religious or alternative community. Another option is to create a community of their own. Whether None parents are raising their children with conventional religion or an alternative worldview, their choice not to affiliate does not mean they must do it alone. Isabel and some other families contacted the minister at her former church and persuaded him to help them run a children's program:

> The minister would come to someone's house once a month and do a study group with the adults, and he would do a children's program before that . . . [with] maybe seven other regular students. And maybe at times as much as fifteen. . . . They sang, and they heard a story. . . . The children loved it. My son liked it lots better than school. He loved the stories and the concept of the spiritual world and that there was a God. He was actually very attracted to the church and its ritual. Like I said earlier, we never actually went to church because we never found one that we liked. But

the few times we did go to church, it was on Christmas or something like that, to see a choir or a play; he really loved it.

The program went on for two years until the minister tragically died. Isabel and her friends never reestablished it. Similarly, Rebecca and Jon reached out to other seeker families to form a community. They would meet occasionally for a satsang [a Hindu gathering] at somebody's house in which the children participated. Eventually this became a weekly event. As Rebecca told me:

> We go to satsang, which is every Saturday; it's a rotation at various houses. There will be one at our house this coming weekend. Forty or fifty people usually come, it depends on the house; if it's a bigger house it may be more people. You basically go potluck. What happens is you do puja [Hindu worship], and then there are devotional songs and then you eat a meal, a vegetarian meal. . . . [The children are involved] as much as they can handle, mostly in story telling and singing. . . . Also when we have the satsang at our house, there are Indian kids. They are so amazing . . . anyway it's nice to have them together.

Like Isabel, Rebecca loves the impact this communal event has on her child. "Aden is so at ease with that," she said, "because it's a different culture. There is one of them who is older, and he loves to sing, and when Aden hears him singing, he is mesmerized. It's amazing, this kid gets all the adults to participate. . . . So now Aden, like when he does karate, he likes to meditate; he meditates before and after, he likes his identity as a vegetarian, he talks about it, and I find them chanting from time to time."

Considering how positive Nones who chose the do-it-yourself option feel about community, I wondered why they insist on doing it alone. Two reasons were commonly given. The first was that these parents tend to be suspicious of institutional religion, which they view as hypocritical or shallow. As Isabel puts it, "I'm often kind of just turned off by churches. Sometimes the churches, I don't know, sometimes the sermon seemed very crass and base. Sometimes even hypocritical." Similarly, Jon said of his Jewish mother: "We know she doesn't believe, but she does all these things and goes through the motions to be a good Jew, like make this perfect seder." Hypocrisy also bothers Vicky, a Seeker who combines elements of Native American and Buddhist practice. Raised in Alabama by a strict Catholic father and a Baptist mother, she had to attend mass every Sunday and watch religious television. Vicky left church because, she said, "it was a place that made me feel really horrible about how I was naturally as a female; and that I should feel bad about every feeling and every thought of that I had in regards to my body." Yet she likes what she called the "energy" of a Catholic mass, so she has considered taking her daughter to a local Catholic church: "We have a really pretty Little Chapel of St. Anthony, which I have fond memories of going there with my grandparents." But her husband is opposed to the idea, especially, as she put it, "after what happened with the priests, he just thinks they are a bunch of hypocrites."

The other reason for not affiliating was not being able to find a community. Despite their misgivings about institutional religion, most of the self-providers I talked to had made some effort to locate a religious or spiritual community. Isabel, for example, went church shopping and then gave up. Jon had a similar experience: "I would take [my son Aden] to a synagogue if I found one that wasn't so goofy." His wife concurs: "We find that every place we go, it turns into a social club." And Vicky points out that institutional options outside mainstream churches are not always readily available, especially in a small town: "They've built a Buddhist temple somewhere outside of Boston and I'd love to take my daughter there to see and experience a ceremony." But Vicky is unsure of the location and whether anyone can just go there. So for now, she continues to do it alone.

Self-providers deeply value integrity or "being genuine" which may be why they are unwilling to compromise and simply settle for a community, religious or alternative, that is a less-than-perfect match. But they are also aware of the benefits of community. Self-providers, more than other parents I studied, were often conflicted about how to raise their children. For example, Jon told me:

> I have really mixed feelings about the idea of religious instruction. . . . I think that a lot of "indoctrination" does help because there are stories, there are songs, there are rituals, and they develop the emotional, affective capacity. . . . So that kind of indoctrination I am in favor of. But very

often it ends up feeling kind of corny? Like if you don't truly have the conviction, it can feel kind of corny. And then what you're really modeling is: go and do things that you don't quite believe. You're going through the motions, like my mom. . . . I feel guilty for not continuing the line of Jews, because so many people tried to exterminate Jews, so I feel I have some sort of duty, I don't know. But I also wonder, is there—it's very easy for me to build castles in the sky, like when I talk to my Orthodox Jewish friends, I think: oh wouldn't that be pretty, every mitzvah has a meaning, and I read a lot of books about the law. But the actual doing, it always kind of strikes me as a pain in the neck, and also I feel like I have a spiritual path which is the real thing so I would be foolish to give it up in order to have something different. But I am conflicted.

For Jon, the conflict seems to be between what he perceives as his obligation to the Jewish community and what he actually believes. For others like Vicky the conflict is rooted in her own uncertainty: she is still sorting out what her beliefs actually are. She admits that religion provides answers to some difficult questions: "I haven't thought of an answer for this yet, but when you think of death, and you do die, is it just the end? Is it just emptiness and that's it? Is it that you're gonna go into the ground and not die and that's a really depressing thought. So I can understand why people would want to have heaven, or hell, or purgatory to go to." Understanding other religions, however, is not enough to make a commitment, much less educate one's child. As Vicky put it, "I can't tell her something I don't believe."

Doubt and conflicted emotions are, of course, not unique to None parents who are attempting to transmit their unique worldview to their children. But without the regular support of a community, such conflicts may eventually lead the parent to give up on the project. Self-providers reported difficulty in sustaining their efforts, especially as children grew older and other activities competed for their interests. Jon admitted that his son was "often bored [with religion]." But unlike churched parents, who are likely to make their kid attend religious education classes at least until confirmation or bar mitzvah, Jon is doing the education himself, and he is not inclined to continue it if his son loses interest: "I'm really not into the notion of forcing them to do it, to the point that they might rebel against it." Vicky also has difficulty in engaging her daughter. She recalls how she took pains to go beyond celebrating Christmas and Easter as "cultural holidays" with gifts and candy egg hunts, like most Americans do. Being spiritually inclined, she wants to do more than that. So she bought a nativity set and explained to her daughter: "This is what people believe, that Jesus was born on Christmas day and Easter is when people believe he died and then came back from the dead." Vicky's use of the phrase *people believe* reflects a self-conscious effort to be honest with her daughter about what religious symbols mean to others, in contrast to what it means to her: that Christmas is a "time to give back" to the world. As she put it: "It's not just about you getting a gift, it's about giving to other people and making sure they know you care about them." But her daughter, like many children, is more attached to the cultural trappings of the holidays (Santa Claus and the Easter Bunny) than the religious meaning. Vicky's daughter's response to the religion lesson was lukewarm. "She's just like, okay, whatever. Now can we do an Easter egg hunt?" Vicky keeps trying, but she admits that "this is hard."

Isabel ceased her efforts at religious instruction after the priest died and the children's program ended. "Yeah, we used to always pray [with my older son] when he went to religious instruction," she said, "and then it stopped being available, and we stopped doing it [because he got interested in sports which took up all his time]." She expressed some regret about what she perceives as the outcome of this: "[My son] informed me tonight that he doesn't believe in God when I told him what you were interviewing me about."

"Were you surprised at that?" I asked.

"I was shocked. I was upset, but my husband thought it was wonderful that he was being an independent thinker. My husband really embraced his courage to say what he felt and thought, rather than focusing on anything else. I didn't say anything. I still don't quite believe it."

Isabel was not the only parent to give up on self-providing. Providing religious, spiritual, or secular worldview education oneself requires a great deal of effort. While parents who choose conventional or alternative communities can leave matters of content and pedagogy to someone else, self-providers must find a way to articulate their religious or secular beliefs and determine how to transmit them. As Vicky put it, "I do a lot of thinking, self-torture." That may explain why self-provision as a method of incorporating religion—although chosen as an option by some parents in all categories (except Indifferent)—was often tempo-rary, as parents shifted to other options.

Letting Others Do It

Although most parents are not as tortured as Vicky, many None parents reported feeling ambivalent about the question of religion. Imagine you, the parent, are not into organized religion but many elements in the society around you—the media, your parents, your friends—are telling you religion is good for your kid. Going back to church, especially if you are secular, will create some cognitive dissonance. Yet, doing nothing can make you feel guilty. One way to deal with this dilemma is through *outsourcing*, that is, letting other people deal with providing religion in your child's life. Like parents who choose the conventional route, most outsourcers will enroll their children in a formal program like the CCD, Hebrew school, or Sunday school. What makes the outsourcers different is that they themselves remain uncommitted—they do not intention-ally incorporate religion or spirituality in the home and they decline to become themselves members of that religious institution.

The outsourcing option was selected by parents with various world-views: Unchurched Believers who did not want to commit themselves and Seekers or Secularists with strong family ties to conventional religion. As noted in my discussion of conventional strategies, the appeal of outsourc-ing becomes quickly apparent if you look at the tremendous resources that are offered by organized religion. And yet, the fact that these parents decline to commit themselves suggests some lingering reservations about organized religion: If religion is good, but not good enough for me as a parent to want to be part of it, why have a child participate? Parents gave various answers to this question, but a common theme emerged: they felt a duty as parents to provide religion, regardless of their personal ambiva-lence about it, because their children "had a right" to this information. Often this was because religion (usually Judaism or Catholicism) was a family heritage that their children ought to know about. Sometimes, par-ents saw religious instruction as providing cultural benefits. And in a few cases, parents followed the interest or inclination of their children.

Ellen, an Unchurched Believer from a Catholic background, is an ex-ample of a parent who is considering outsourcing in order to preserve a family tradition. At thirty, she's married and staying at home with an infant and a toddler. Her parents have raised the baptism question, but she does not want to join a church because it is boring and has no relevance to her life: "They just make you fall asleep." She does not agree with Catholic Church teachings: "I get really mad about [the church's opposition to] gay marriage and how they can't use birth control in Africa. . . . There is nothing about it that's appealing to go there." And yet, she told me she would "love to find a good church with a good priest," so she can send her children there. She has not spent much time looking for one, however, because her husband is against it. Instead, she plans to enroll her children in Catholic school to learn about religion. She admitted: "Maybe it's my parents influence. I want to give my children what I had even if I don't personally connect to it anymore." Outsourcing serves Ellen's need to offer her family's religion to her children without having to recommit herself.

Commitment also seems a challenge for Susan, whom I introduced earlier to illustrate a Seeker type that combines elements of Buddhism and Judaism. Susan is torn about how to raise her two-year-old son. On the one hand, she proudly calls herself a pluralist and would like to raise her son that way. To that end, her child plays with a stuffed Torah and a toy Buddha, and she has Christian iconography in her home as well. "He learns about all of [religions]," she said. On the other hand, she feels a special obligation toward Judaism, her family's tradition (she was raised by her Orthodox grandmother). "I do want him to learn foremost about Judaism before he makes up his mind about what he wants to be," she explained. "I have this little fear that Judaism will die, and I think Judaism is . . . a beautiful and humble religion and it's also ground of all monotheistic religions, and I simply believe it should be alive and well." Still, she does not want to be formally affiliated with a synagogue because she does not want to pay the membership fee and also is "not comfortable with the ideology there." Instead, she is enrolling her son in a Jewish preschool to give her son some exposure to her heritage.

Parents may also let the extended family take care of passing on the religious heritage, as is the case with Samantha and James. We saw in chapter 4 how their parents (hers Jewish and his Catholic) moved them from religious indifference to greater appreciation of their heritage and a desire to pass it on to their children. At the time of my interview they had not been able to settle on an appropriate community. So the kids learned both traditions by visiting with both sets of grandparents. In Samantha's words, "Hanukkah parties and Rosh Hashanah dinner with my parents, Christmas with my husband's family." For Passover they went to her parents' house for a seder. Her parents explained to the children "a little bit about what it meant, same with Yom Kippur." Christmas Eve mass was spent with her husband's parents. Samantha concluded: "So I would say there is some religious content, more than just chocolate and presents. My mother-in-law will get the children books, and so will my mother, and there is some education and talk about what these holidays are. The kids love it." With grandparents taking charge of introducing children to family religious heritage, it seems that Samantha and James are off the hook, at least for now.

The family heritage argument for outsourcing was usually made by Nones of an ethnic Catholic or Jewish background. Other parents outsource religious instruction because they think it confers certain benefits such as a morality or cultural literacy that they themselves have already acquired but children still need to learn. One mom who was personally indifferent to religion was nonetheless considering sending her little boy to Sunday school because, she said, "there's value in religious ed, knowing about the Bible, having basic understanding about stories, events in it. My little brother and sister who didn't go to church, I notice they don't know these things, and it's important to know that because most of America does. You need those cultural references." Fran, described earlier as a self-provider, and her husband Jeff experimented with outsourcing as well. They sent their kids to a Unitarian Universalist Sunday school, without affiliating themselves, because, as Jeff put it, "you need to know other people's reference points. And ethical foundation, understanding what that is in various cultures and religions. And knowing how to figure out if someone is following their own code of ethics, or if they are being hypocritical." Similarly, recent studies report on atheists who send their children to conventional Christian Sunday school in order to expose them to diverse religions or provide them with an ethical framework.[16]

Most None parents who outsource do so because they see some sort of value in learning about religion, be it due to family heritage or to acquire cultural literacy. For a few parents, outsourcing was a way to respond to a child's interest in religion. Roxanne, introduced earlier as an Unchurched Believer, said she and her children celebrated Christmas and Easter with their Catholic grandparents, and she would "dig out the Bible" when her daughters asked about the meaning of Christmas, but she did not herself engage in any systematic effort to incorporate religion in their home. Roxanne said she decided to enroll one of them in Sunday school only because the child wanted to go. She expressed surprise at her daughter's "natural spirituality" which she contrasted with her own ambivalence about religion. Like parents who feel compelled to provide music lessons to a gifted child, Roxanne felt she should not deprive her daughter of religion. "We tried different places that people recommended," she said. "One was a Methodist church that was supposed to have a really great kids group, but Jillian didn't like it all that much," so they stopped sending her there and are currently looking for a more suitable program.

Among the parents I studied, outsourcing tended to be a transitional option. It was a way for None parents, ambivalent about transmitting religion to their children, to try out the idea of joining a community, either conventional or alternative. Once they got their feet wet, they may eventually affiliate themselves, as happened to Beth, also introduced earlier, who decided to join a Unitarian Universalist congregation. As she put it, "I'm just starting to understand that religion doesn't have to be a bad thing." The experience of outsourcing, however, also may intensify the parent's skepticism about religion, leading them to try to transmit an alternative worldview themselves (Fran and Jon did) or to drop the project entirely, a subject I will consider next.

Doing Nothing

Some parents chose to do nothing. By this I mean that they took no action to transmit any particular worldview, religious or secular, to their children. They do not enroll their children in institutional religious or alternative worldview education program; they remain unaffiliated; and they do not take any actions to introduce religion, spirituality, or a secular philosophy such as Humanism into their home life. While these parents often do celebrate holidays such as Christmas or Hanukkah, the meaning of these events is cultural: it is about setting up a tree, hunting for candy eggs, and getting presents; or it may be family history, an opportunity to cook grandma's special recipe for roast lamb, for example. The religious meaning is not explained. When visiting such families I never saw religious books or toys in the home and there was no religious symbolism on display in the house. I refer to these parents as *nonproviders* because they do not provide instruction or involvement in either religion or a secular philosophy. Not surprisingly, all of the parents categorized as Indifferent were nonproviders. But the category includes a Secularist, a Spiritual Seeker, and several Unchurched Believers as well.

You might think, as I did initially, that doing nothing about transmitting religion was a deliberate assertion of the parent's identity as a None. But you would be wrong. The common theme that emerged from my interviews with nonproviders was that they were too busy with other things to give much thought to how to deal with religion in the lives of their children.

Two examples are Jared and Peter, introduced earlier as Nones who are Indifferent to religion. Both were raised Protestant and have very positive memories of that experience, but they drifted away because religion ceased to have any relevance in their lives. Unlike other parents described in this chapter, having children did not alter their indifference. When their own parents asked about the children's religion, each considered outsourcing, but then decided not to go through with it. Jared claims to see value in religion because he "really loved Sunday school when [he] was a kid" and because "there are a lot of things you learn in church that are useful" such as "cultural references, singing, speaking publically . . . and exposure to different kinds of people." His commitment to actually provide such education, however, is vague: "Maybe when [my son] gets older . . . but I don't think that's going to happen because we spend too many weekends out of town. . . . [*Laughs.*] And even if we were here we wouldn't go." Peter is similarly nonchalant. He and his wife had their three children baptized because, he said, "her parents wanted it, and it seemed like the right thing to do at the time." But when asked if he had considered sending them to Sunday school, he responded: "Fleetingly. . . . I let the thoughts pass out of my head." Instead, he spends hours every weekend on his and the boys' true passion, baseball.

Neither Jared nor Peter engages children in religious activity in the home. When I visited them, evidence of the activities that engaged them was vividly on display: Jared's skis and snowboards in the mudroom, photos of the smiling family on a mountaintop; Peter's sons' baseball trophies on the bookshelf, piles of sneakers, and mitts at the door. Symbols of religion or spirituality such as I had seen in some other None homes—a communion photo, a Bible, a Buddha image—were conspicuously absent. Although both families celebrate Christmas and Easter as cultural holidays with gifts and egg hunts, they do so because it is fun, it brings the family together, and "the kids love it." There is no attempt to incorporate religious content in these events.

Peter and Jared's indifference to religion makes doing nothing a logical choice. But even parents who are Unchurched Believers or who replace their childhood religion with a Secular or Seeker-style worldview will sometimes take no action to transmit that to their children. Isabel, an Unchurched Believer who tried self-providing, is now, in her words, "doing nothing with religion," mostly because her children lost interest. Robert, a Secularist, briefly joined a Unitarian Universalist congregation so his young children could be part of their worldview education program. But after a couple of years, he left because his kids no longer wanted to go and he did not want to force them. Eileen, a Seeker, said she would like for her children to "have a spiritual community" but she cannot find one. She has tried out some places she hoped would be open-minded, most recently the Quakers, but did not feel comfortable there because she is a single mom and "it was all married couples." A mother of twin twelve-year-old boys, she has tried talking to them about spirituality, with mixed results: "They are interested, when I tell them a story, but not too much; they have always been very resistant to my telling them anything." So for now, she is doing nothing, mostly because she is too busy. She works full-time as a paralegal. "It's [about having the] time, really." Three years later she had given up entirely.

Doing nothing to transmit religion to children would seem like the default option for None parents. In my research, however, it was the least common strategy. There's a methodological reason for this: I was conducting a study on how and why None parents do or do not incorporate religion in the upbringing of their children. Parents for whom religion or spirituality or a secular philosophy is important enough that they want to raise their child that way are more likely to be interested in the research question and therefore to participate in the study. National survey data suggests that roughly one-third of today's adult Nones were raised without religion,[17] so it stands to reason that doing nothing remains a common option. Yet, surveys tend to oversimplify that picture: only conventional religion is counted; parents raising a child in an alternative community such as the AHA would be defined as "doing nothing." Clearly, more research is necessary to determine how many None parents are doing what with their children.

This chapter has explored five different ways that None parents approach the question of transmitting religion or a secular philosophy to their children. My sample is too small to say anything about which of the options described here is the most popular strategy. What this study does show is that there is more variety in how Nones raise their children than existing research would imply. It is not just a choice between doing nothing and going back to church. None parents may also find an alternative worldview community, or outsource religious instruction, or try to transmit a religious or alternative worldview without institutional support.

The picture is further complicated by the fluidity that characterizes contemporary American religious life. As Roof has shown in his work on religion among the baby boomers,[18] recent generations of Americans are much less likely to maintain lifelong loyalty to a particular denomination. Instead, they experiment and explore, go church shopping to find what they like. They may "try on" a community for a while and then switch to another or drop out entirely when it no longer suits them. This kind of fluidity was characteristic of the None parents I studied as well. There was considerable movement and flux between these five strategies described in this chapter. Parents may outsource religious instruction and, after a few years, go back to church or synagogue themselves. They may experiment with providing religious or secular worldview education themselves and then, finding it difficult, move toward outsourcing. They may reaffiliate with conventional religion, get frustrated, and eventually drop out again and do nothing with their children. They may, as Jeff and Fran did, cover all the bases: When their oldest two children were in elementary school, they sent them to Sunday school (outsourcing). Two years later they pulled the children out and experimented with creating their own meaning and moral structure (self-providers). Five years later the family moved to another city and joined a Unitarian Universalist congregation (alternative community); during this time two additional children were born. Another three years later, Jeff and Fran had dropped out and were doing nothing to transmit any particular worldview to their children. In short, whatever the numbers tell us that None parents are doing with their children, they may not be doing it for long.

Returning to my daughter's question—"What are we, Mom?"—it appears that None parents give no single answer. They respond in different ways and their answers change over time. And given the lack of precise survey data on the subject, we can't even say which of the many options presented here is most common, normal, or typical of None parents. This inconclusive conclusion can be interpreted in different ways. On the one hand, it is consistent with the understanding of None, discussed earlier in this book, as uncommitted. If Nones identify as such because they do not want to commit to a particular tradition or institution, one would expect to see a high degree of diversity and fluidity among this population. On the other hand, there is some order beneath the chaos. In chapter 3 I showed that many Nones hold substantive spiritual or secular worldviews that are functionally equivalent to religion. In this chapter, I have argued that None parents use clearly identifiable strategies to transmit those worldviews to their children. Those strategies, albeit diverse, are all ultimately powered by a similar motive, which is the topic of the next chapter.

6

The Meaning of Choice in Religion

Nones are changing the American religious landscape, and the way they raise their children amplifies that change. That change does not signify widespread secularization (at least not yet), but neither is it merely about believers rejecting institutions. It is about choice. One of the central arguments of this book is that what makes Nones distinctive from churched Americans is their insistence upon *worldview choice*. Not affiliating with organized religion is about asserting the right to make one's own choices. Unchurched Believers who choose to be Christian or Jewish in ways that may not fit with the dogma of a particular church or synagogue; Spiritual Seekers who combine elements of various religions, rather than committing to any of them; Philosophical Secularists who think it is up to the individual to create his or her own meaning in life— for all of them, having a worldview is a deeply personal choice. Carrying on one's family tradition, affiliating with a particular institution, or even selecting a religious preference on a public opinion survey is perceived as problematic because it limits that choice in some way.

The celebration of personal choice in religion is, of course, not limited to Nones; indeed, the majority of Americans claim to affirm personal choice. Nones, however, take worldview choice further than most. They are, in that sense, at the cutting edge of contemporary religious trends. In this chapter, I will look more closely at the trend toward worldview choice: how the language of personal choice is reflected in the decisions None parents make about their children, and what impact this may have on the next generation and on the culture at large.

Maximizing Our Children's Choices

None parents make different kinds of decisions. Some go back to church, some join a community that welcomes doubters, some self-provide knowledge about religion or a secular philosophy, some outsource religious instruction, and some do nothing. Yet regardless of which path they choose, the decision is always framed as a way to help the child make his or her own choices. I say *always* because there were no exceptions among my respondents. When I asked parents why they chose a particular option for their child, they offered various reasons. But one reason cut across the board: the parents I talked to claimed the option selected would ultimately help their children to choose their own worldviews.

The use of a *choice narrative* is not surprising among parents who employ the "do nothing" strategy, those who take no action to raise their children with religion, spirituality, or a secular philosophy. Natalie is an example. She is a Spiritual Seeker, her husband is a secular Jew. Their son is still in preschool, and both parents work full-time. Like many parents who select the do nothing option, they admit they are just too busy to deal with the religion question. But they also frame their inaction as a way of letting their child decide. Natalie puts it this way: "I think it is good for a parent to provide the model of 'I don't know all the answers,' or 'I know some of the answers for me, but I don't know all of the answers, and certainly not for everybody.' You need to find your own way. Some of what is in my path I think is good for you too, but it is your choice ultimately." While some would dismiss this as mere rationalization for doing nothing, such a judgment assumes that parents *should* take actions to help their children make choices about religion.

One would also expect to hear choice narratives from parents who educate their children about a variety of religious and secular worldviews. Beth, whose young daughter is enrolled in a Unitarian Universalist worldview education program in Florida, said: "They are getting a good education there. And that's what I want for her. I don't want her to be spoon-fed one idea—even paganism [which along with Buddhism is Beth's preferred path], that's not the only idea I want her to have. I want her to pick her own path. I teach her to question everything, I teach her to form her own ideas about spirituality." Jay, a Colorado parent with a teenage son in a similar program, said: "So it is sort of the foundation I would like to provide, not a religious faith, not a 'here's what you have to believe' kind of thing, more like, 'here is a lot of information and you decide what you want to believe.'" In California, Jon and Rebecca are raising their son with a combination of Jewish and Hindu tradition.

They tell him: "You have a choice, you are not automatically born into a tradition because your parents are. Your parents will raise you with a particular tradition but you are not automatically in a tradition; you have to make a choice sometime." For parents who are educating their children about a plurality of traditions, both religious and secular, the choice narrative is a logical corollary: they are offering various options, so the child can choose.

More surprisingly, choice narratives were also employed by parents who deliberately raise their children in a particular tradition. Denise, an Unchurched Believer who returned to synagogue to raise her daughter with Judaism, said she tries hard to maintain the child's freedom to choose: "Kids that age are so open, and that's why you also have to be careful, when you have certain beliefs; you want them to also be able to make up their own minds and decisions, you want to sway them but not direct them." Jennifer, an Unchurched Believer in Massachusetts who went back to church when her son was six, insists that she is not directing him: "I would not want to force Zach into anything, like if he did not want to do Sunday school then he wouldn't go . . . if he was old enough to stay home, he could watch some TV." Like many None parents, Jennifer contrasts her attitude with that of her own parents, who were strict, church-going Catholics: "I notice the difference between when I was a child and when I look back now. The forcing you to go to church, that's what everybody did back then, about everything not just church." She recalls how during the blizzard of 1978, "everything was shut down, and still [they] walked downtown to church." She thinks the lack of choice is what eventually caused her to leave church: "I think that's the worst thing you could do to a child. When they are really little, of course, they go with you everywhere, but as they get older, that's when you teach them something and don't force them into it." Nicole in Colorado is also wary of imposing her worldview. Although her own path is that of a Spiritual Seeker, she feels it would be wrong to raise her two teenagers outside a church: "I didn't want to make that choice for my kids. I feel like by taking them to church on Sundays I am allowing them to keep their options open and I am sure that when they are in college or young adults they will have a period in their lives when they choose not to go to church. And that's fine, but at least they will have this memory of something that they used to do and they can choose whether to do that again." None parents who reaffiliate so their kids can attend Christian or Jewish Sunday school or who outsource their children's religious education to a church or synagogue are, objectively, limiting their children's choices. Yet, they do not see it that way. They think they are offering guidance that the children can choose to follow or not.

The story we tell about what we do may or may not reflect what we actually do. The majority of None parents do, in fact, restrict their children's choices. This is true not just of those who raise their kids as Christians or Jews. Those who provide a pluralistic worldview education typically offer a rather one-sided, liberal perspective that does not include, for example, fundamentalist Christianity or Orthodox Judaism as a viable option for their child. Those who do nothing are not exposing their children to any options. As Nicole put it, "My experience is that, generally, people raised without religious traditions as children do not have religious traditions as adults. And the parents say I will let my kids decide if they want to go to church when they're adults, but my experience is, you're making that choice for them as children. Because kids who don't go to church as kids won't do so as adults, so you're kind of sending them on the 'don't go to church' path whether you realize it or not."

Several parents acknowledged this tension between the narrative of choice and the reality of more limited options. Robert, a Philosophical Secularist, feels it is near impossible not to impose your own worldview on your children. "I was careful. I was not a crusading atheist, so it wasn't like atheism was my kind of antitype to religion where I told them, there is no God." When his children asked questions, he would say: "some people believe this, but I don't believe there's a God." Of course, those people did not get to explain to Robert's children why they believe in God. And Robert is a caring, morally upstanding individual who has a loving relationship with his children. This biases the outcome, and Robert admitted as much. "The problem that I saw is just that children are children, they don't have a mind of their own at that point, so even though I had this kind of illusion that they would make up their own mind, they just followed behind me." Rebecca puts it more bluntly. Although she hopes "that [she has] given [her son] enough material and freedom that someday he will choose for himself," she admitted: "No matter what I am doing I am going to brainwash, no matter what, because we will teach [our children] what we know, what we believe to be true." We influence our children's choices in the path that we choose, through the options to which we expose them, and in the way that we present the alternatives to them.

There were a few parents who tried very hard to avoid even such unintended influence. Instead of choosing a path for their children, they claimed to follow the children's lead as to whether or not and how to explore various worldviews. I met several parents of younger children who said they had no plans to raise them with any particular worldview, but who predicted that they might explore religious education if the child expressed an interest. Natalie, the seeker I cited earlier, is doing nothing with her son for now. She said: "I don't know if that will change once he reaches an age where he starts asking questions. But the only way I see it changing is if he wants it to. . . . Yeah, if he was interested in going to a synagogue or church or whatever, yes I would be interested in going with him." This kind of choice language was also common among parents of older children who said they had chosen a particular path but the child was losing interest. Robert placed his daughter in the Unitarian Universalist worldview education program during the sixth and seventh grade. But the last year she was in it, in "the so-called affirmations class, which is the Unitarian analogue to what would be a confirmation class in some other church, she decided that she did not want to go on into the high school group . . . she decided that she had other things to do." If you follow the child's lead into religion, you also follow it out of religion.

The idea of leaving the choice to the child was particularly striking among parents with two or more children and who decided to raise one child with religion and another without it. Unlike his daughter, Robert's son never attended any kind of religious education program because "he didn't want to do it and [the parents] didn't have any real agenda or need to push him." So too with Roxanne, whose older daughter was not raised with any particular religion while the younger daughter attended church. Roxanne is an Unchurched Believer who chose the outsourcing option in response to her daughter's interest: "During that time when I wasn't feeling comfortable with any church, and when I personally . . . did not have the need for a church, and so if one of the children were voicing a concern or a need for a church then yes, I definitely wanted to respond to that." Roxanne resents the lack of choice about religion in her own childhood: "I felt like I had been ripped off because I don't remember my baptism at all. . . . [Being Catholic] was not an active choice . . . it was chosen for me." But just as her parents should not have imposed religion on her, she does not want to impose "no religion" on her child.

Following a child's lead can be challenging when he or she chooses a path that is different from that of the parent. Consider Rosario, an Unchurched Believer whose personal orientation is recognizably Christian. She and her four children attended a Mormon church, but ended their affiliation when she divorced several years ago. When I spoke with her, Rosario claimed she had no religion and was not raising her children in any particular tradition. The kids sometimes attend Mormon Church with their father on the weekends they stay with him. But she said they are not particularly interested in religion. Except for one of them, she said: "My 10 year old son, he's concerned and interested in exploring religions. . . . He is by far, of all four of them, the most spiritually minded. Or maybe just more philosophical than the other kids. He is a creator. I think this is something that comes up in his natural process." So Rosario wants to support him in his interests: "We went to the library a couple of weeks ago, and we got a book on Buddhism, he wants to understand." Buddhism is not her path (she still believes in the Christian God) but she does not want to impose her path on him, or on any of her children. Or consider Brenda, the Philosophical Secularist who raised her children without religion—until they became born-again Christians during their teens. She recalled: "[The] greatest challenge was probably holding back, not criticizing them when they became Christian, not directing, because that's what I felt was the important thing to do. In fact, it was probably a direct response to the way I was raised. I felt that my parents were imposing their belief system on me, so I wanted to do the exact opposite." Doing the opposite initially meant raising her children without religion. Now it meant supporting her children in their religion. Not an easy task, especially for a Philosophical Secularist for whom a conversion to religious fundamentalism represents a total rejection of the parent's worldview. So Brenda's experience is a real test of the choice narrative, and her restraint is impressive. We all want for our children to have freedom of choice—until they make choices we do not like.

Roots of the Choice Narrative

Allowing your children to choose whether and how they may be exposed to religion or some alternative worldview may seem extreme, but it is rooted in a much more widely held perception that religious choice is good. Most Americans believe that religion should be a matter of personal choice,[1] a view that has held steady for nearly half a century and that is reflected in high levels of religious switching and intermarriage even among the churched population. The choice narrative, as Sheena Iyengar persuasively argues, has become the lingua franca of America.[2]

This was not always so. For my grandparents and generations before them, religion was something you inherited rather than selected, something that determined whom you would marry and how you raised your children. Religion was like a family relationship or a job: people did not always enjoy it, but they lived with it. A few people became atheists because they rejected religion intellectually, but nobody expected religion to make you feel good or fit in with your lifestyle as we do today. The normative narrative about religion was that of duty; it did not occur to most people that they had a choice. Then came the 1960s and everything changed. Okay, I'm exaggerating a bit, but most serious scholars of religion in America suggest that the rise of the choice narrative is a product of the mid-twentieth century.

The narrative of choice in religion can be understood as part of a long-term trend toward greater individualism and commodification of all aspects of American life. Its most obvious roots are in American individualism. As Robert Bellah argues in *Habits of the Heart,* individualism is the "first language" of American culture that provides a "common moral vocabulary" to express how we think of success (as a matter of individuals making the right choices), freedom (as individual freedom from others), or justice (individuals have equal opportunities guaranteed by fair laws).[3] Individualism, however, is not our only common language. Bellah reminds us that earlier periods of American history were guided by other cultural narratives: the Biblical narrative of the Puritans, who understood themselves as creating a new promised land guided by God, during the colonial period; and the Republican narrative of Washington and Jefferson who emphasized political equality and freedom, and the individual's responsibility to participate in representative government. Those earlier narratives, Bellah argues, still resonate but have been largely displaced by a new moral language, modern individualism, which takes two forms. The first, or what Bellah calls *utilitarian individualism*, emerged in the late nineteenth century with industrialization and America's emergence as an economic powerhouse. Rooted in Benjamin Franklin's notion that God helps those who help themselves, this narrative asserts that it is the individual's disciplined and vigorous pursuit of his own interest that will lead to the good society. The second variation, *expressive individualism*, arose in the mid-twentieth century with the rise of the counterculture and the identity rights movements (for blacks, women, gays, and other oppressed groups). This narrative, as expressed in the ideas of Walt Whitman, sees the ultimate purpose of American independence as exploring and expressing one's true inner self. The good society is one that facilitates this freedom for every individual.

The moral language of expressive individualism shapes all aspects of contemporary American life. A good education allows us to explore our interests; the best job gives expression to our talents; the ideal marriage is personally fulfilling. Women should not have to stay home and raise children if they want a career; a son should not have to take over his father's business if he has other interests; gays and lesbians should not have to pretend they are straight. These are the kinds of truisms that almost everyone today, especially the young, accept without question. We should not be surprised, then, that religion too is increasingly about individual expression.

Sociologists of religion trace the rise of individualism in religion to the cultural revolution of the 1960s.[4] Clark Roof's research showed how boomers dropped out of church in record numbers to seek a spirituality that resonated with them personally. Religion became a personal quest, where attendance and dogma no longer matter, but freedom and choice are core values.[5] Robert Wuthnow describes this change in religious orientation as a shift from a *dwelling spirituality* to a *seeker spirituality*. In the former, spiritual beliefs and practices are housed in the institutions of organized religion, and religious identity is typically ascribed by the family. In the latter, spirituality is sought in personal experience, and every individual negotiates his or her identity.[6] The move toward individualized religion was precipitated by various factors: the civil rights revolutions exposed racism and sexism in religious institutions; rising rates of higher education exposed more people to new ideas (especially Eastern religions); a wider range of options (post-Vatican II Catholicism; the New Age, Evangelicalism) lead to more religiously eclectic habits; and the complexity and mobility of modern life (people live in one town, kids go to school in another, and play sports in yet another) made commitment to church impractical. While many people still do attend church, of course, they tend to select a community based on their individual preferences (e.g, rousing music, a conservative theology, a woman minister) rather than the tradition they inherited.[7] Religion, for better or for worse, is increasingly perceived as a personal choice.

The choice narrative is an expression of individualism, to be sure. But it is more than that. It also reflects the power of the market and the commodification of all aspects of life, giving rise to a new cultural framework: consumerism. In this framework, increasing aspects of human life are (and should be) made available through the market that offers a wide array of options from which individual can (and should) choose.

Americans today expect to have markets not just for objects and services supplied for profit (e.g., food, clothing, automobiles, electrical repairs, or legal advice) but for expertise or care traditionally provided by nonprofit institutions such as healthcare or education. Because the market is competitive, advertising and branding becomes increasingly important in the quest to persuade consumers to choose a particular product. Thus it is not just car dealerships and fashion houses that aggressively advertise, but universities, hospitals, and state and local governments that seek to brand themselves in an effort to attract customers. Our very identity is defined by consumption. We express who we are through the style we wear, the car we drive, the way we decorate our homes, and others identify us by our consumption choices. In today's society, *class* has little meaning as everyone considers him- or herself middle-class. Instead, social distinctions are based on generations of consumers whose identities are defined by their consumption habits (e.g.,Yuppies, Gen Xers, or DINKS for Dual Income, No Kids).[8] The consumer, as Celia Lury notes, has become the "master category of collective and individual identity" in contemporary American society.[9]

As with individualism, this was not always so. Although human societies have always consumed objects and services, we began to *iden-*

tify as consumers only in the nineteenth and twentieth centuries. James Twitchell traces the rise of consumer culture in America to the success of the industrial revolution and the emergence of surplus production, which in turn gave rise to advertising. The purpose of advertising is, of course, to get us to consume. But advertising, writes Twitchell, is also about meaning. In a competitive market offering a wide array of very similar products, advertisers seek to persuade Americans to consume by associating a product with meaning and status (youth, beauty, adventure) rather than its actual characteristics (this cereal is made with oats). Thus advertising transforms the act of consuming from a pragmatic economic action (I am hungry, so I buy a box of cereal) to a meaning-making act (I choose to buy this cereal because it is organic and locally produced). Consumption, in this context, feels empowering because we consume by choice rather than from need, and because it is limited only by money, rather than pre-existing status such as family, gender, race, class, or religion.[10] Small wonder, then, that more and more Americans would begin to identify as consumers and to use the language of consumer culture to frame all aspects of their lives.

Religion, of course, cannot escape from this. Religion has become something we choose from a wide array of options in the market place of ideas based on our personal preferences. Surveys show more than half of all Americans changed religion at least once,[11] and that increasing numbers go church shopping to find a community that fits our preferences.[12] Some want emotional fulfillment, others seek social connection, still others seek moral guidance and assistance with problems in their lives. Religious institutions, in turn, are responding to market demands. Churches and synagogues today offer various services (e.g., day care for children, afternoon programs for teens, singles mixers, baseball leagues, or drug addiction support groups) that are intended not to serve the poor but attract middle-class individuals to become members. And an increasing number of religious institutions have begun campaigns to brand and advertise themselves to potential customers (many religions, of course, have a long history of seeking out new members, but it is only recently that religious institutions have adopted consumer language).[13]

Indeed, some scholars have argued that the market has itself become a religion, displacing more traditional worldviews such as Judaism, Christianity, or even secular humanism.[14] Over the last two centuries, science has steadily chipped away at religion's traditional function, to offer a meaning system that explains how we should live in the world. Consumerism has stepped in to fill the gap. As James Twitchell writes, "Western culture had to accept that we are not the center of the universe (thanks, Galileo), not the center of God's creation (thanks, Darwin), not the center of a coherent self (thanks, Freud), and so rather than cast our lot with the moody existentialists and admit we are but mites on dust bunnies skittering around the universe," we willingly embrace the order and meaning offered by consumer culture.[15] That meaning, Twitchell asserts, is driven by advertising, which sells the packaging—an image, a life style, a promise of fulfillment—rather than the product itself. We buy the product because we want that meaning. In the postmodern world where religion no longer assigns us a role or duties to perform, we construct a self and choose a lifestyle by consuming. The market, as David Loy writes, is not merely *like* a religion, it *is* a religion, in the sense that it shapes our values and actions far more than Christianity or some other traditional religion does.[16]

At the core of modern consumer culture is the idea that we always have a choice. Everything in life—food, clothing, healthcare, entertainment, education, love, religion—is provided by markets that offer options from which individuals can choose based on their particular preferences. Nothing is fixed or final. If you are tired of driving a sensible Subaru station wagon, you can buy the sporty Mini Cooper. If you have spent the last twenty years cutting hair, you can still retrain and become an accountant or a yoga teacher. If your parents raised you in one religion but it no longer resonates, you can shop around and find another worldview, or create your own from the many different options that are available. It is this emphasis on preferences and options that consumer culture contributes to the choice narrative. American individualism tells me I have the power to choose; consumerism promises there will be many choices.

Consumer culture and individualism are distinct yet complementary cultural frameworks that both privilege the narrative of choice. We can see both strains of this narrative in the stories presented in this book: Each parent believes she chose her own worldview from an array of options (consumer religion) based on what works best for her (utilitarian individualism) and what speaks most directly to her true self (expressive individualism). Parents want their children to choose their own world-view as well. Given the larger historical context, we can understand the growth in Nones as the inevitable outcome of individualization and commodification in religion. Declaring yourself to be None is the pen-ultimate expression of personal worldview choice, a declaration that you are unique and will not be defined by somebody else.

The Cultural Impact of the Choice Narrative

The choice narrative has become the dominant ethos of our time.[17] It is so deeply embedded in our culture that we take it for granted; we rarely question it, and we look with suspicion at those who do. The nar-rative is used by both ends of the political spectrum, from liberals who believe we can choose our gender identity to conservatives who assert that homeless people have made poor choices. Even the academic study of religion is pervaded by narrative of choice. The dominant theoretical framework for understanding religion nowadays (especially in the social sciences) is rational choice or market theory, which analyzes religious behavior as a rational cost-benefit calculation made by individuals, and the emergence, rise, and fall of religious institutions as a response to those calculations.[18] The choice narrative liberates; it is respectful of individual differences; it holds individuals accountable. Like freedom or justice, it has become axiomatic that choice is good, and by extension that more choice is better.

Yet as Sheena Iyengar reminds us, there are other types of cultural narratives, such as the narrative of destiny common in many religions, or the narrative of chance embraced by science. And not all societies glo-rify individual choice as ours does. Iyengar distinguishes between *indi-vidualist* cultures such as the United States and more *collectivist* societies such India. In individualist cultures, people are encouraged to choose, and having preferences and exercising choices is considered important beginning at a very young age. It is commonplace for American par-ents to ask preschoolers if they want cereal or toast for breakfast. Most teenagers expect to choose where to attend college and what to study. And everybody, of course, will choose whether and whom to marry. This is not the case for people (like Iyengar's parents) whose marriages were arranged by family and whose courses of study and occupation are still often determined by caste. In such collectivist cultures, people are encouraged to do their duty, as determined by the community, and violations are strongly sanctioned. Although such a system seems deeply oppressive to many Americans, Iyengar's parents are happy in their marriage and satisfied in their careers because they frame their story differently. Marriage is understood as a uniting of two families. One's profession is a way of carrying on a family tradition or of giving back to the family who has sacrificed so much to educate their son, for example. By contrast, families in America are seen as a fulfillment of the individual. Because we are socialized in either the collectivist or individualist mode from early on, the cultural scripts for both types of cultures are deeply internalized, and we may not even be aware we are using them.

A growing chorus of voices, however, has criticized the choice narrative, or at least its dominance in our society. These critics assert that the increasing individualization and commodification of our culture is a problem for America that ultimately threatens the very freedom we hold dear. Perhaps the best-known example of this criticism is Christopher Lasch's best-selling book, *Culture of Narcissism,* originally published in 1979. Lasch offered a stinging critique of our society's glorification of personal choice, claiming that it not only undermines community but ultimately also leads to pathology. Using a clinical definition, he asserted that most Americans today have developed a form of narcissism, a preoccupation with self that derives from dependency and weakness of ego and requires continuous external validation. He questioned the notion that maximal freedom of choice is liberating, describing, for example, how the modern university's system of "endless electives" actually undermines a coherent education, how corporate advertising manipulates us to seek and express identity through our purchases, or how the market for self-improvement plays to our insecurities and makes us dependent on experts. In the culture of narcissism, he writes, the self becomes a "performer under constant scrutiny of friends and strangers" (he would be absolutely horrified by the existence of Facebook).[19]

Lasch blamed both the right and its veneration of unfettered capitalism and the left and its celebration of identity politics for creating a hyper-individualist culture that has weakened family and community ties. That argument, made more than thirty years ago, has been bolstered by more recent interpretations. Robert Putnam's 2000 book,

Bowling Alone, presents reams of statistical data showing that Americans have become increasingly disconnected from friends, neighbors, and community institutions such as parent teacher associations, political parties, and churches.[20] He asserts that the loss of these social bonds is a serious threat to our society. Declining family bonds and community ties mean the most vulnerable members of society, such as children and the poor, are less likely to get the support they need. Declining civic engagement by ordinary people means our government will become less representative of the mainstream America and give more voice to moneyed interests or extremist voices. Declining participation in church and synagogue means we spend less time volunteering to help others, and perhaps more importantly, are rarely reminded that we should put others before ourselves.

America's embrace of the personal choice narrative in religion has been subject to particular criticism because organized religion has long served as an important counterweight against the human tendency to be self-centered. As Robert Wuthnow argues in *After Heaven,* the classic religious traditions call on individuals to abide by rules and discipline set by a higher authority that has ultimate wisdom. By contrast, personal choice–based spirituality does not demand much of us; the self becomes the only arbiter of what is right or wrong. An example frequently cited by sociologists of religion is Bellah's interview (in *Habits of the Heart*) with a young nurse named Sheila who claimed she believed in God but did not attend church and described her religion as "Sheilaism. Just my own little voice. It's just love yourself and be gentle with yourself. You know, I guess, and take care of each other."[21] Critics like Bellah and Wuthnow point out that the classic religious traditions ask us to commit to institutions to which we give of ourselves (e.g., through regular attendance, tithing, or volunteering), whereas personal choice spirituality requires no such commitment (hence attendance and donations are way down). The classic religious traditions call on us to be our brothers' keepers; while in personal choice spirituality we are no longer responsible for larger social problems because gender, racial or economic inequality can simply be blamed on the poor choices made by other individuals. This is not to say that individuals will not engage in charity or social activism outside of organized religion. Even when people care about others, however, the critics point out, it can be difficult to harness personal spiritual ideals to transform society without the help of institutions. As the temperance movement and the civil rights movement remind us, individuals need organizations to effect change. The culture's movement toward personal choice spirituality, in short, robs religion of much of its moral and social power.

From this perspective, None parents' celebrations of personal choice are a problem, yet another step down the ladder to narcissism. I think the critics have a point. As a long-time community organizer in my adopted city of New Haven, I am well aware of how difficult it can be to get people civically engaged these days, and after some twenty years of teaching undergraduates, I am sick and tired of hearing my students cop out of difficult discussions and essays by adopting a lazy and uncritical stance of cultural relativism. But critics such as Lasch, Wuthnow, and Bellah may also overstate their case. It is easy to forget how oppressive and intolerant the Christian-dominated American culture could be in the past and to overlook the role that organized religion played in legitimating that value system. The churches and synagogues of old, for example, did provide a counter-weight to selfishness. But they also taught (and some still do) that a woman's place is in the home raising children, that a man loving another man is a terrible sin that must be punished, and, in some parts of the country, that God created black people to live separately from whites. The narrative of choice allows me to reject such narrow options—not because I'm narcissistic or shallow but by giving me permission to question authority, to trust my own experience, and to seek out other ways to read a sacred text and to explore alternative worldviews (secular humanism, Paganism) that exist outside the religious establishment of this society.[22] It may or may not be a coincidence that most of the critics of the culture of personal choice are middle-age, middle-class, white, straight, and male—in other words part of the establishment whose values were long supported by the civic-minded moral communities that are now declining. What is clear is that the rise of the personal choice narrative has served to radically decentralize authority in religion. And that, to me, is not such a bad thing.

The rise of the choice narrative, then, is ambiguous in its impact on our culture. It has fractured our society, to be sure, but it has also liberated some of us. In so doing, it may reflect the inevitable tension between what is best for the individual versus what is best for society. The choice narrative's impact on the individual, by contrast, would seem un-ambiguously positive. After all, the narrative empowers the individual. Rather than dutifully carrying on a family religious tradition, I can select a worldview that best expresses my own personal identity or most effectively works to accomplish my goals. Rather than imposing a tradition on my children, I encourage them to choose their own. It is intriguing to consider how having such choices might shape our children. On what basis will they make such choices? How will they feel about having that choice? And are they really free to choose? Let's look more closely at what research tells us about this.

The Personal Impact of Choice

Psychologists have long been interested in why and how individuals make choices, and the impact that this process has on their emotional well-being. Some aspects of making choices appear to be innate. Studies have shown that both animals and humans prefer having some choice over no choice, even when the no-choice option is better. The *desire* to choose thus seems to be a natural drive, perhaps because it allows us to maintain a sense of control over the world around us.[23] Other aspects of choosing are learned.

Animal and human studies suggest that the ability to perceive choices is a learned process. Iyengar gives the example of people from former communist Russia who were asked to pick one of seven popular sodas. They declined to choose, perceiving the seven flavors as one option, soda. When she put out water and juice in addition to the seven sodas, they perceived it as three options. By contrast, to Americans, who are accustomed to having many options, the variations among sodas mattered a great deal. Learning from our perception of choices and options applies to many less trivial matters; it explains why women who experienced abuse as children will often not leave a violent marriage, or why gifted low-income children are less likely to apply to an Ivy League college than children from well-off families.

Learning also shapes the criteria by which we make choices. Iyengar's distinction between individualist and collectivist cultures illustrates this. One study she cites reported that Anglo-American children performed significantly better on a given task if they were able to choose it themselves, compared to children who were told their mothers or a teacher had chosen the task for them. Asian-American children, by contrast, performed best when they believed their mothers had chosen the task, second best when told the teacher did. The first-generation children, Iyengar concludes, apparently were influenced by their immigrant parents' approaches to choice: "[For them] choice was not just a way of defining and asserting their individuality, but a way to create community and harmony by deferring to the choices of people whom they trusted and respected. If they had a concept of being true to one's self, then that self, most likely, [was] composed, not of an individual, but of a collective. Success was just as much about pleasing key figures as it was about satisfying one's own preferences. Or, you could say that the individual's preferences were shaped by the preferences of specific others."[24] The study also illustrates how the emotional benefits we derive from choice are influenced by experience. The Asian children performed better on tasks chosen by their mothers, because they were happier and less anxious when deferring to authority, in contrast to the Anglo children, who perceived such authority to be oppressive. Even if the desire to choose is innate, this does not necessarily mean that greater happiness comes from individuals rather than communities making choices.

The extent to which making choices is learned raises interesting questions about None parents and their children. They, as well as other Americans, embrace the choice narrative because it expresses deeply held values: the right of each individual to be free and to be happy. Freedom is perhaps most important. It is enshrined in the nation's founding documents, enforced in our laws, and invoked by leaders on both sides of the political spectrum as what makes this country special. We all like to think of ourselves as free, and employing the choice narrative helps us do that. By framing my life as a series of choices that reflect my preferences, I assert my freedom to define who I am as opposed to conforming how family, colleagues, or society defines me.[25] But recent research on the psychology of choice suggests we may not be as free as we think we are.

The Illusion of Choice

Americans have more options than ever about what kind of worldview will guide our lives, but the availability of options does not necessarily translate into freedom of choice. To begin with, we often don't know what we want. As psychologist Barry Schwartz explains in *The Paradox of Choice,* knowing what we want depends partly on past experience of various options and those are often biased. He cites research by Daniel Kahneman and colleagues that demonstrates that our memory of a past experience is mostly determined by how it felt at its peak (the funniest part of the movie, the most painful moment of surgery) and how it felt when it ended. Because the peak-end rule influences whether people want to have the experience again, our stated preference will often be irrational. Would I really prefer surgery that involves intense pain followed by mild pain to surgery that involves only intense pain? Would I really prefer a one-week vacation that ends in a glorious day to a three-week vacation that ended in a five-hour traffic jam? Probably not. The disjunction between logic and memory suggests, we do not always know what we want.[26]

Even when we do know what we want, our choices are shaped by our familiarity with various options (the exposure effect), how the options are presented (framing), and the meanings we associate with various options (associations). Studies show that the more we are exposed to an object or idea, the more we like it (assuming we are neutral to begin with).[27] This is why people will vote for a candidate whose name they remember from the ads on television even if they know nothing else about him, or why people prefer Mom's cooking even if her food is objectively unremarkable. Americans' increased support for gay rights has been linked to greater exposure to positive gay images in the media. And, as discussed in chapter 3, the media's frequent coverage of the growth of the None population may have inadvertently contributed to further growth by familiarizing us with the concept, making it easier for individuals to choose to leave church.

Researchers have also examined how framing affects the choices we make. Barry Schwartz gives the example of two gas stations that both list the same prices, $1.45 per gallon for cash and $1.55 for credit, but one gas station has a sign that reads "Discount for Cash" while the other advertises "Surcharge for Credit." The impact on the customer's wallet is identical, but people have very different reactions: they prefer to buy something when it is framed as a discount. And then there is the famous trolley problem: Imagine a runaway trolley is hurtling toward five people who are tied up and unable to move. You can pull a lever which will switch the trolley to a different set of tracks, but there is one person on the side track. It is impossible to operate the lever in a way that would cause the trolley to derail without loss of life. Most respondents to this hypothetical scenario chose to save five people, rather than one person. But responses change when the dilemma is framed differently. As before, a trolley is hurtling down a track toward five people. You are on a bridge under which it will pass, and you can stop it by dropping a heavy weight in front of it. As it happens, there is a very fat man next to you— your only way to stop the trolley is to push him over the bridge and onto the track, killing him to save five. Should you proceed? Most people who approved of sacrificing one to save five in the first example do *not* approve to do so in the second example.[28] Although in both scenarios one person is killed to save five, people tend to frame the first killing as a side effect of the attempt to save a life, whereas they frame the second example as an intentional act of killing. Framing also helps explain why some Nones understand themselves as cultural outsiders while others do not, regardless of the actual number of Nones present in the region where they live.

Both the framing and exposure effect are, of course, widely used by advertisers in crafting messages to get us to choose the products they promote. But the most common method of seeking to influence our choices is by harnessing the power of association. Studies have shown that our brains store information based on association. People are much better able to remember a random series of numbers and letters when they associate them with meaningful visual images. This is why master poker players or competitors at the US Memory Championships deliberately practice such associations. It is also why tying a string to your finger helps you to remember to call mom on Mother's Day—unless, of course, you use that trick too often and create too many associations. Advertisers use the power of association when they pay famous actors or athletes to endorse a particular product: we see Michael Jordan wearing Nikes and we associate the positive feelings we have about him with that brand. Numerous studies show people are willing to pay significantly more for a particular brand, even when its objective qualities are indistinguishable from other brands. In blind taste tests, respondents preferred wines with expensive sounding labels to wines presented as cheap, or bottled water to tap water, or a can labeled as Coca Cola to other sodas—even when the beverages they were actually drinking were the same.[29] The Coca Cola Company has made particularly effective use of the association effect. For many people, Coke has become a symbol of America, it tastes better because of what it means. The association effect is clearly at work among Nones for whom no religion means they are free thinkers rather than sheep that follow along with the herd. Claiming membership in religion, for them, is associated with conformity to particular institutions or ideas. As I have argued, Nones may or may not have a religion (they may be Unchurched Believers, Spiritual Seekers, Philosophical Secularists, or just Indifferent), but by claiming no religious preference, they are sending a message that they are different from other Americans, that they are not conforming to the norm.

The various ways in which our decision-making can be shaped by factors like exposure, framing, or association should make us wonder how much freedom we can really give our children. Even with the best intentions, most None parents are shaping their children's choices. Because we believe in our own worldviews, we take pains to create positive associations for it, telling stories or creating fun family celebrations like a puja or a Christmas tree with Micky Mouse on top. As Robert pointed out, his children were more likely to adopt his own atheist worldview than that of their fundamentalist Christian grandparents, no matter how hard he tried to be fair and respectful in presenting other worldviews. The parents I interviewed were all in some way limiting the worldviews their children were exposed to. People who take the traditional route and go back to church or outsource religious education are presenting their child with only one option, whereas those who do nothing are presenting no options. Those who opt for the alternative worldview education model do expose multiple options to their children, but they tend to frame them in rather slanted ways: worldviews like Buddhism, Neopaganism, or Jewish humanism are framed in positive ways while fundamentalist Christianity or Islam are framed as irrational and dangerous. And it was a common pattern among all parents to frame their own decisions as maximizing children's freedom in contrast to the decisions of others, which they often judged as restrictive. Parents who did nothing claim that this allows their children to choose for themselves, rather than restricting them to a particular path as church-going parents do. However, parents who return to church framed the do nothing option as coercive and the traditionalist strategy as offering options that their children can take or leave as they wish. The narrative of choice, in short, may be somewhat self-serving.

The Tyranny of Choice

Freedom of choice in religion may be somewhat of an illusion. Yet, we as Americans love the narrative of choice, not only because it connotes freedom but also because we associate it with happiness. The pursuit of happiness is our birthright, and the best way to pursue it is for *me*, not other people, to make decisions about *my* life. Since we have different preferences, the more choices there are, the more likely it is that each of us will find an option that makes us happy. Recent research, however, suggests that conventional wisdom may be wrong.

Making choices can be stressful. As psychologist Barry Schwartz noted in an interview, many people are overwhelmed with the choices they have. We must make decisions about trivial things, "like what cereal to buy, what pain reliever to buy, and about important things like what 401(k) funds to invest in, whether to get married, when to get married, whether to have children, when to have children. And the cumulative effect of all of these choices creates a kind of stress and anxiety level that I think contributes to the three-fold increase in depression that's occurred in the last thirty years."[30] He and others assert that such stress is reduced when choices are more limited—either by turning decision-making power over to others, or by limiting the number of options available.

Research consistently shows that restriction in the number of options actually benefits us. In Iyengar's famous jam study, people who were presented with many different choices of jam to taste were actually less likely to make a purchase and less happy with the choice that they made than people presented with only a few options. Similar results were reported in another study where employees were less likely to participate in company-sponsored retirement plans the more options they were given.[31] From car buying to making decisions about childcare or surgery, people faced with multiple options were less happy: they experience more stress in the choosing process and express more regret over their decisions.

The stress of having too many choices is worse for some people than for others. Schwartz differentiates two types of decision-making styles: *Maximizers* expend a great deal of effort on exploring and evaluating their options. Even when they find an item that fits what they want, they keep looking around to make sure they do not miss items that may be even better. They seek and accept only the best. *Satisficers* search only until they find an option that meets their criteria; then they stop—not because they have lower standards, but because they settle for good enough and do not worry about the possibility of other, better options. Although maximizers seem to make the perfect choice, Schwartz found they tended to be less happy than satisficers not only about the choice they made but about their lives in general. "Maximizers," writes Schwartz, "worry the most about regret, about missed opportunities, and about social comparisons, and it is maximizers who are most disappointed when the results of their decisions are not as good as expected."[32] Indeed, people with very high maximization scores also had higher rates of clinical depression. Schwartz sees a causal relationship between choice maximization and happiness, arguing that maximizers seek a level of perfection for themselves and the world that cannot be met.[33] In their quest for perfection, they are unable to limit their options. Satisficers, by contrast, set voluntary limits on their options by stopping the search when they find what is good enough.

If limiting the number of options is one route to happiness, so is allowing others to choose for us. Iyengar reports on several studies showing that ceding control over some decisions to others (parents, experts, God) will sometimes make us happier than trying to make every decision ourselves. This makes intuitive sense in contexts where we lack expertise: I would rather let the plumber decide what kind of valve to put on the dishwasher pipe than trying to figure it out myself. But delegating decision-making also increases happiness in realms of life that are more personal. Several studies have shown that people in arranged marriages report greater levels of marital satisfaction and lower divorce rates than people who chose their partners.[34] This may be because the former had different expectations of marriage, seeing it as a source of financial and social support and stability, rather than as a means to personal fulfillment as many Americans do. But it may also be because parents are more likely to select a partner who is compatible (intellectually or socially) than a young person in the throws of sexual attraction. Similar findings have been reported about people in conservative religions. In traditional religions, both trivial and important choices are decided for us such as what to wear, what to eat, or whom and how to marry. The conventional wisdom that we are happier when we can decide for ourselves would predict that the members of the most restrictive religions (e.g., Orthodox Jews, fundamentalist Muslims, or Amish Christians) would be the least happy. It turns out the opposite is true: followers of restrictive religions report much higher levels of happiness and life satisfaction than followers of liberal religions or secular people.[35] Delegating at least some of our choices to others relieves us of what sometimes can be a burdensome responsibility (and it also gives us someone to blame).

It is interesting to ponder the implications of what Schwartz calls the "tyranny of choice" for Nones in America. Religion in our culture is perceived as a personal choice, rather than a duty or tradition, and this can be liberating as I seek or create a worldview that truly expresses my authentic self. But it can also be overwhelming. As Clark Roof noted in his study of baby boomers who became seekers, it can be very difficult (if not impossible) to find a religion you can totally believe in. For many young people especially, self-identifying as Nones is a way of saying, "there are many choices and I don't want to make a decision right now."

As Nones get older and start families of their own, they often do make a choice (even if some continue to claim no religion). Schwartz's model of different kinds of choosers may help shed some light on why Nones choose the way they do. Some of my respondents exhibited the characteristics of maximizers, spending a great deal of time exploring various different worldviews, and when they did choose one they continued to second-guess themselves. Maximizing was common among Nones who are Spiritual Seekers and those parents who opted to be self-providers of their children's worldview education. Take Vicky, for example, who has spent much of her adult life exploring various religions and claims she would like to find a spiritual community to raise her child. But she has been unable to find the right fit. She likes the energy of her mother's revivalist church: "It is so alive, the energy in the room, people singing and getting the spirit." But she rejects their intolerant theology. She feels drawn to Buddhism, but does not want to drive an hour to the nearest Buddhism center. So she is doing her best to transmit her own worldview to her daughter, but is continuously doubting her own lack of expertise and her ability to give her daughter what she needs.

Other None parents sounded more like satisficers. They were less inclined to shop around, and whatever decision they made did not appear to trouble them much. This was a common pattern among Unchurched Believers and those parents who opted to either raise their children in the tradition they had left or outsource religious education—like Denise, who drifted out of Judaism when she was a teenager and then reaffiliated, at her mother's urging, not because she no longer had doubts but because she decided that she wanted religious community for her child and her mother's synagogue was good enough. Or like Renee who dropped out of the Catholic Church in college and then reaffiliated because she thought church provided a good enough way to teach values to her children. The church is not perfect (Renee was deeply concerned about the priest scandal) and she acknowledges that there are other options (her sister was raising her kids Jewish, and Renee approved of that choice), but she chose Catholicism because it is what she knew.

During my research, I did not have access to the instrument Schwartz used to differentiate maximizers and satisficers; therefore I cannot say definitively that my respondents represented these types. Nevertheless, the patterns are striking and surely merit further investigation. These patterns also raise questions about whether or not None parents' stated intention to maximize their children's choices will actually make their children happy. If adults can feel overwhelmed by the process of choosing the right worldview, this may be even more true of children. And if my child turns out to be a maximizer, telling him to choose his own religion may just be setting him up for misery. Fortunately, as I have shown, the narrative of choice is exactly that, a narrative. It seems that whatever Nones tell themselves about choice, most parents do, in fact, restrict their children's choices—and this is probably a good thing.

7

The Risks and Benefits of Raising Children without Religion

Our children will eventually choose their own worldview, just as we did. Yet, that does not prevent many None parents from worrying about their choices. Most Nones, having been raised with religion themselves before stepping away from it, have personal experiences with both the strengths and weaknesses of organized religions, and they are acutely aware of the limitations of parental influence. They would like to give their children the good things they remember—a sense of awe for something greater than we are, a moral compass, the joy of a family tradition—but, as one of my interviewees put it, "without the garbage" of beliefs and practices that no longer made sense to them. They want to offer their children a choice of worldviews that they themselves typically did not have, and yet they want to do what they can to transmit their own values to them. As one parent bluntly stated, "we try to be liberal and we want to let them find their path on their own, but of course we are still happiest when they choose a path we recognize." There is a tension here that is perhaps irreconcilable and that is amplified by the newness of the None path. I heard many variations of this story.[1]

Parents deciding to raise their child in one tradition, usually by returning to church or synagogue, often expressed concern about repeating the mistakes of their own parents and indoctrinating their child. As one Unchurched Believer remarked, she was "trying out" Hebrew school for her six-year-old but did not want to commit to the process: "I'll introduce her to the first couple of years of it and then see if she wants to continue. Because I was never really given that choice and I was really upset about that as a child. . . . I don't want to box her in." Another parent who had affiliated with a church after her elder daughter expressed an interest declined to enroll the younger daughter because the child did not want to. The mother feared that if she "pounded religion into their heads," as her parents had done, she would only turn the child away from spirituality. While these parents are clearly narrowing their children's options, they still worry that it will backfire.

Parents who offer their children a wider range of options also worry. Those raising their children with multiple worldviews or without religion—usually by going it alone or affiliating with an alternative community—speculated about how the lack of a unified worldview and structure might inadvertently harm their children. One Spiritual Seeker parent was raising her child as a "Buddhist Jew" but worried that what she did at home was not enough: "During times of difficulty you need some kind of structure, and I want that to be available, even if you don't use that all the time. Being a seeker is great, but when the rubber hits the road all human beings need a structure. It's meant to help us." Yet, although she had spent several years shopping appropriately open-minded Jewish communities, she had thus far been unable to find one. A Philosophical Secularist parent who had raised his two children in an alternative (humanist) community expressed some dismay that the teenagers had become completely indifferent to the kinds of big questions that animated him. "I feel it's good to reject traditional religion but you still want to be spiritual, you don't want to be one-dimensional . . . so I guess I do feel, gee, I have left them without any sort of spiritual resources." The magnitude of the decision to raise a child outside of church felt scary to one couple I interviewed. The wife, a Spiritual Seeker, talked at length about the importance of imparting a "moral framework" for their child: "We are responsible for this kid forever, and to me that's the frightening thing about trying to go about this on our own." The husband, a Philosophical Secularist, chimed in: "If we raise them in a traditional religious environment . . . there's help, and if we really kind of botch it, then there is someone else there to catch the slack." Yet he was not ready to put his child in such an environment because he told me, "I can't find a place that I would be comfortable with."

As mentioned previously, many Seeker and Secularist parents, especially those who live in places where fundamentalism dominates the culture, worry about their kids going over to the other side and becoming religious fundamentalists. One Seeker mom who was raising her ten-year-old daughter in multiple traditions, speculated what path the girl might choose as an adult: "We all want our kids to have a little bit of us. If she chooses Christianity . . . or Judaism, or part of it, or Paganism . . . it will still be a part of our family. [But] when it's not something you know you get scared, like if she became an Evangelical Christian." Another parent, a Philosophical Secularist whose teenagers had become born-again Christians, worried about their future while trying hard to remain true to his commitment to worldview choice. The hardest thing as a parent was, as he remarked, "not to criticize them when they became Christian." Instead, he hoped "the children will find their way back [to something closer to the parent's worldview] when they go off to college."

On the other side of the spectrum, Unchurched Believer parents often worried when their children showed no interest in religion. Parents who allowed their child to choose whether to attend religious education classes would second-guess that decision when the child opted not to. One parent said of his son: "He doesn't seem to show any sign of interest in religion of any sort, and it's kind of hard not to feel like, hmm, did I make a mistake." Another parent, whose son had attended religious instruction, was shocked when he told her that he did not believe in God. When I interviewed her, she told me, "I still can't quite believe it . . . it may have something to do with being a teenager" (in other words, she hopes it's just a phase). Yet another parent, who had turned away from church after getting a divorce, expressed concern that only one of her four children was receptive to her efforts to transmit spirituality in the home. The others, she told me, "either don't want to talk about it or kind of pacify me by saying, 'Oh, I think I'll read my scriptures.'" She asserted that her oldest daughter "goes to church for her dad." But to her mother the girl admitted: "I don't care, I don't believe, I don't know. I don't really want to think about it. I don't want to talk about it." So her mother has concluded that religion is "not necessarily something that she would pursue on her own." The mother is disappointed "because I have this wonderful vision" of sharing a family faith. It is also challenging because of the mother's commitment to choice: "Do I just let it go so that they can find their way without me interfering?"

This is a good question and one that I think is particularly salient to None parents. Worrying (in the sense of speculating how children might choose and reflecting on our own influence on that process) is, of course, not unique to Nones; it is part of being a parent. My daughter, Sheila, knows to look right and left before crossing the street, but we live in a city and I still worry a little bit every time she walks two miles to her friend's house. Her Internet use at home is closely monitored, but I am still wary about what she may choose to watch while hanging out with other girls. I buy organic food and cook healthy, balanced meals for our family, but I remain skeptical that Sheila will select fruits and veggies over chips and soda when she goes off to college. We all hope to instill good habits and values in our children, but we have limited control over their choices once they leave the house.

Choosing a worldview, however, is different from other kinds of decisions, and worrying about that choice may be a particular burden for None parents. Our friends who are raising their kids Catholic or Jewish have little doubt that they are doing the right thing. I am raising my daughter without religion, and I often wonder if that is the best decision. Although this may be a personality trait (I chose to write this book, and parents who chose to participate were those who tend to worry about this type of thing), there are also good reasons why Nones might worry more.

For example, Nones take the choice narrative so seriously. Unlike churched parents, whose default decision is to raise the kids in their own tradition, most Nones feel very uncomfortable about what they see as "choosing for our child." Thus, as discussed in the previous chapter, they seek ways (or tell themselves they are seeking ways) to give their children options and allow them to choose for themselves. In short, because None parents *expect* their children to choose, it makes sense that they would give more thought to what that choice might be.

None parents pondering the question of how kids will choose is intensified by the fact that they remain a minority. Although having no religion is a more common option today, especially among the young, American culture still largely reinforces the message that religion is good for children. Children are naturally spiritual, psychologists tell us, and religion offers comfort and meaning, especially in situations of suffering that are difficult to explain to a child. Children need clear rules and limits, and religion provides a widely shared and time-tested set of values and morals. Children do best if they have the support of a community of caring adults, and churches, synagogues, and mosques give them just that. Religion can have its downsides (brainwashing, rigid behavior, abuse), but those are exceptions to the rule (the vast majority of Catholic priests did not partake in sexual abuse of children) or the province of extremist religions (think fundamentalist Mormon child brides), which is not the route most Americans would go anyways. If the parent is sane and the religion moderate, we are told, children are better off with religion than without it.

But are they really? Is religion truly natural and beneficial for children? Or is it just that popular media and best-selling psychologists are catering to majority opinion, that is, churched Americans who, of course, would want to believe that. There is a large and growing research literature exploring the impact of religion on children. In this chapter I will look more closely at what this research does and does not tell us.

Are Children Naturally Spiritual?

One argument that is often made for raising children with religion is that they are naturally inclined to be spiritual.[2] The research supporting this argument tends to use the terms *spirituality* and *religion* interchangeably, in the sense of believing and wanting protection from supernatural powers or seeking a transcendent meaning of life. Spirituality, in this view, is like imagination or play: an inherent and healthy psychological need that parents ought to meet rather than try to quash, and engaging a child in organized religion is a time-honored way of doing that. One variation of the "children are naturally religious" thesis is found in humanistic psychology; another in evolutionary psychology.

Humanistic psychology has its roots in the early twentieth century when various thinkers began to challenge the dominant Freudian paradigm. Freud thought that beliefs in God are rooted in children's feelings about their fathers, a mixture of fear and awe of an all-powerful being who controls their lives. He argued that religion is a form of projection that meets deep emotional needs but ends up causing repression, guilt, and neurosis.[3] Among the first to question this view was Carl Jung, a student of Freud, who had a more mystical take on religion. Jung believed that all humans share in a collective unconscious containing universal psychological patterns or archetypes (such as the anima, a feminine aspect in men, the animus, a masculine aspect in women, or the inner child), which may be in conflict with each other or with the demands of society. His study of Christianity, Hinduism, Buddhism and other religions led him to understand their symbols and stories as expressions of such archetypes (e.g., the divine child is a symbol of the developing personality or human potential). He further argued that humans are motivated not just by sex and aggression, as Freud had thought, but by a deep need for psychological wholeness: an integration of opposing aspects of the psyche in order to realize the authentic self. This search for self-realization, a process Jung called "individuation," is the mystical heart of all religions; the journey to meet the divine is a journey to meet the self.[4]

The idea that the quest for self-realization is an inherent psychological need was further developed by Abraham Maslow, widely considered the father of humanistic psychology and what later became the human potential movement. Maslow asserted that humans are motivated by a hierarchy of needs, often depicted visually as a pyramid. The most popular version has five levels, with the lower four designated as deficiency needs and the top as growth needs. At the base of the pyramid are physiological needs (food, water, warmth, sex); once those are met, we are motivated by longer-term safety needs (security, order), then social needs (love and belonging), and then esteem needs (recognition, power). At the very top of the pyramid was what Maslow called the need for self-actualization (realizing our human potential) and self-transcendence (becoming one with the unity of all beings), which historically have often been met by religion. In a wealthy and stable society like the United States, where many people's basic needs (i.e., safety, love, and esteem) are taken care of, attending to the psychological need for transcendence may be particularly urgent.[5]

While Maslow was not a child psychologist, others have applied his ideas to children. One of the best known is Robert Coles who has written extensively about children's spirituality. Based on his interviews with hundreds of children from families of different worldviews (including atheists), he concluded that children are naturally spiritual. By spiritual, Coles means that they have questions about finitude, space, and time; they want to know why we are here and what happens at death. If they are raised with religion they wonder about the nature of God; if not, they wonder what other people believe about God. Coles argues that children's understandings of God do not merely parrot what their parents have taught them, suggesting that spirituality—in the broad, metaphorical sense of searching for meaning making—is inherent.[6]

The humanistic psychology argument that children are naturally spiritual is often criticized for its fuzziness. Although Coles's samples were large, he did not perform any controlled studies. More importantly, he and other humanistic psychologists tend to define spirituality so broadly (a need for meaning, the quest for self-realization) that the claim that children are inherently spiritual becomes kind of a truism, an assertion that is unfalsifiable but also much less interesting. By contrast, researchers in evolutionary psychology seem to be making a more precise claim about children's inborn religiosity. They assert that religiosity is a product or a by-product of evolution, or as Catherine Caldwell-Harris put it, belief in and worship of God or other supernatural beings "may be the default setting for our species."[7]

The evolutionary psychology of religion emerged at the end of the twentieth century, although some of its ideas hark back to nineteenth-century thinkers like Edward B. Tylor or Emile Durkheim.[8] One school of thought is that religion itself is adaptive because it conferred some kind of evolutionary advantage. This view emphasizes the role of religion in promoting cooperation and group cohesion, for example, through rites of passage that assign particular social roles to adults or to children, and through moral commandments that encourage charity and prevent murder or incest. Membership in such a group enhances an individual's chances for survival and reproduction, and as groups compete over scarce resources those with religion do better than those without.[9]

The other school of thought is that religious beliefs and behaviors emerged as by-products of other evolved traits, such as the tendency to over-attribute agency to phenomena. Attributing agency refers to the human inclination to presume the purposeful intervention of a sentient or intelligent agent in situations that may or may not involve one. It is postulated that the tendency to attribute agency evolved as an adaptive strategy because it motivated humans to take precautions in situations where one is unsure of the presence of an intelligent agent, such as an enemy or a predator. The perils of living in an environment we cannot control eventually led to religion and its beliefs in gods and spirits and rituals designed to get these supernatural powers to do our bidding or at least spare us from disaster.[10]

It is one thing to hypothesize about the origins of religion; it is another to say that religiosity evolved into a trait that is hardwired in the human brain, as some evolutionary psychologists do. Thus Justin Barrett links belief in God to our evolved ability to recognize mental states in others; he sees such belief as a natural part of human cognitive development. He asserts that children's facility for agent-based reasoning, the instinct for purpose-driven explanations of how the natural world works, and an innate belief in superpowers predispose them to become religious without any cultural influence.[11] Children, as he puts it, are "born believers" which implies that it would be useless and possibly even harmful for parents to resist that tendency. Barrett's thesis also implies that atheism is unnatural and therefore deviant.

Evolutionary psychology of religion is a relatively new and contested field, and the hypothesis that children are born religious is at this point still a hypothesis—there is insufficient data to back it up. Barrett's assertion in particular, that children will naturally be inclined to believe in God even without cultural influence, has never actually been tested. Indeed, it is unclear that this hypothesis can be tested on children, given that by the time they are old enough to answer a researcher's questions about their beliefs or practices, they have already been molded by their parents to either be religious or not. Studies of adults, meanwhile, provide evidence that both religious and secular inclinations are natural variations in human beings. Catherine Caldwell-Harris has shown that an individual's inclination to believe or not believe in supernatural agency can be predicted by variations in personality such as individualism or low sociality, a preference of logical reasoning over intuition, and a focus on here-and-now problem solving instead of a concern for transcendence.[12] She and others point out that the so-called naturalness hypothesis is not deterministic but probabilistic, that is, people are likely to attribute supernatural agency to events they cannot explain but this does not mean people will always do so.[13]

Even if we assume that children are, in fact, naturally spiritual, it does not necessarily follow that we should raise them with organized religion. When humanistic psychologists like Maslow or Coles talk about spirituality they are using the term in a broad, metaphorical sense to refer to the quest for meaning, and they acknowledge that organized religion may or may not adequately fulfill that human need for meaning. Thus Coles's research on children's spirituality included atheist children who made sense of the world and their lives on secular terms, and Abraham Maslow reported that some of the most highly self-actualized individuals were those who had rejected religion.[14] Indeed, many parents in this book became Nones precisely because they felt organized religion failed to give meaning to their lives.

Finally, just because something is natural does not mean that it is good. Kids have all sorts of inclinations (e.g., eating with their hands, hitting others, breaking things, and making a mess) that will not serve them well in later life, and much of a parent's role is to nurture more civilized behaviors. The more important question therefore may not be, are kids born to be religious but what will religion do for them in the future?

Does Religion Cause Positive Outcomes in Children?

Many studies have associated religious involvement with positive outcomes in the lives of children and youth, showing, for example, that kids raised with religion are less likely to use drugs or engage in risky sexual behavior, have lower rates of depression and suicide, and do better in school.[15] One of the largest and most comprehensive studies of this kind was the National Study of Youth and Religion conducted in 2003 by sociologist Christian Smith and his colleagues.[16] Smith reports on their findings as well as those of related research in *Soul Searching: The Religious and Spiritual Lives of American Teenagers*, which makes a passionate and often convincing argument that religion has a positive impact on youth. He asserts that religion actually plays a causal role in these outcomes, and that it is organized religion in particular that has this impact. His argument is worth presenting in some detail.

The core of the argument is found in chapter 7, "Adolescent Religion and Life Outcomes." In it, Smith divides respondents into four "ideal types" of religious and nonreligious teens: (1) those who are devoted to religion (they attend services weekly or more, do same for prayer and scripture reading, claim faith is extremely important to them), (2) those who are regularly involved but somewhat less devout (they attend weekly or a couple times a month, faith ranges from very to not very important), (3) those whose involvement is sporadic (they attend monthly or a few times per year, faith ranges from somewhat to not very important), and (4) those who are disengaged from religion (they never attend religious services, pray or read scripture a couple times per month or less, faith ranges from somewhat to not important in life). Smith then correlates these types with various life outcomes and finds that more religious teens (the devoted and the regulars) consistently have better life outcomes than less religious teens (the sporadics and the disengaged).

His data suggests that religious teens are better able than nonreligious teens to avoid various risky behaviors (smoking cigarettes, drinking, marijuana use, cutting class, low grades, suspension from school). Religious teens also engage in less media use (watching television during the school week, watching R-rated movies, viewing Internet porn, or playing video games). They have more conservative sexual views and are less likely to be sexually active than nonreligious teens. They express higher levels of emotional well-being (i.e., are more likely to have positive body image, less likely to feel depressed and misunderstood), have stronger adult ties (i.e., are more comfortable talking to adults other than parents and relatives and know more adults who care), and feel closer to family and siblings than nonreligious teens. Religious teens exhibit higher levels of honesty and moral reasoning (i.e., are less likely to cheat on exams or lie to their parents) and show more compassion for the poor and vulnerable (not just in their beliefs, but in actual behaviors such as volunteering service and donating their own money). Although some of the differences are very small (e.g., 14 percent of religious teens reported that they frequently cheated on tests, compared to 15 percent of nonreligious teens), others were quite large (e.g., 28 percent of religious teens had sexual intercourse compared to 49 percent of nonreligious teens), and taken together they are certainly significant.

Smith claims that the differences between religious and nonreligious teens hold, even after controlling for various demographic factors that might affect these outcomes (e.g., kids who come from poverty or divorce). Although he acknowledges that some of the results may be due to other factors, such as personality or reverse causation, he asserts that these do not explain away the differences between religious and nonreligious teens. Rather, he argues, there is a clear causal connection between religion and these outcomes. Some of this causal effect is direct in the sense that there's something about religious beliefs or practices themselves that promotes positive outcomes; some of the effect is indirect in the sense that churches or synagogues provide a social context that facilitates such outcomes.

Smith then goes on to propose nine specific causal mechanisms by which religion exerts such influence. The first three involve what he calls "moral order": Religion provides (1) moral directives of self-control and personal virtue grounded in the authority of a tradition; (2) spiritual experiences that help young people internalize those values; and (3) adult and peer group role models of positive behavior. The next three causal mechanisms occur via "learned competencies": Religious involvement offers (4) service opportunities where teens gain community and leadership skills; (5) beliefs and practices that develop coping skills in stressful situations (e.g., meditation or prayer, or trusting that God will resolve a difficult situation); and (6) educational opportunities to acquire cultural capital (e.g., biblical literacy or musical skills). The final set of causal mechanisms work through "social and organizational ties": Involvement in religious institutions provides (7) social ties that are not age-stratified, allowing youth to develop close relationships with caring adults beyond their immediate family; (8) network closure, allowing caring people to convey information about youth to their parents; and (9) extra-community links since most American religions are part of larger (regional, national, or international) structures that connect youth to valuable resources such as summer camps, mission projects, and trips to Israel or Mecca. Smith admits that not all religious communities provide these mechanisms to the same degree, and that some of them can be provided by nonreligious communities. But he and others insist that churches and synagogues do better a better job of facilitating these causal mechanisms than other types of communities.[17]

The data presented is impressive and the arguments are plausible, so it is not surprising that Smith's thesis will be compelling to many churched American parents. It may also be convincing to some None parents, especially those who are on the fence about religion, like Unchurched Believers, Indifferents, or Spiritual Seekers. And it will likely be reassuring to those Nones who decided once they started a family to reaffiliate themselves with an institution, especially if it is a traditional church or synagogue. After all, Smith's arguments speak directly to many parent worries about the choices their children will make and the limited control we have over that. Parents do not want their children to start smoking cigarettes, do drugs, drop out of school, or become depressed; and parents need all the help they can get in trying to prevent such outcomes. The apparent protective impact of religion also raises interesting questions for those None parents who more affirmatively reject religion, such as Philosophical Secularists, who reject religion as irrational, or those Unchurched Believers who view all institutional religion as corrupt. Is it possible that, at least for children, religion's benefits outweigh the costs? How important is the transmission of what I believe to be true compared to the practical outcomes my child could gain from organized religion? And if I believe, as most Nones do, that my children must choose for themselves anyway, then why deprive them of what seems to be such a wonderful resource? Before we all go running back to church, let's consider some of the downsides.

Just as there are many studies pointing to religion's benefits, there is also plenty of research showing organized religion to put children at risk. Numerous studies have associated religion with psychological and physical abuse of children, with long-term consequences for the victim's lives. The best-known recent example is probably the clergy sex abuse scandal in the Catholic Church—although many would argue that religion per se was not a causal factor here: whatever the abuses of authority and administrative oversight, sexual contact between clergy and children is clearly forbidden by church teachings, and incidents of abuse were the exception not the rule. However, the research literature suggests several instances where religious teachings and practices themselves do seem to be implicated in causing harm to children.

Religion has been shown to encourage physical abuse by providing a moral framework that legitimates often severe corporal punishment. Several scriptural passages sanction the beating of children: "He that spareth his rod hateth his son: but he that loveth him chasteneth him betimes" (Proverbs 13:24) and "Withhold no correction from the child: for if thou beatest him with the rod, he shall not die. Thou shalt beat him with the rod, and shalt deliver his soul from hell" (Proverbs 23:13–14). The widely held Christian doctrine that children are born with a "wayward or distorted will" and the belief that God would punish earthly pleasure with torture in hell also motivates parents to use physical punishment.[18] Such punishment is often meted out by otherwise caring parents with good intentions. They understand spanking to help rebellious children to "joyfully submit themselves to God" and take "the injunction to break the will as mandate to inflict severe physical punishment."[19] The result is that religion-based physical child abuse is not uncommon, yet it remains underreported and is often exempt from legal intervention because it is protected by the First Amendment.[20]

Although the link between religion and physical abuse is found mostly among fundamentalist Christian sects, this does not let moderate or liberal religious parents off the hook. Even when children are not beaten, studies show religion may foster emotional abuse by promoting ideas that cause emotional torment.[21] Many people tend to think it is comforting to children to know that God watches over them. But the idea that God watches your every act and is aware of all your thoughts can be terrifying to children, especially when combined with traditional religious teachings about sin and punishment. Minor infractions of rules such as eating forbidden treats, or using and accidentally breaking objects belonging to an adult, as well as emergent sexual feelings become sources of guilt, shame, and fear. Even well-meaning parents may inadvertently use religion to cause children to feel alone, stressed, or worthless.[22] Some experts argue that such emotional damage has more long-lasting effects than physical abuse related to religion, and the former is certainly more common although we are loath to admit it.[23] As Betty Bottoms and colleagues note, the media brings public attention to fringe cults who abuse their children in the name of God and are then "rejected by society with much self-righteousness." Yet those "beliefs and practices may differ only in degree from those of mainstream religious groups such as Methodists, Baptists, and Catholics."[24]

My point here is not to argue that religion is inherently abusive to children—although some have gone that far.[25] Rather, I want to remind readers that religion can and often does have a negative impact on children, just as it often does have positive outcomes. [26] It is true that religion's negative outcomes are mostly characteristic of more conservative traditions (fundamentalist Christians or Muslims, or Orthodox Jews). But the same argument could be made to dismiss Smith's claim about the benefits of religion. After all, religion's protective impact on children is greatest for those most intensely committed to it: those who take its teachings more literally or believe more of traditional doctrine; those who pray daily and attend services several times a week; those who go to Bible camp and mission trips—all of these behaviors are far more characteristic of religious conservatives than of other individuals.

There are other reasons to be skeptical of studies like Smith's. Critical reviewers of the literature on religion's positive outcomes have pointed to various problems with the methodology and analysis that raise questions about the predictive value of those findings. In particular, they warn against extending such findings to make predictions about secular persons.[27] One problem is what sociologists call *construct validity*, that is, our ability to define accurately what it is we are trying to measure—in this case the impact of religion or religiosity. Since there is no universally agreed upon definition of what exactly constitutes a religious person, most studies, including Smith's, rely on proxy variables such as frequency of church attendance and prayer, or the respondents' claims about the depth of their faith or relationship with God. Although such variables are crude but largely fair indicators of religiosity for the churched Christian population (e.g., some people attend church purely for social reasons but most do not), they are problematic when applied to anyone else (e.g., many devout Buddhists never attend services). This critique is particularly relevant to the None population, which is quite diverse in terms of what might be defined as religiosity or nonreligiosity as I have shown.

Another common problem has to do with sampling. A recent review of the literature cautions that too many studies linking religion with health and well-being rely on volunteer samples who may or may not reflect the general population. More problematic, particularly in its relevance to Nones, is the lack of secularist comparisons. Studies claiming positive outcomes for religion have mostly focused on people with at least a minimal level of religiousness, comparing those who are more religious with those who are less so, and either excluding or undersampling nonbelievers.[28] As Karen Hwang and colleagues have pointed out, "there is a near universal absence of atheist control groups," so we cannot draw valid conclusions about this subgroup. This problem is particularly evident in the National Study of Youth and Religion. Smith compared teens who are committed to organized religion (the devout and the regulars) to those who are less committed or alienated from it (sporadic attenders and the disengaged). Many of these less religious teens were raised by churched parents, but for some reason the children no longer found religion to be meaningful. Smith does not consider teens who may have been actively raised in some alternative worldview or who are affirmatively secular. In other words, he is comparing those who have religion to those who lack it, and ignoring those who may have replaced religion with something better.

As of this writing, there are no studies of children that make such a comparison. In the few studies that compare religious adults with atheists and secularists (rather than just with the less religious), the supposed benefit conferred by religion is often absent.[29] Samuel Weber and colleagues recently reviewed hundreds of articles claiming a link between religion and well-being and found ten quantitative studies that included atheist controls. Of these, two articles found more psychological distress among the atheists than among the religious, and seven showed them to have comparable or less stress than the religious. Several studies suggest that what seemed to cause distress was not religion or the absence of it, but personality or the strength of individual conviction.[30] Ironically, what caused most distress among atheists was the negative perception that others have about them.[31]

Such misattribution of causality points to a third problem with the positive outcome of religion research: the studies often do not demonstrate that religion (rather than, say, the friends one makes at church) is a causal factor. As we all know, a correlation does not make a causation. If it did, we might have to conclude that religious people are happier because they are less intelligent, or that devout teenagers stay out of trouble because they are conformist and lack imagination.[32] Research has frequently found such associations but sociologists of religion generally decline from drawing causal inferences.[33] The same is true of recent scholarship on secularism. Studies have repeatedly shown that people living in Scandinavian countries, which are the most secular nations in the world, report the highest levels of personal happiness. Yet we rarely hear scholars assert that Scandinavians are happy because they lack religion. Instead, they conclude that Swedish and Danish well-being probably results from neither secularism nor religion but from the fact that they live in societies with relatively low income inequality and strong social ties.[34] Most social scientists know better than to assert causality— yet they often do imply it. The repeated assertion of that implication and the use of implications made by other researchers amplifies its impact, creating a kind of multiplier effect where a large number of positive associations is taken to mean a causal relationship exists.

This is also a problem with Smith's *Soul Searching*. Smith is a careful scholar and acknowledges that some of the positive outcomes found among religious teenagers may be due to other factors. Personality is likely to play a role. For instance, teens who get into trouble by stealing or using drugs may just be risk-takers, a personality trait that is less common among the highly religious. So it is risk-taking, rather than religiousness, that explains why some teens engage in such behavior and others do not. Reverse causation can also be a factor. Consider a sexually promiscuous religious teen who drops out of church because she has come to disagree with its doctrines on sexuality and knows the people there will disapprove of her behavior. Researchers will count her as "disengaged" and mistakenly assume that it is her nonreligiousness that caused her sexual behavior, when causation actually runs the other way around. To his credit, Smith clearly describes these limitations of his findings, admitting that "the observed positive association between greater teen religiosity and positive life outcomes cannot be explained by one simple causal mechanism" and admitting that religion is only "part of what helps produce" them.[35] Having stated this caveat, however, Smith uses the remainder of the chapter to launch into a lengthy and passionate explication of why religion does play a causal role and what the exact causal mechanisms are, supporting his argument with reference to the multiplier effect of previous studies that imply causation (Smith cites hundreds of studies correlating religion with positive outcomes). Unless you are a skeptical reader, it is easy to overlook that eight of the nine causal factors are things other than religion, or that the large body of previous research also fails to prove a causal link. The chapter ends with the story of an African American inner city youth whose life could have ended up badly but whose faith community helps keep him out of trouble. It is compelling because of its emotional appeal and because it speaks to what many people already believe—but it is not a strong causal argument.

In the end the question of whether organized religion causes positive outcomes in children remains unresolved. As with the debate over whether religiosity is innate, there is plenty of data that proponents of either side can use to support their position, but careful analysis suggests (as it often does) that the picture is more complex.[36] To say, as humanistic psychologists do, that children have a need for meaning is highly plausible but offers no particular mandate for raising them with religion, as there are many other sources of meaning available. The claim made by some evolutionary psychologists that children are born with an inclination to believe in supernatural beings lacks empirical support; and even if it could be proven, it does not follow that parents should encourage such belief through immersion in organized religion. The positive outcomes that sociologists like Smith have associated with religion must be balanced against limitations and flaws in the research and against risk of negative outcomes.

So where does all this leave us? For the majority of American parents (those who are affiliated with religion), the upsides of raising children with religion would seem to outweigh the downsides. Whatever children's innate characteristics, religious socialization offers them many benefits, especially if parents can avoid traumatizing their children with religious threats. Even if most of the benefits of religion could be had elsewhere, it makes sense that parents who are already affiliated would take advantage of what their church or synagogue has to offer. And for parents convinced of religion's truth there is the added moral responsibility to transmit that worldview to their children.

The path is less clear for None parents. For Unchurched Believers and some Spiritual Seekers, affiliating with a religious community to help raise their children seems to be a sensible option. If you as a parent can affirm the teachings and practices of that community, it does not matter if all of the positive outcomes associated with religious involvement flow from sources other than religion itself—as long as they keep flowing. But what if you cannot affirm those teachings and practices?

For those Nones who reject traditional religious (read conservative Christian or Jewish) values, the pragmatic argument is less compelling. Most Philosophical Secularists and some Spiritual Seekers will not want their children to be indoctrinated into a worldview that they believe is irrational, sexist, arrogant, or demonstrably false—regardless of how many positive role models, caring adults, or opportunities for learning useful skills that community offers. In addition, they—and even many Unchurched Believers—may not agree that all of the supposed benefits of religion actually *are* benefits. Take the issue of premarital sex. Smith seeks to demonstrate religion's beneficial influence on teens by asserting: "Nearly all Devoted teens believe in waiting for marriage to have sex, compared to less than a quarter of Disengaged teens who believe the same. Likewise, only 3 percent of the Devoted believe it is okay for teenagers to have sex if they are 'emotionally ready for it,' compared to 56 percent of the Disengaged."[37] He then goes on to show that, although beliefs are not always matched by actions, devoted teens are less sexually active (or at least less likely to admit to sexual activity) which Smith clearly thinks is a good thing. My reaction when I first read this passage was: Excuse me? What century are we in? Parents do no want their children to engage in risky sexual behavior. But (outside of conservative religious circles) it is widely accepted that young people *will* have sex before marriage, and most Americans not only do not disapprove of premarital sex but think some level of premarital experience is actually beneficial.[38] What many parents do want their teen to avoid is pregnancy and disease.[39] Yet there is no discussion in Smith's research of birth control or the role that religion might play in encouraging or discouraging teens from practicing safe sex. Instead, he assumes, without evidence, that saving sex for marriage is a positive outcome and that premarital sexual activity, even among emotionally mature teenagers, is a negative outcome. Surely, many contemporary parents—and not just Nones—would disagree.

So is it better to raise your children with or without religion? The research literature, at this point at least, cannot definitively answer that question, especially not for Nones. In the absence of expert recommendations, the answer will depend on who you are and what your own worldview is. As most parents know, children have powerful sensors for detecting what our actual values are, regardless of what worldview system we try to transmit to them. So integrity may be what matters most. And if, like most Nones, you believe that children make their own choices anyway, then the system may matter even less than you think.

Conclusion

Writing this book marks the completion of a project that engaged both my professional and my personal life for many years. I have learned a great deal: from the families who generously shared their stories with me; from other scholars whose work I explored in books and articles, at conferences, and in personal conversations; and from my daughter whose questions first prompted this research ten years ago. Sheila is thirteen now, on the cusp of adolescence, an apt juncture to look back on the past and to ponder the future. So I will use the pages that remain to reflect on the significance of this research—both from a scholarly angle and from my personal experience as a None parent—and to address new questions it may have raised.

The Scholarly Perspective

When I began this project nearly a decade ago published research on None parents did not exist. There were surveys on Nones, and much discussion of demographic trends but no focus on parents in particular. You could find how-to books for atheists and seekers, but no scholarly research on the broader None parent population. Thus the original purpose of writing this book was simply to get information about them and to answer the questions that sociologists of religion and Nones themselves have about the meaning of None parenting. Now ten years later, I have armfuls of data, a few answers, and, of course, many more questions. In what follows I will review some of the more important findings of this study and the implications they have for future research.

Unity and Diversity among Nones

None parents are more diverse than expected but they are also more distinct from their churched counterparts than is usually acknowledged. In this book, I have offered a conceptual framework to better understand the diversity of None worldviews. Previous studies have described Nones as either religious (unchurched believers) or not (secular), or something in between (spiritual but not religious). The worldview categories used in this book—Unchurched Believer, Spiritual Seeker, Philosophical Secularist, Indifferent—expand existing typologies by distinguishing those who affirm a secular philosophy (such as humanism, skepticism, atheism or even agnosticism) from those who are simply indifferent to either religious or secular worldviews. The distinction between what I have called Philosophical Secularism and Indifference is not merely a refinement of existing categories in the field but an essential reconceptualization of what is meant by None.

The Philosophical Secularist category helps us appreciate forms of secularism that function as substantive alternative worldviews, rather than just the absence of religion. While some of these movements originate in their rejection of religion, they have not stopped there. Secular philosophies such as humanism or Freethought provide meaningful explanations for human existence and purpose. They offer a rational basis for moral behavior and compassion to others. Philosophical Secularists have created institutions where members can gather as community to affirm their history and values and celebrate important individual or group events and organize for social action. They have also begun to create programs for children. While Philosophical Secularists share a rejection of the supernatural, they hold diverse perspectives and divide into various schools of thought that differ in ideology and practice, just as religious sects do. Although Philosophical Secularists may not always affiliate with an institution, this is no different from Unchurched Believers whose substantive worldview has long been acknowledged by sociologists of religion. It is time we respect Philosophical Secularism for what it is, a substantive alternative to religion.

A small but growing literature on secularism has begun to do so. Scholars are beginning to categorize the varieties of Philosophical Secularist groups and movements,[1] the ways that secularist philosophies confer meaning as well as moral guidance,[2] the process by which individuals acquire a secularist identity and worldview,[3] and the establishment and growth of Philosophical Secularist institutions.[4] We need more studies of this kind. Taking Philosophical Secularism seriously as a substantive worldview is also an important part of comparative research. As several scholars have pointed out, too many studies claiming positive outcomes for religion rely on comparisons of the devout with those who are less religious, rather than comparing religious people with those who affirm a secular philosophy.[5] We need to address what Hwang calls the absence of atheist control groups, not just in studies of adults but also in those of children and adolescents.[6] Now that more children are being raised affirmatively secular, there are even fewer excuses not to do so. Previous research, as well as my own, has tended to describe atheism and other forms of Philosophical Secularism as an achieved identity because the vast majority of such individuals were raised with religion and then rejected it. However, as more children are raised as secularists, it will be interesting to explore how atheism functions as an ascribed identity.

While Philosophical Secularists have replaced religion with an equivalent but non-religious system of beliefs, practices, moral principles, and organizations, Indifferents have not. I created this category to draw attention to those individuals who are neither religious nor secular; nor do they fit in the in-between Spiritual Seeker category because they are not searching. Debates over the existence of God or the supernatural which constitute the core tension between religion and Philosophical Secularism leave Indifferents cold; experimentation with alternative spiritual practices and experiences like yoga or meditation that so compel Spiritual Seekers seem to Indifferents like a waste of time. Finding coherent answers to what all the other categories would call the big questions (why are we here, what happens after we die) is not something to which they give a lot of thought because, as they see it, these questions are not relevant to their lives. This does not mean they lack purpose in life, but rather that they are not looking for it in religion, a secular philosophy, or in some alternative spirituality.

Indifferents are interesting for several reasons. First, if we consider Philosophical Secularism as a functional substitute for religion, then Indifferents are in some sense the true Nones. Second, there is ample evidence that many of those counted as religious or churched are only nominally so, suggesting there may be many Indifferents among them.[7] If this is the case, then current surveys which count only the unaffiliated as Nones may be severely undercounting None growth. I would like to see future research developing better measures of religiosity that distinguish Philosophical Secularism from Indifference, and identify Indifferents among those who do claim a religious affiliation. We should also investigate what that affiliation means to them. I remember talking to my husband about this book and referring to him as a None, and he responded, "No, I'm a Christian." When I pointed out that he did not believe in God and thought religion was a hoax, he said, "Well, you have to be something, and I'm British, so I'm Christian." For him the religious label was part of a cultural identity. But there are other possible reasons, like conformity to a peer group or political ambition that may also cause Indifferents to claim affiliation. If we want to make valid claims about religiousness or secularity in America, we ought to explore those reasons.

As diverse as Nones are, they are unified by more than just a refusal to identify with organized religion. This book has argued that Nones, although not a coherent movement, share a deep commitment to personal worldview choice that distinguishes them from many of their churched counterparts. We see this in the narratives about how they arrived at their own worldview (chapter 2), a process they see as contrasting with that of churched Americans. While "those people" inherit their religion, Nones—be they Unchurched Believers, Spiritual Seekers, or Philosophical Secularists—see themselves as constructing their own. We see the language of choice even more clearly in the decisions they make about transmitting worldviews to their children and the way their narratives make sense of those decisions (chapter 6). Regardless of which strategy they employ—going back to church, finding an alternative community, outsourcing, self-providing, or doing nothing—parents frame it as helping their children choose their own worldview. None parents want to maximize their children's choice options, and some even follow their children's lead.

While the idea of choosing one's religion has deep roots in the larger culture and resonates well beyond the None population, it often remains rather theoretical for churched Americans who were raised in one religion, never explored anything else, and "choose" to stay there. They then indoctrinate their children in that religion, believing if those children carry on, they too have chosen. By contrast, Nones, most of whom left the religion they were raised in, must eventually make a decision: to go back, select something else, or just do nothing. In that sense, they are actually living out the idea of choice. Choice empowers the individual; however, previous research has called attention to some of the limitations on that empowerment. In reviewing recent findings in the psychology of decision-making, we saw that choice can be illusory, it can be overwhelming, and it may or may not improve our lives.[8] How people experience choice is also influenced by their decision-making styles, such as maximizing or satisficing.[9] Although None parents do not always give their children as much choice as they think they do, it would be interesting to compare the life outcomes of children who were raised to choose their own religion with the outcomes of those who were not. I would also like to see future research to test the hypothesis that Spiritual Seekers are more likely to be maximizers.

Parenthood and Identity

Nones' worldviews are characterized by a great deal of fluidity over time and are shaped by their relationships with others, especially their children. This book explores how the meaning of individuals' None identity changes when they become parents. Before starting a family, identifying as None can often serve as a placeholder for young, uncommitted individuals who have left religion but do not feel ready to commit to something else. Having children compels them to think about what being a None means, to articulate what a None's worldview is rather than what it is not (chapter 3). Childrearing also pushes parents to discuss that worldview with those who are close to them—partners and extended family—and who may themselves have a stake in what will be transmitted to the children. Although previous research has emphasized how None family formation often results in accommodation to religious spouses, this book has shown how becoming a parent may also serve to consolidate an individual's secular identity. My data pool is small, and more research is needed to explore this process. Previous research has focused almost exclusively on the impact that parents' religion or affiliation has on their children. By contrast, this book has drawn attention to the way that children may influence their parents' worldviews. Children ask probing questions (challenging us to reflect more deeply on our worldview), they mimic parent behavior (which may clash with our professed beliefs), and they interact with peers who may have different worldviews. We need more research on how, when, and why children influence parents' religious or secular identities.

I began this project because so little was known about how None parents deal with the question of religion in their children's lives. The existing literature focuses mostly on Nones who return to church when they start a family. This book shows that there is more variety in how Nones raise their children; it is not just a choice between doing nothing and going back to church. None parents may also find an alternative worldview community, outsource religious instruction, or try to transmit a religious or alternative worldview without institutional support (chapter 5). These five options for incorporating worldviews into the upbringing of a child could, theoretically, be applied to churched parents as well, and future research may draw comparisons between churched and None parents in this regard. Of particular interest is the outsourcing option, which, based on anecdotal observation, is not uncommon among parents who do claim a religious affiliation (e.g., so-called inactive Catholics who send their children to CCD). It would be fascinating to compare the narratives used by such so-called religious parents to those of so-called None parents to justify outsourcing and to reflect on the implications for how we measure religion and secularity. We also need to study the impact that these various options have on children. As noted in chapter 7, many positive claims have been made about raising children in church but it is not clear if those benefits come from a caring community or from religion per se. It would be great to see a controlled study comparing the outcomes of raising children in a Philosophical Secularist community with raising them in church.

Nones as Cultural Outsiders or Insiders

Nones are growing, but they remain a minority. This book has shown that many Nones perceive themselves as cultural outsiders. I have argued that outsidership is partly a function of where Nones live and partly a deliberate choice (chapter 4). American culture is regionally diverse, and there are some parts of the country where Nones may feel less welcome than others. Although surveys show Nones to cluster in certain zones (like the Pacific Northwest or New England), I suggested that it is not the relative size of the None population but certain characteristics of the local public culture (such as variations in religious diversity, the relative strength of religious institutions, and the extent of privatization of religion) that make Nones feel accepted or in tension with the larger community. My argument here is supported by previous research demonstrating the influence of place on perceptions of cultural outsidership.[10] However, further research is necessary to test the causal role of these and other factors.

Nones may also choose to see themselves as outsiders, as other religious minorities have, because it confers certain benefits. I suggested that in places where Evangelical Christianity dominates the public culture, claiming outsider status gives Nones (who hold very diverse worldviews and are mostly not organized into a coherent movement) a clear sense of positive identity. *None* comes to mean more than just someone who is unaffiliated and instead signifies an independent thinker who is tolerant of others (in contrast to the majority churched population whom they see as rigid and conformist). The positive outsider identity helps Nones resist accommodation and to seek out or create community among other people with no religion. Being an outsider justifies affiliation with an organization because it helps them in transmitting to their children the language and symbols of their nonreligious identity, be it Seeker or Secularist. Affiliation, in turn, reaffirms the plausibility and salience of their nonreligious worldview, making it more likely that they will remain Nones in the future. By contrast, None parents living in places where religion is more privatized do not claim outsider status or the benefits that go with it. How will this affect their children? Future research will determine the long-term impact of this difference.

There is an extensive literature on religious outsiders, especially on what is sometimes called high-tension religions (religions whose beliefs, values, and practices substantially conflict with those of mainstream culture). The religions studied tend to be culturally conservative (e.g., fundamentalist Christians, Orthodox Jews, or polygamist Mormons). It is only recently that some scholars have begun to consider subsets of Nones, especially atheists, as a high-tension worldview. For example, several recent studies show how atheists face strong prejudices and sometimes discrimination, as other minorities have.[11] We need more research on how Nones are similar to or different from other minorities. Will the findings of studies showing children raised in high-tension religions to be more likely to retain their worldviews carry over to children raised as Philosophical Secularists?[12] Will cultural tension lead secularists to organize, as Evangelical Christians did a generation ago?[13] Under what conditions will secular Nones accommodate to the religious majority, and under what conditions will they resist?

Finding New and Better Ways to Study Religion and Secularism

Nones challenge our preconceived notions of what is religion, what is secularism, and how these worldviews should be studied. Americans commonly define religion in terms of beliefs about ultimate meaning and purpose (which usually include God or supernatural beings), values, and customs or practices (e.g., prayer, meditation, dietary rules, or sexual norms) that give expression to those beliefs, all of which are shared by a particular community (including leaders and followers). Secularism is usually defined as the absence of these beliefs, values, and customs. Such definitions work pretty well when applied to religious or secular institutions; for example, in discussions about the separation of church and state in American politics. They work less well when applied to individuals.

One problem is how the definition reifies affiliation as normative. Since many people find meaning through religion, it is easy to assume that those who do not have religion, the Nones, must lack such meaning. But as I have shown in this book, most Nones do have substantive worldviews, including a coherent set of beliefs, values, practices, and sometimes even community that lend meaning and moral order to their lives. Another problem is how we measure an individual's religiousness or secularity. If an individual claims to hold religious beliefs, participates (even minimally) in religious practices, and belongs to a community, we count them as religious. If they do not, we count them as secular. The study of Nones demonstrates that we should also consider how much an individual's worldview *matters* to him or her (worldview salience) and the extent to which it actually shapes their lives (lived religion). I suggested earlier that Indifferents (who are found in the ranks of both the churched and the Nones) may be a better indicator of secularism in America than atheists or humanists are, and a recent study by British sociologist Lois Lee provides empirical support for this.[14] I do not want to refer to Philosophical Secularists as another type of religion because they reject that term. But it may be time to develop a new terminology that includes both religious and Philosophical Secularist worldviews.

We should also encourage more inclusive methodological approaches. This book has drawn on qualitative research to provide much needed empirical data on how None parents deal with the question of religion in the lives of their children. There are limits to this approach, mostly because sample size tends to be small, which is why I frequently call for more and larger studies to confirm some of my findings. But the qualitative approach also has clear advantages, especially when studying a minority worldview such as the Nones. Because of the negative stigma associated with the term *atheist*, respondents to surveys will often not identify as such, even when they hold what is, by all objective standards, an atheist worldview. By contrast, that worldview will become apparent in qualitative research that records the individual's own words and actions. The term *spiritual* also is problematic when used in surveys because it means different things to different people. However, when we allow research subjects to explain what *spiritual* means to them, we can interpret and categorize their responses more effectively. By listening to people tell their stories, I was able to discern important patterns, like the narrative of choice or the outsider narrative which would not have come through in a survey. By visiting with people where they live and observing them interact, I could appreciate the influence of relationships, like married couples who have different worldviews, and social context, like the large number of churches with crowded parking lots in the Colorado Springs neighborhood where I interviewed several Seekers and Secularists. Although I would love to see more large quantitative studies of Nones—especially the kind that take seriously the distinction between secular and Indifferent—some questions, particularly those regarding children, may better be addressed in smaller, more direct settings.

My Personal Journey, a Decade Later

There's a tradition in the sociology of religion, still followed by some, that researchers should keep themselves separate from their academic work in order to approximate the ideal of the neutral observer. This ideal is reflected in the use of impersonal language (writing "fifty individuals were interviewed for this study" or "this research has found," rather than "I interviewed fifty individuals" or "my conclusions are"). It is also reflected in the structure of academic articles and books that locate the origin of the research question in the relevant literature and are often silent about the scholar's personal experience or interest. While it is laudable for scholars to try to be objective, especially in religion, complete neutrality is usually elusive. Most scholars' research interests, in fact, are somehow connected to their lives (as a recent book by Zuckerman and Hjelm has shown), and this can often have a positive impact.[15] These connections may facilitate access to a particular research population, provide sensitivity or insight that otherwise might be lacking, or in some cases offer additional data. To acknowledge these connections, rather than hide them behind impersonal language, helps rather than impedes the goal of neutrality by alerting readers to potential slants in one's research and allowing them to weigh the conclusions accordingly. It is in this spirit, and to share my experience with those readers who are parents themselves, that I will end the book by returning to my own story.

Readers may be wondering where my family fits into the typology of None worldviews proposed in this book. Applying the criteria laid out in this book, I began this project as a Spiritual Seeker but by the end, I had moved closer to the Philosophical Secularist camp. My husband was and has remained Indifferent. He does not believe in God and thinks religion is a crutch. Churches exist to brainwash people for financial and political gains. But he will not identify as an atheist (because, he said, "there's probably something out there") and has no interest in secular philosophies or communities. When I raised the question of incorporating religion in Sheila's life, he was surprised I even asked: "Why would you do that?" When I explained why we should at least explore the options, he was open to letting me do so but did not want to become involved himself.

At the time I was much more worried about the whole question of religion than I am now. Sheila was three, an age when she started to ask questions, which prompted me to look at what other people are doing. My husband's family and relatives back in England are Evangelical Christians who sent their kids to church, Bible school, and mission trips. My sister is unchurched but she had her children baptized and was raising them Christian; they also received religious instruction as part of their private school education. Our closest friends with similar age children are Catholic and Jewish, and they enrolled their kids in CCD and Hebrew school. Add to that the fact that I am a religious studies professor and felt that I should be doing something about religious education—if only to educate Sheila about other religions—I had no excuse not to explore other options.

One of the beautiful experiences about doing this research was all the ideas it generated for what I might do with Sheila. Over the years, I considered all of the various strategies I described in this book. The traditional route of going back to church was the most obvious choice. There was a part of me that would have loved to go back and give Sheila what I had as a child. I adored the frilly lace dress I wore for my baptism (I was nine when my mother decided to affiliate with church). I was awed at the mystery of receiving communion in a darkened incense scented room. I eagerly anticipated the magic of a Christmas holiday that is based not on getting every item on your list but on faith that this is the time when God entered the world. As a child religion gave me the security that comes from knowing your place in history: that God created the world and placed humans in it; he made a covenant with the Jews; he sent his son, Jesus, into the world who then was crucified yet saved humanity in the process; Christianity spread to Europe, which is where my ancestors came from. Religion offered the comfort of knowing God is watching over you and will make everything right. But I could not offer this to Sheila because I no longer believed. Some of my European ancestors were Nazis and God did not make everything right. Christianity, like all major world religions, has deep strains of misogyny that conflict with modern egalitarian values. There are too many teachings—creationism, the virgin birth, Jesus rising from the dead—that strain the credulity of a modern, scientifically educated person. And if you consider that there are multiple other religions with conflicting truth claims, all of them unprovable, the whole idea seems even more implausible. My mother had religious faith; I do not. Going back to church with Sheila would be a lie that I could not live with and that she would ultimately see through.

Then again, why hold her hostage to my own doubts? After all, we encouraged her to believe in Santa and the tooth fairy, plus there is the whole family heritage of which she ought to have some knowledge. So, for a while, I decided to outsource. A friend, a conservative Catholic with a young son Sheila's age, told me she had found the perfect religious education program called "The Catechesis of the Good Shepard." It a Montessori-based two-year program for preschoolers and kindergarten age children that allows children to choose from various religion-themed play activities rather than imposing a unified curriculum on them. The teacher leading the program was a lovely woman, gentle and non-dogmatic and so good with kids. My husband was initially opposed to any kind of church-based education, but I convinced him to give it a try. The program was based at St. Mary's Catholic Church in New Haven, Connecticut, and I enrolled Sheila for the first year. She loved it. She learned to dip her fingers in holy water and make a sign of the cross. She would play with wooden Jesus and sheep figurines and then make paper flowers, and she would hear a Bible story at the end. When we went to England for Christmas, my husband's family was duly impressed with Sheila's knowledge of religion.

At the end of the school year, however, the doctrinal basis of the program became more clear. The first year curriculum, geared to very young children, was centered on the idea that God is a good shepherd who will take care of you—a fairly generic religious concept that I could accept. By contrast, the second-year curriculum involved teaching children the Catholic creed and preparing them for first communion. I did not feel comfortable with that. Parents were encouraged to attend church with their children, and in talking to other parents I realized that everybody else was actually doing that. I felt like a fraud. So the next Sunday, I went to mass and I took Sheila with me. St. Mary's cathedral is in the heart of the Yale campus, an old gothic building made of stone with stained glass windows and wooden pews. It is cool inside and dark, your eyes unavoidably drawn upward to the source of light. The organ played and it smelled like incense. I felt like I was travelling back in time to when I was a child in Germany. But reality quickly set in once the service began. There were rousing hymns singing glory to God, prayers, a reading from the Bible, a homily on a topic I cannot remember, people lined up to receive communion. The hymns struck me as militaristic, the Bible reading felt irrelevant to my life, and the prayers reminded me that I do not believe in God. Sheila was bored and fidgety. I was bored and alienated. It was clear this was not the right path for us. I was disappointed, but also relieved.

I realized I needed to own my worldview, which at the time most closely resembled that of a Spiritual Seeker. I believed all religions (well, most of them) contain some truths and positive values and affirmative rituals, and I liked the idea of selecting those that resonated into my own personal spirituality. I liked the way I feel after doing yoga or meditation. I see a lot of wisdom in Buddhist philosophy, in the Jewish ritual of Shabbat, and in some mystical Christian writings. I bought a book about the Buddha, and another that rendered the biblical creation story to emphasize the presence of God in all of nature. Stewart, Sheila, and I would pause briefly before dinner to say "blessings on the meal" acknowledging our gratitude for nature's bounty. But the ritual soon became rote, and reading stories from a couple of books to a child is not the same as celebrating annual holidays, eating special foods, and gathering with others. Like other parents trying to self-provide the transmission of a spiritual worldview, I struggled for time and consistency.

I was excited to hear parents in several of my interviews discuss the option of education via an alternative community, enrolling your child in a worldview education program, such as that offered by the AHA or Unitarian Universalist communities, that teaches children about multiple religions, as well as humanism and atheism, and allows them to choose for themselves. The curriculum is designed for particular age groups and runs on Sunday mornings, concurrently with adult programming (such as Unitarian services or AHA lecture or discussion groups). What a great idea! I searched online to locate the local Unitarian congregation, and discovered that they had such a program and that everyone was welcome to drop in. On a Sunday morning in early summer we drove out to a handsome modern building on a wooded campus. We were directed by a friendly staff member to a basement room full of preschool-aged children where a young woman led my daughter to a round table covered with cotton balls. "This week we will be exploring our connection with nature," the woman said. I was not sure how this was related to the balls, but Sheila was fascinated with them and she seemed happy to be with other little kids, so I left and went upstairs to the adult program. The meeting room was spacious, light, and modern, and almost every seat was taken. Teenagers and older children sat together near the front of the room. The program opened with a jazz quintet playing a set of contemporary instrumental pieces. There were some announcements and a moment of silence honoring someone's death. The teens and children performed a song, then they left to attend their classes. The pastor now commenced a lecture on international human rights. The lecture was interesting and resonated with my progressive leanings, the jazz was cool, the people were friendly (and I recognized some of them from the local environmental activist community). Unlike my experience at St. Mary's, I was neither alienated nor bored by what I experienced. Yet something was missing. Even now it is hard for me to articulate what it was. It is an emotional thing. The space was pleasant but it did not inspire the awe and mystery I feel in ancient churches and temples. I love hearing jazz but I prefer it in a bar over a glass of bourbon. The lecture was intellectually satisfying but it did not move me. I realized that being moved, being touched, and having a spiritual experience was essential to me, and it did not seem like I was going to find my needs met here.

It was another disappointment. By this time Sheila was almost six years old, and I had considered and rejected most of the strategies None parents normally use to deal with religion. I knew I could not return to church, so I experimented with outsourcing but it felt inauthentic. I had tried self-providing a kind of worldview education but found it difficult to sustain on my own. I explored an alternative community but found it did not meet my spiritual needs. The only option left, it seemed, was to do nothing. Maybe my husband was right. We do not want organized religion in our lives. Secular replacements are unnecessary. Sheila can learn about all the various religious and nonreligious philosophies in school or in college. And we can transmit a positive value system to her without the formal framework of a particular, named system of thought or practice. Eventually she will figure it out on her own, as we did. Let it be.

And that is pretty much what we did for the next six years. We have not enrolled Sheila in any more programs, and we have taken no intentional actions to incorporate religion, spirituality, or a secular philosophy into our home life. Based on the criteria set out in this book, it appears we are "doing nothing," at least from the outside. If you look closer, however, you might perceive a different picture. You would notice that, although I no longer read religious stories to Sheila, we talk about many different worldviews. You would see that, although we do not have a schedule of rituals or services, she has frequently participated in those of others. Several of her friends are Jewish, and attending their Hanukkah parties and bat mitzvahs became an occasion to experience and talk about Judaism—"Why is the Hebrew Bible written backward? What is that big scroll they carry around and why do they kiss it?" My husband and I choose not to have a television set in the house but we subscribe to the Sunday edition of the *New York Times*, which remains on the breakfast table all week. Religion frequently makes the headlines, raising more questions: "Who is the pope? Why do these people wear that (the Muslim hijab)? Why do Hindu gods have so many arms, and how come this one has an elephant head?" As I answer these questions, Sheila is learning a great deal about the religions of others.

She is also learning about her parents' worldview. Although my husband is disinclined to discuss such matters, Sheila and I have had several deep and wide-ranging conversations about "the big questions." We have talked about the biblical creation story (and those of various other religions) and why I think the scientific account is more compelling. We have talked about women and children in various religions and why they are subjected to male authority and often abuse. One day, as part of a world religions unit, her teacher had assigned them to read several passages from the Bible. Sheila came home mystified at its content. "God seems so mean and arrogant," she said. "He's always telling people to worship him, and then he goes and smites people who don't follow his rules." I explained that the text authors, who lived several thousand years ago, probably imagined God as a larger version of the authorities of their times, powerful kings who made absolute rules and demanded absolute loyalty. "So why would people still follow this religion today?" she demanded. That is a good question, and I am not sure of the answer, but it offered an opportunity to explain the difference between religious progressives (like Congregational Christians or Reform Jews) and religious conservatives (like the Southern Baptists and orthodox Jews), and families we know that exemplify both types.

I have shared with Sheila why I do not believe in God, but that I am inclined to think there is a spiritual dimension to life. A kind of life force that animates nature, a storehouse of wisdom we can draw on when we meditate, a kind of cosmic energy permeating the universe from which we come and to which we must return. I suspect the various gods and goddesses of the world's religions are just different labels people in various cultures have given to this energy. One day, after attending funeral services for the relatives of friends, she and I pondered the question of what happens after death, and whether some spiritual aspect of the individual survives. I admitted that I would like to believe there is something like a soul, if only so I can still watch over her after I die. Sheila smiled at me and said, "Yeah, I'd like that too. But if your body is dead, then your brain is dead, and without a brain you would have no awareness of watching over me. That makes no sense." Out of the mouths of babes, as they say.

Sheila's rejection of the eternal soul, her critical reflection on the God of the Bible, her playful invention of a goddess Olisama to whom she has erected a secret rock garden in the evergreens behind our house—all this suggests that even parents who *think* they are doing nothing about transmitting their worldviews to their children are, in fact, shaping their children's views. Yet it is important to remember that children also shape their parents' worldview. Sheila was right about the brain and awareness, of course, but somehow I had never bothered to address that problem. Now I did, and I realized my discomfort with it—and how religion and later spirituality was a way of avoiding that discomfort. Glossing over inconsistencies is a common habit in religion, of course, but there is something about a ten-year-old calling you out on it that has an impact. I began thinking and reading about the finality of our lived experience in this world, the reality that, as the Zen philosophers put it, right now is all you have. I have tried in the two years since that conversation to make peace with that reality, and in the process my worldview has changed. The blending of religious ideas that comprised my Spiritual Seeker identity (the great goddess of nature, Buddha-Moses-Muhammad-Jesus as wise teachers, a soul that reincarnates until we too become wise) is giving way to a simpler, more secularist philosophy. Ten years ago I thought becoming a parent might restore my faith in religion. It has not. But it has given me something better: a faith in the process of choosing our own worldview.

APPENDIX: SOURCES AND METHODS OF RESEARCH

I have come to this research as an academic who is a None parent, and my experience as such has enriched my work in important ways. The goal with this study was to go beyond my experience and explore what parents elsewhere are thinking, saying, and doing. Thus the data gathered for this book was based on a formal process that included culling existing survey data and doing my own qualitative research. The latter included conducting in-person interviews and collecting demographic information, as well as observing respondents' activities and context, and then coding and analyzing the data thus gathered. I already commented briefly on the basic research process in chapter 1. For interested readers, here is more detailed information about my sources and research methods.

Survey Data

Several major surveys have analyzed demographic and some belief characteristics of Nones. My research has relied heavily on the American Religious Identification Surveys (2001 and 2008) and the Pew Religious Landscape Survey (2008). Full reports on both (as well as links to other surveys) are available at commons.trincoll.edu/aris/ and at religions. pewforum.org/.

Qualitative Data

Most of the qualitative data (interviews, observational data, demographic information) presented here were gathered over a period of two and a half years, starting in early 2005 and ending late 2007. I began transcribing, coding, and interpreting this data in 2006 and finished in 2008.

The project was advertised and data was gathered in eight locations: the Greater Boston area; Hartford and New Haven, Connecticut; Jacksonville, Florida; Denver and Colorado Springs; San Francisco and Los Angeles. Participants were recruited via flyers posted at community notice boards, schools, preschools, and day care centers, as well as by circulating e-mail and by word of mouth. People interviewed were asked for the names of others who might be interested in participating, creating a snowball sample.

In order to focus on the current generation of None parents who are in the process of raising their children, the sample was restricted to respondents who self-identified as having no religious affiliation and who had children under eighteen living in their homes. Parents who were expecting their first child were included, but those whose children were already grown were excluded. Respondents selected ranged in age from twenty-three to fifty-five, with an average age of thirty-eight. Two-thirds of respondents were women, and all but six were married. Most were white and had completed at least some college; all were employed or supported by someone who was employed (I did not ask questions about income, but people's homes and neighborhoods often gave clues to their economic circumstances). Almost all respondents had themselves been raised with religion; their religious backgrounds included Catholic, mainline Protestant, conservative Protestant, Jewish, Mormon, Unitarian, and Bahai.

Interviews

I conducted forty-eight formal interviews, plus many additional informal conversations with None parents. By informal conversation I mean the kind that is unsolicited and unplanned and does not follow a particular structure. The conversation might have occured at a social event, where I met another None parent and we started talking, and they said something really interesting, so I told them about my book project and asked: would it be okay if I incorporated our conversation in my research? If they said yes, I started taking notes. By formal interview I mean the kind that is solicited, scheduled, structured, and recorded. Respondents were invited to participate, given information about the questions motivating the project, and they consented to the process ahead of time. The conversations were scheduled for a specific date and time and were guided by a structured set of questions intended to take about forty-five minutes. My goal in using these questions was not to limit the conversation but to make sure we covered certain topics. In practice, respondents often strayed from the guidelines to share other information that turned out to be interesting, and talks frequently lasted for an hour or two. Thus the difference between the two types of interview was not as dramatic as the description might imply; my goal in both cases was to listen to None parents tell their stories. All conversations were taped and then transcribed, and all respondents were assigned pseudonyms.

Interview questions covered two areas: parent worldview and the process of raising children. Information about the presence, proximity, or influence of grandparents, in-laws, and other extended family was not systematically gathered, but frequently emerged from the interview.

The list of questions about a parent's worldview included the following:

- Were you raised in a religious faith? If no, why not? If yes, did this involve participation in organized religion? For either, tell me about what that was like.
- When and why did you disengage or disaffiliate from religion?
- Do you consider yourself spiritual or religious? What do these terms mean to you? Do you believe in God, or a higher power? Do you engage in any kind of practice you would call religious or spiritual?
- Have you ever explored religions, spiritual, or philosophical paths other than the one you were raised in? If not, why not? If yes, which ones?
- Are you considering affiliation with any organized community that represents a particular spiritual, religious, or secular worldview? If no, why not? If yes, why and why this one? For how long have you been engaged with this worldview, and how actively are you involved?

The list of questions about raising children included the following (if the respondent was expecting his/her first child, questions were directed at plans for the future):

- Do you intentionally incorporate religion, spirituality, or a particular secular worldview into your child's upbringing?

- Do you celebrate holidays with your children in the home? If no, why not; what kinds of events *do* you celebrate? If yes, which ones, and how do you celebrate these events?
- Do you participate in any kind of religious, spiritual, or other worldview community with your children? If no, why not? If yes, which ones and why?
- Are you providing any kind of education about religion or other worldviews to your children? If no, why not? If you have not yet made a decision, what options are you considering? Why these options? If yes, why this one? Did you consider other possibilities?
- If you do provide any kind of education about religion or other worldviews to your children: Who provides the education (you or an organization)? If the parent provides, how and what do you teach your child? How is your child responding? What do you find most challenging about providing religious instruction to your child? If an organization provides, what is your reaction to what your child is learning in this community? How is your child responding? Has there ever been a discrepancy between what the child is being taught and what you believe or practice? If so, how did you react? How did the child react?
- Who is the primary decision-maker with respect to the question of incorporating religion, spirituality, or some other worldview to your children? Has there ever been any disagreement in your family about this? Has the extended family tried to influence your decisions in this area?
- Has having no religion ever made you feel different from other parents?
- As you think about the question of religion, spirituality, or some other worldview in your child's life, what is it you want to give him or her?
- How has becoming a parent impacted your own worldview? Has it changed or stayed the same? If you participate in a community with your child, how does this contribute to your own development? If you do not, how do you pursue your own growth?
- Is there anything else you would like to mention that I did not ask about?

Observational Data

Gathering observational data is more complex, involving observation of respondents' behaviors and settings, and sometimes participation in respondents' activities. For this research, I made a point of visiting institutions with which parents were considering affiliating, especially those that offered alternative educational programs for children (e.g., AHA and UUA). I visited at least one such institution in each of the locations where I did research, and took notes on who attended and what happened. I also spent time driving around my interviewees' neighborhoods. I would count the number of churches and synagogues and check if the parking area was full or empty on weekend mornings or Wednesday evenings. I noted any religious billboards. In every city, I collected copies of the local paper and looked at the religious ads, as well as articles about religion or secularism, and noted the editorial slant. At people's homes, I would look for bumper stickers on their cars that reference a particular worldview, and note any artifacts or books around the house that convey a religious, spiritual, or secular message.

Taking notes on all of these observations generated reams of data on what some scholars have called "the material culture" of religion (or in this case nonreligion). While the study of material culture was not a primary focus of this research, it supplemented what I was learning through interviews and library research. It often provided vivid illustrations of experiences reported by None parents and sometimes offered cues to follow-up questions I needed to ask.

Demographic Information

All respondents were given a questionnaire asking them to provide name, age, gender, city of residence, ethnicity, education, occupation, marital status, and number and age of children. Names were used for research coding purposes only; all names used in this book are pseudonyms.

Interpreting the Data

Transcribed interviews were manually coded for thematic content. Responses were then analyzed and categorized based on these emerging themes. Sampling of additional respondents continued during the coding process until thematic saturation was reached. During coding, demographic characteristics (such as religious background or geographical region) and certain objective responses (e.g., yes or no, in response to questions like, "Do you intentionally incorporate religion, spirituality, or a secular worldview into your child's upbringing?") were entered into an Excel spreadsheet. Observations about respondents' behaviors or their material environment were noted to provide a context for the patterns that emerged.

Interpreting qualitative research is complex and time consuming. Transcribed interviews (especially if they last an hour or two) comprise many pages. People use language in idiosyncratic ways and touch upon various topics, especially when you use a semistructured format as I did. Although computer programs can aid in the identification of frequently occurring words such as *choice, atheist* or *Sunday school,* there is much they ignore. Ultimately, nothing beats the painstaking process of carefully reading each transcript, in order to analyze it for important patterns or themes.

Some themes were built into the interview. For example, I designed certain questions because I wanted to test Fuller's model of different types of Nones and identify respondents as Unchurched Believers, Spiritual Seekers, or Secularists. Others themes emerged from the data. For example, the ubiquity of what I call choice language, the use of outsider narratives, or the various strategies (e.g., traditional, alternative, or outsource) that parents use to deal with the question of religion in their children's lives. Once I had identified such a pattern or theme, I would go back and define the characteristics and variations of that particular theme. For example, a parent who says, "I want my son to make his own choices about religion" is obviously using choice language. But there are many other formulations that can also be coded as choice language, such as: "I don't want to impose my worldview on my child," "I want my daughter to have lots of options," or "I think it's important for my kids to be exposed to many different worldviews and figure it out for themselves." Having identified patterns, I would then look for how they cluster with certain demographic characteristics, for instance the preponderance of outsider narratives in certain regions. I would also look for how various themes cluster together, which resulted in the categories of worldviews presented in chapter 3 and the types of parenting strategies presented in chapter 6.

The Role of the Researcher

The commitment to the kind of formal process I have described here, combined with transparency about who we are, helps scholars be neutral and balanced—whether we are doing mostly quantitative or qualitative research, and whether those we study are similar to or radically different from us. The conventional wisdom is that scholars should be outsiders, or at least act as such, although that wisdom is often applied rather selectively (e.g., a Muslim author of a book about Christianity will be suspected of bias, whereas Western scholars who happen to be Christian are presumed to be able to write objectively about Islam). In the sociology of religion, however, there is increasing acknowledgment that insidership is not necessarily a liability. I believe that my experience as None parent researcher actually enhanced this project in various ways. Identifying myself as such made it easier to gain access to and trust from other None parents, especially because I am employed as a professor of Religious Studies at a Catholic university, a position that might otherwise cause respondents to suspect me of having some kind of religious agenda. Once I had begun the project, my identity as a fellow None parent facilitated keeping in casual touch with some respondents, and these subsequent interactions provided a continuous stream of additional data, against which I could compare my emerging findings. Finally, being a None parent sensitized me to the problem of negative labeling and the need to pay attention to secularism as a substantive and affirmative worldview.

NOTES

INTRODUCTION

1. Pew Forum on Religion and Public Life, *US Religious Landscape Survey.*
2. Baker and Smith, "The Nones," 252–263; Kosmin and Keysar, *American Nones*, 17–20. This is a marked contrast to previous generations, when race in particular was a very strong predictor of religious affiliation. See Welch, "The Unchurched," 289.
3. Fuller, *Spiritual, but Not Religious*; Stark, Hamburg, and Miller, "Exploring Spirituality," 3–23.
4. See Jamieson, *A Churchless Faith*; Jamieson, *Church Leavers*; Altemeyer and Hunsberger, *Amazing Conversions*; Altemeyer and Hunsberger, *Atheists*; Ecklund and Schultz Lee, "Atheists and Agnostics Negotiate Religion and Family"; Pasquale, "A Portrait of Secular Group Affiliates"; Smith, "Becoming an Atheist in America"; and Zuckerman, "Atheism: Contemporary Numbers and Patterns."
5. Strauss and Corbin, "Grounded Theory Research," 3–21.
6. Kosmin and Keysar, *American Nones*, 17–20.
7. Secularization theory predominated among American sociologists of religion until the second half of the twentieth century. For a classic statement see Berger, *The Sacred Canopy*; or Luckman, *The Invisible Religion*. Proponents of secularization theory argued that religious pluralism and privatization in America undermines the plausibility of any religion. Their argument was challenged by proponents of the so-called market theory of religion, which asserted that competition between multiple religions actually reduced secularization because individuals have more choices, and churches must try harder to attract them. Articulations of this theory may be found in Stark and Bainbridge, "Towards a Theory of Religion"; or Finke and Stark, *The Churching of America, 1776—2005*. Like secularization theory before it, the new market theory of religion has also become a bit of a dogma. The media, of course, are less subtle in their arguments and more obvious in their biases. Thus newspaper headlines reporting on the increase in Nones included titles such as "The Decline of Christianity in Australia and America" by Kirkwood in *Eureka Street*; and "The Good News about Evangelicalism: It Isn't Shrinking and the Young Are Not Becoming Liberals" by Johnson in *First Things*.

CHAPTER 1. WHO ARE THE NONES?

1. Gallup, *The Unchurched American*; Gallup, *The Unchurched American—10 Years Later.*

2. Pew, *US Religious Landscape Survey.*

3. See, for example, Roof, *A Generation of Seekers*; Roof, *Spiritual Marketplace*; Wuthnow, *After Heaven.*

4. See, for example, Wright, "Post-Involvement Attitudes"; Peter et al., "The Dynamics of Religious Defection among Hutterites;" and Bromley's edited volume, *Falling from the Faith.* In "Linking Social Structure," an article written a decade later, Bromley refers to people leaving cults as *apostates* and reserves the term *defectors* for those leaving more mainstream churches. But this use of the terms does not seem to have taken hold in the literature.

5. Marler and Hadaway. "'Being Religious' or 'Being Spiritual' in America"; Ashley, "The Spiritual, the Cultural, and the Religious."

6. Zuckerman, *Society without God.*

7. In the last decade several American Religious Identification Surveys have been conducted by Barry Kosmin and Ariela Keysar at Trinity College in Connecticut. Information is available at www.trincoll.edu/aris.

8. The American Religion Data Archive has been renamed The Association of Religion Data Archives. Information is available at http://www.thearda.com.

9. Putnam, *Bowling Alone*, 65–74.

10. Gallup, *Unchurched American*, 2.

11. Roof, *Generation of Seekers*, 151.

12. Fuller, *Spiritual, but Not Religious*, 4.

13. Kosmin and Keysar, *American Nones*, 21.

14. Hoge, Johnson, and Luidens' study of unchurched Protestants, *Vanishing Boundaries*, divides them in to four types: those who maintain church membership but don't attend, those who attend but never become members, seekers, and seculars.

15. Pew Forum on Religion and Public Life, *Global Religious Landscape Survey.*

16. Kosmin and Keysar, *American Nones*, 21.

17. Stump, "Regional Variations." While many people think of cities as more secular, there is no clear evidence that this is actually the case. Some studies suggest that religion thrives in urban areas while others do not; see Welch, "Community Development."

18. Kosmin and Keysar, *American Nones*, 18–19.

19. Ibid.

20. Ibid.

21. Pew Forum on Religion and Public Life, *Faith in Flux.*

22. Gallup, *Unchurched American*; and Gallup, *Unchurched American—10 Years Later.*

23. Statistics cited are from Kosmin and Keysar, American Religious Identification Survey, but other surveys, like Pew's *US Religious Landscape Survey*, show similar results.

24. See, for example, Edgell, Gertais, and Hartman, "Atheists as Other"; Jenks, "Perception of Two Deviant and Two Non-Deviant Groups."

25. Luo, "God '08."

26. Volokh, "Parent-Child Speech"; Council for Democratic and Secular Humanism, "Atheists Still Remain Black Sheep," 29.
27. For a review of feminist and multicultural critiques of science, see Lorber, *Gender and the Social Construction of Illness.*
28. Pals, *Eight Theories of Religion.*
29. Purpora, *Landscapes of the Soul*; Putnam and Campbell, *American Grace.*
30. Fuller, *Spiritual, but Not Religious*; Pasquale, "Secular Group Affiliates."

CHAPTER 2. WHAT DO NONES BELIEVE AND PRACTICE?

1. Defining religion and religiousness is a problem that has vexed scholars for centuries, and there is still no consensus. For a good overview of the issues, see McGuire, *Religion: The Social Context*, 8–14.
2. Religiosity is usually measured as it relates to institutional or official religions such as belief in the doctrines of or participation in the rituals of Catholicism or Islam. It is more difficult to capture elements of popular religion such as beliefs in lucky charms or the practice of getting a "message" from random openings of the Bible.
3. Stark, Hamburg, and Miller, "Exploring Spirituality."
4. Hout and Fisher, "Why More Americans."
5. Jones, Daniel Cox, and Juhem Navarro-Rivera, *The 2012 American Values Survey.*
6. Hout and Fisher, "Why More Americans."
7. Berger, *Sacred Canopy*; Luckman, *Invisible Religion*; Putnam, *Bowling Alone.*
8. Stark, Hamburg, and Miller, "Exploring Spirituality," 4.
9. This problem is illustrated in the 2012 American Values Survey. The report describes Nones as comprised of three subgroups: 23 percent are unattached believers (those who describe themselves as religious despite having no formal religious identity); 39 percent are seculars (those who identify as secular or not religious); and 36 percent are atheists or agnostics. By this accounting, the vast majority of Nones (i.e., the secular plus the atheist/ agnostic categories) appear to be secular—a dramatic contrast to the assertions of Rodney Stark and others that most Nones are Unchurched Believers. A closer look at these categories, however, suggests reality is more complex. Seculars are defined as secular *or* not religious, which makes them seem equivalent even though they often are not. For example, somebody who describes him- or herself as "not religious" may be an atheist, a Wiccan or a Buddhist who perceives him- or herself as spiritual rather than religious. Similarly, the atheist *or* agnostic category is likely to include many agnostics who believe in a spiritual dimension but perhaps to with lesser certainty than theists do.
10. Fuller, *Spiritual, but Not Religious.*
11. Ammerman, "Spiritual but Not Religious?," 262–275.
12. Roof, *Generation of Seekers*, chap. 3. *See also* Wuthnow, *After Heaven.*
13. Ammerman, "Spiritual but Not Religious?," 275.

14. Scholars have made distinctions between different kinds of defectors from religion, but these too are focused on the individual's relationship with organized religion. For example, Armand Mauss distinguishes between intellectual apostasy (those who reject religious beliefs), social apostasy (those who lose social connections to church), or emotional apostates (who react to perceived hypocrisy or hurt by religion). Brinkerhoff and Mackie distinguish between ritualists (who no longer believe but continue to attend services and maintain affiliation with a religious community), outsiders (who believe but do not belong), and true apostates (who neither believe nor belong). Phil Zuckerman distinguishes between shallow apostates (those who do not totally reject religion because they are spiritual) and deep apostates (those who completely reject religion). See Mauss, "Dimensions of Religious Defection"; Brinkerhoff and Mackie, "Casting off the Bonds of Organized Religion"; Zuckerman, *Faith No More*.

15. Pasquale, "Secular Group Affiliates."

16. Fuller, *Spiritual, but Not Religious*; Zuckerman, "Atheism"; Jones, Daniel Cox, and Juhem Navarro-Rivera, *The 2012 American Values Survey*.

17. The "new atheist" writers such as Sam Harris and Richard Dawkins are famous examples of this; but sociological research shows many ordinary atheists also hold negative attitudes about religion, usually because they have been hurt by it. See Zuckerman, *Faith No More*, chaps. 3 and 5.

18. Lim, MacGregor, and Putnam, "Secular and Liminal."

19. This category should not be confused with Indifferentism, a worldview whose adherents are called Indifferentists. Indifferentism refers to a belief that all religions are equally valid. By contrasts, *Indifferents*, as I define it, refers to individuals who are indifferent to the very question of religious validity. The question of which, if any, religion is true, just doesn't matter to them.

20. The criteria listed were used as guidelines to code individuals as one type or another, and most respondents were placed in a category because they met the majority of its criteria. For respondents who seemed to fit more than one category, more weight was given to how they labeled themselves, and additional factors such as behavior or the presence and perceived meaning of symbolic objects in the home were also considered.

21. Bellah et al., *Habits of the Heart*, 221.

22. Lee, "Secular or Nonreligious?"

23. Sociologists refer to this phenomenon as "belonging without believing," a pattern that is quite common in Europe. In Scandinavian nations such as Denmark and Sweden, for example, over 80 percent of the population are members of Christian churches, but only 62 percent believe in God (Luchau, "Atheism and Secularity," 177–178). See also Grace Davie, "Vicarious Religion."

CHAPTER 3. THE IMPORTANCE OF TIME

1. Pew, *US Religious Landscape Survey*.

2. Jones, Daniel Cox, and Juhem Navarro-Rivera, *The 2012 American Values Survey*, 7–8.

3. Pew, *US Religious Landscape Survey*, 36–37; Kosmin, Meyer, and Keysar, *The American Religious Identification Survey 2001*, 1.

4. Putnam and Campbell, *American Grace*, 72–75.

5. Jones, Daniel Cox, and Juhem Navarro-Rivera, *The 2012 American Values Survey*. According to this survey, the other frequently cited reasons for leaving religion are antipathy toward organized religion (16 percent), negative personal experiences with religion or life experiences in general (11 percent), perceptions that religion is at odds with scientific principles or logic (8 percent), and perceptions that religion or religious people are hypocritical (8 percent).

6. Hout and Fisher, "Why More Americans."

7. Ibid.

8. In the 2012 election, 60 percent of Americans under thirty voted for Obama (Roper Center, *How Groups Voted*) as did 70 percent of Nones (Pew, *How the Faithful Voted*).

9. Baker and Smith, "The Nones," 258–259.

10. Putnam and Campbell, *American Grace*, 74–75 and 120–123. See also Chaves and Anderson, "Continuity and Change in American Religion."

11. Kosmin and Keysar, *American Religious Identification Survey 2008*. The 2012 American Values Survey reports that only 7 percent of today's Nones were raised without religion.

12. As Music and Wilson put it, "few people switch to make their marriage a secular one." Their analysis of national survey data shows the unaffiliated and liberal Protestants were the most likely to switch for marriage reasons, while those raised Catholic were least likely (Music and Wilson, "Religious Switching for Marriage Reasons," 267). For additional discussion of Nones who go back to church, see Glenn, "The Trend in 'No Religion Respondents'"; Greeley and Hout, "Musical Chairs"; Roof, *Generation of Seekers*, chap. 3; Woodward, "A Time to Seek."

13. Kosmin and Keysar, *American Religious Identification Survey 2008*.

14. Bainbridge, "Atheism."

15. Hout and Fisher, "Why More Americans."

16. Music and Wilson, "Religious Switching for Marriage Reasons."

17. Baker and Smith, "The Nones."

18. Ecklund and Lee, "Atheists and Agnostics," 737.

19. Ecklund and Lee note that spouses of atheist respondents in their study tended to be female because their sample consisted of scientists at elite universities who were predominantly male. However, the gender gap among seculars is confirmed by other studies such as ARIS 2001 and 2008 that are based on larger, more representative samples.

20. Argue, Johnson, and White, "Age and Religiosity"; Ingersoll-Dayton, Krause, and Morgan, "Religious Trajectories"; Petts and Knoester, "Parents' Religious Heterogamy"; Wilson and Sherkat, "Returning to the Fold."

21. Ecklund and Lee, "Atheists and Agnostics."

22. Phillips, "Assimilation, Transformation."

23. Putnam, *Bowling Alone.*
24. Barber, "Are We Ready."
25. One widely studied example is Willow Creek Community Church, located in South Barrington, a Chicago suburb, which was founded based on a marketing survey inquiring why the unaffiliated stayed away from church. The effort of such churches to reach the unaffiliated has led some scholars to label them as "seeker churches." See for example, Sargeant, Seeker Churches.
26. See, for example, Woodward, "Time to Seek."
27. Kosmin and Keysar, *American Religious Identification Survey 2008.*
28. Putnam and Campbell, American Grace, 148–149.
29. Kosmin and Keyzar, *Religion in a Free Market*, 98; Pew, *US Religious Landscape Survey*, 34.
30. Zuckerman, *Faith No More*, 121–125.
31. Starks, "Exploring Religious Self-Identification."
32. Chaves and Anderson, "Continuity and Change."
33. Banerjee, "Religion Joins Custody Cases."
34. Kosmin and Keysar, *Religion in a Free Market.*
35. Adler and Wingert, "A Matter of Faith," 48.
36. Kosmin and Keyzar, *Religion in a Free Market*, 103.
37. Jocelyn E. Strauber, "A Deal Is a Deal."
38. According to Pew's *US Religious Landscape Survey*, 27 percent of all Americans intermarry but 59 percent of the unaffiliated are married to someone of a different faith. Another study finds that members of liberal religion and secular people of any religious background are the most likely to marry someone of another religion; see Sahl and Batson, "Race and Religion in the Bible Belt." Another study finds that the importance of religion to a person is a more significant predictor of intermarriage opposition than what religion they belong to; see Sherkat, "Religious Intermarriage in the United States."
39. Copen and Silverstein, "Transmission of Religious Beliefs."
40. Vern L. Bengtson and his colleagues have conducted extensive research in this area: Bengtson, "Beyond the Nuclear Family"; Bengtson, Copen, Putney, and Silverstein, "A Longitudinal Study"; Bengtson, Biblarz, and Roberts, *How Families Still Matter*; Casper and Bianchi, *Continuity and Change in the American Family.*
41. These programs, officially titled the Confraternity of Christian Doctrine but colloquially known as CCD or catechism, provide Catholic religious education to children attending secular schools. Like Protestant Sunday school, CCD classes usually meet weekly and are often staffed by lay people.
42. See, for example, Dudley and Wisbey, "The Relationship of Parenting Styles"; Dudley and Dudley, "Transmission of Religious Values"; Stolzenberg, Blair-Loy, and Waite, "Religious Participation in Early Adulthood"; Myers, "An Interactive Model of Religiosity Inheritance." For an overview of the literature, see Hyde, *Religion in Childhood and Adolescence.*

43. One notable exception is an article by Gallagher, "Children as Religious Resources." However, this article does not address the question of individual parent-child relationship. Rather, it focuses on the role children play in religious congregations, that is, how the integration of children in the worship service and other activities affected adult religious identity in those congregations.

CHAPTER 4. THE IMPORTANCE OF PLACE

1. Pew Forum on Religion and Public Life, *Growth of the Non-Religious.*
2. It is interesting to note in this regard that Britain has included an atheism curriculum in its state-sponsored religious education program. See Watson, "Can Children and Young People Learn."
3. Bellah et. al., *Habits of the Heart*, chap. 2.
4. McKinley, "Texas Conservatives."
5. Farkas, Johnson, and Foleno, *For Goodness' Sake.*
6. Ironically, a local newspaper in Colorado Springs actually ran an article on the topic during the time that I was interviewing local Nones; see Asay, "Who Is God?" Similarly, a recent story on Fox News reports on a study that religion is good for children; see http://www.foxnews.com/story/2007/04/24/study-religion-is-good-for-kids/.
7. Unsurprisingly, many of these books and articles are written by and for Christian conservatives. However, several liberal academics impart a similar message: that children are naturally spiritual and that teaching them about god will enhance their lives. See for example, Coles, *The Moral Life of Children*; Coles, *The Spiritual Life of Children*; or Heller, *Talking to Your Child about God.*
8. The Public Agenda Poll, conducted in 2001, cited in Farkas et al., *For Goodness Sake*, 10–11.
9. Edgell, Gerteis, and Hartmann, *Atheists as Other.*
10. Harper, "The Stereotyping of Non-Religious People"; D'Andrea and Sprenger, "Atheism and Non-Spirituality."
11. Barton, "America's Most Biblical Hostile US President."
12. Similar numbers were reported for 2008 in Pew's US Religious Landscape Survey and in Kosmin and Keysar's "American Nones."
13. Pew Forum on Religion and Public Life, *Nones on the Rise.*
14. The *American Religious Identification Survey 2008* breaks down the proportion of Nones by state: Massachusetts (22 percent), Colorado (21 percent), Connecticut (14 percent), and Florida (14 percent).
15. Mormons, Muslims, and Jews are relatively large religious minority groups that illustrate differential growth and mainstreaming patterns. ARIS reports that in 2008, 1.2 percent of the US population identified their religious affiliation as Judaism, 1.7 percent as Mormonism, and 0.6 percent Muslim. Both Mormons and Muslims have experienced significant growth rates, partly because they discourage intermarriage and tend to have large families. Judaism, with high rates of

intermarriage and small families, has decreased, but is culturally accepted as more mainstream American than either Islam or Mormonism.

16. See, for example, Smith, *American Evangelicalism*. This phenomenon applies even to nonminorities. For example, one study found that white Evangelical Christians were more likely to vote Republican when there were many secularists where they lived; see Campbell, "Religious 'Threat' in Contemporary Presidential Elections."

17. The 2013 Pew *Growth of the Non-Religious* survey reports that Evangelical Christians hold the most negative attitudes toward Nones, and Evangelicals hold a culturally dominant position in both Jacksonville and Colorado Springs. The issue of cultural tension is also addressed by Cimino and Smith, "Secular Humanism and Atheism."

18. For further discussion on defining religion and culture, see Geertz, "Religion as a Cultural System"; Ann Swidler, "Culture in Action."

19. The results of their investigations are discussed in an eight-volume book series, Religion by Region, edited by Mark Silk and Andrew Walsh and published by Alta Mira Press in Lanham, MD.

20. Kosmin and Keysar, *American Religious Identification Survey 2008*.

21. Outsiders may succumb to the dominant religion. One study found secular Jews living in Israel were more likely to become religious, and the authors cite previous studies showing similar effects among seculars living in Christian societies; see Lazerwitz and Tabory, "National Religious Context."

22. See, for example, Karim, *American Muslim Women*.

23. Herberg, *Protestant, Catholic, Jew*.

24. See Silk, "Religion and Region," 267.

25. Ibid.

26. Nugent, "The Religious Demography."

27. McGuire, *Lived Religion*.

28. Berger, *Sacred Canopy*.

29. Silk, "Religion and Region," 265.

30. Walsh and Silk, *Religion and Public Life in New England*.

31. Wilson and Silk, *Religion and Public Life in the South*.

32. Silk speculates that Evangelicalism's strong hold over the public culture of the South may lead to Nones being undercounted: "In most parts of the country this two-to-one ratio holds: twice as many people claim a religious identity as are claimed by a religious organization. The one exception is the South, where the ratio is three to one" because southerners feel themselves under stronger cultural pressure than other Americans to identify themselves to surveyors as "having a religion" ("Religion and Region," 266).

33. Berger, *Sacred Canopy*.

34. Moore, *Religious Outsiders*, xi.

35. Ibid., 44.

36. Garcia, "The Social Context of Organized Nonbelief."

37. Peter Berger coined the term *plausibility structure* to designate the social base (interactions within a network of persons who share a particular meaning system) that is required for a religion to remain plausible. Several empirical studies supported this idea; see, for example, Roof, *Commitment and Community*.

38. One of the best-known studies is Kelley, *Why Conservative Churches Are Growing*. More recent work has applied this concept to Nones. For example, Smith, "Creating a Godless Community."

39. Religion scholar Randal Balmer describes how one megachurch, Willow Creek Community Church, was designed on the basis of a market research survey about what would bring the unaffiliated back to church; see Balmer, *Mine Eyes Have Seen the Glory*. Since then, many churches have jumped on the bandwagon, and various pastors have published books expressing the need to reach out to this population; see, for example, Stetzer, *Lost and Found* and Hunter, *Megachurch Methods*.

CHAPTER 5. WHAT ARE WE, MOM?

1. Kosmin, Meyer, and Keysar, *American Religious Identification Survey 2001*.

2. Hunsberger, "Background Religious Denomination"; Hunsberger and Brown, "Religious Socialization"; Hood et al., *The Psychology of Religion*.

3. Ingersoll-Dayton, Krause, and Morgan, "Religious Trajectories," 64; Wilson and Sherkat, "Returning to the Fold," 154.

4. Gunnoe and Moore, "Predictors of Religiosity," 614.

5. An abbreviated version of the findings presented in this chapter were previously reported in Manning, "*Unaffiliated Parents*."

6. Ecklund and Lee, "Atheists and Agnostics."

7. Ingersoll-Dayton, Krause, and Morgan, "Religious Trajectories"; Alwin, "Religion and Parental Childrearing Orientations"; Ellison, Bartkowsky, Michelle Segal, "Conservative Protestantism"; Fay, *Do Children Need Religion?*; Johnson and Mullins, "Moral Communities."

8. For more information, see the website of the American Humanist Association, http://www.americanhumanist.org.

9. Hsu, "Rallying the Humanists," 46.

10. The full list of seven principles is listed under "Beliefs and Principles" on the website of the Unitarian Universalist Association, http://www.uua.org.

11. Kochhar, *Establishing Humanist Education Programs*.

12. Mitchell, "Rational Sunday School"; Lee-St. John, "Sunday School for Atheists," 99.

13. Grossman, "Camps Sign up Freethinkers," http://www.campquest.org. See also Uchtman, "Camp Quest 96."

14. McGowan, *Parenting Beyond Belief*; Hanh, *Planting Seeds*; Starhawk, Baker, Hill, *Circle Round*.

15. The same pattern holds for advice books on parenting within a particular worldview.

16. Ecklund and Lee, "Atheists and Agnostics."

17. Kosmin and Keysar, *American Nones.*

18. Roof, *Spiritual Marketplace.*

CHAPTER 6. THE MEANING OF CHOICE IN RELIGION

1. Even back in 1978 a Gallup poll found 80 percent of Americans agreed that "an individual should arrive at his or her own religious beliefs independent of any churches or synagogue" (quoted in Bellah et. al., *Habits of the Heart*, 228). See also Marler and Roozen, "From Church Tradition to Consumer Choice." in *Church and Denominational Growth*, 253–277.

2. Iyengar, *The Art of Choosing*, chap. 2.

3. Bellah, *Habits of the Heart*, 22–26.

4. Phil Hammond described this revolution as the third disestablishment of religion, the first being the separation of church and state as articulated in the First Amendment to the Constitution, and the second being the replacement of the Protestant establishment by a more diverse (Protestant, Catholic, Jewish) concept of mainstream religion. See his *Religion and Personal Autonomy*, 8–18.

5. Roof and Gesch, "Boomers and the Culture of Choice." See also Roof, *Generation of Seekers*, chaps. 2 and 3.

6. Wuthnow, *After Heaven*, chap. 1.

7. Ibid.

8. Twitchell, *Lead Us into Temptation*, 47–49.

9. Lury, *Consumer Culture*, 9.

10. Lury asserts that in traditional societies, totems (natural objects like plants or animals) symbolized group identity and those totems were used to exclude outsiders (*Consumer Culture*, 13–24). Similarly, Twitchell points out that in feudal and Renaissance Europe, consumption was limited by class. For instance, only members of the aristocracy could wear certain fashions while peasants could not, regardless of their wealth (*Lead Us into Temptation*, 13–14). By contrast, in modern societies cultural objects (clothing, cars) confer such identity, and anybody who can afford to can choose to acquire this identity.

11. Iyengar, *Art of Choosing*, 83; See also Roof, *Spiritual Markeplace.*

12. See Roof, *Generation of Seekers*, 155–156; Music and Wilson "Religious Switching." Although most religious switching occurs within a faith tradition (e.g., from Catholic to Protestant, or from Reform to Orthodox Judaism), such moves often reflect real differences between communities, not just in liturgy but also in theology, gender ideology, or even political orientation. For an extended discussion of such differences, see Hunter, *Culture Wars.*

13. Einstein, "The Evolution of Religious Branding"; Strobel and Webster, "Should Churches Market Themselves," 1049; Coleman, "Appealing to the Unchurched," 77.

14. Foltz, "The Religion of the Market."

15. Twitchell, *Lead Us into Temptation*, 56.

16. Loy, "The Religion of the Market." For an excellent review of diverse perspectives on this topic, see Richard Foltz, "The Religion of the Market."

17. Gauthier, Martikainen, and Woodhead, "Religion in Consumer Society." *Social Compass* 58, no. 3 (2011): 291–301.

18. The relative lack of secularization in America, at least compared to Western Europe, is explained by rational choice theorists as the result of a freer religious market allowing constant emergence of new sects to meet unmet religious preferences. Among the most avid proponents of this theory are Roger Finke, Rodney Stark, and Larry Iannacone; Steve Bruce is one of the most vocal critics. For a review of the issues, see Johnson, "From Religious Markets," and McKinnon, "Ideology and the Market."

19. Lasch, *Culture of Narcissism*, 90.

20. Putnam, *Bowling Alone, chaps. 2–4*.

21. Bellah, *Habits of the Heart*, 221.

22. McGuire, *Lived Religion*.

23. Iyengar, *Art of Choosing*, 10.

24. Ibid., 47–51.

25. Ibid.

26. Schwartz, *The Paradox of Choice*, 49.

27. Iyengar, *Art of Choosing*, 149.

28. Singer, "Ethics and Intuitions," 340.

29. Iyengar, *Art of Choosing*, 67.

30. Interview with Barry Schwartz, *Anderson Cooper 360 Degrees*, CNN, aired on January 9, 2004, transcript available at http://transcripts.cnn.com/transcripts/0401/09/acd.00.html.

31. Ibid, 184–187, 194–200.

32. Schwartz, *Paradox*, 225.

33. Schwartz (chap. 4) distinguishes maximizing in decision making from perfectionism in our work: an artist or athlete who diligently practices his or her craft in search of perfection does so with the awareness that he or she will never actually be perfect, whereas a maximizer actually expects to make the very best decision.

34. See, for example, Iyengar, *Art of Choosing*, 42.

35. Ibid, 26–29.

CHAPTER 7. THE RISKS AND BENEFITS OF RAISING CHILDREN WITHOUT RELIGION

1. Occasionally we also find such stories in the popular media. See, for example, Tierney, "Coveting Luke's Faith," 66; Jones, "Among the Believers," 13; Lalli, "Am I Raising Atheist Children?," 11a; Pearson, "Mommy, Is Santa Jesus's Uncle?," 20–25.

2. Ridgely, "Children and Religion."

3. Pals, *Theories of Religion*, chap. 2. The perception that Freud was antireligion obscures the extent to which he acknowledged its emotional power and social utility. He argued that the projected existence of a loving, all-powerful being

fulfils deep emotional longings for unconditional love and the fear of death; at the same time, religious rules help to restrict sexual and aggressive behavior for the sake of civilization.

4. See Campbell, *Portable Jung*, 121–138 and chap. 13; also Crowley, *Jung: A Journey of Transformation.*

5. Maslow first articulated this idea in his article "A Theory of Human Motivation."

6. Coles, *Spiritual Life of Children*, chaps. 5, 6, and especially 13, "The Child as Pilgrim."

7. Caldwell-Harris, "Understanding Atheism/Nonbelief," 5.

8. For an excellent overview of these and other nineteenth-century thinkers and their influence on contemporary theory, see Pals, *Eight Theories of Religion.*

9. Dunbar and Barret, *The Oxford Handbook of Evolutionary Psychology*, chap. 44.

10. Guthrie's book *Faces in the Clouds* is often cited as the first to articulate this theory. For additional discussion, see Morgan, "Untangling False Assumptions."

11. Barrett, "Born Believers," 38.

12. Caldwell-Harris, "Understanding Atheism/Nonbelief," 6.

13. Morgan, "Untangling False Assumptions," 17–18. See also Loeckenhoff et. al., "Five-Factor Model;" Dickinson, Geertz, and Markússon, "Religion Is Natural, Atheism Is Not;" Saroglou, "Religiousness as a Cultural Adaptation."

14. Maslow, *Motivation and Personality*, 169.

15. See, for example, Cochran and Akers, "Beyond Hellfire"; Krause et al., "Church-based Social Support"; Regnerus, "Shaping Schooling Success"; Thornton and Camburn, "Religious Participation."

16. Smith, *Soul Searching.*

17. See Martin and Mullins, "Moral Communities."

18. Capps, "Religion and Child Abuse," 3. See also Greven, *Spare the Child*; Bottoms et al., "In the Name of God"; Ellison and Sherkat, "Conservative Protestantism."

19. Capps, "Religion and Child Abuse," 3–4.

20. Cooper, "Confronting Religiously Motivated Psychological Maltreatment of Children," 34–37.

21. Simonič, Mandelj, and Novsak, "Religious-Related Abuse in the Family." Simonič and her colleagues identified common forms of religion-related emotional abuse as "spurning (rejecting or degrading behavior), terrorizing (threatening injury, death, or abandonment), isolating (refusing opportunities to interact), exploiting/corrupting (encouraging engagement in inappropriate behaviors), and denying emotional responsiveness (ignoring human needs for interaction and affection" (341).

22. Capps, "Religion and Child Abuse," 4–5; Cooper, "Confronting," 6; Simonič, Mandelj, and Novsak, "Religious-Related Abuse in the Family," 342.

23. Studies suggest religion-based emotional and physical abuse often go together; see Simonič, Mandelj, Novsak "Religion-Related Abuse," 341–342.

24. Bottoms et al., "Religion-related Child Physical Abuse," 89.

25. Dawkins, one of the New Atheists, makes this argument in *"Religion's Real Child Abuse."*
26. A study by Nelsen and Kroliczak revealed that when parents use the threat "God will punish you" as a disciplinary tool, children tended to engage in more self-blame and were more obedient, which suggests that the very benefits of religion are linked to its costs; see Nelsen and Kroliczak, "Parental Use of the Threat 'God Will Punish.'"
27. Hwang, Hammer, and Cragun, "Extending Religion-Health Research"; Herzbrun, "Loss of Faith."
28. Weber et al, "Psychological Distress among Religious Nonbelievers."
29. Zuckerman, "Atheism, Secularity, and Well-Being."
30. On personality causing distress, see Loeckenhoff et al., "Five-Factor Model Personality Traits." On individual conviction causing distress, see Wilkinson and Coleman, "Strong Beliefs and Coping in Old Age."
31. Weber et al., "Psychological Distress."
32. For instance, a recent analysis of two national data sets, the National Longitudinal Study of Adolescent Health and the General Social Surveys, show that adolescent and adult intelligence significantly increases adult liberalism, atheism, and men's (but not women's) value on sexual exclusivity. The authors conclude that "more intelligent individuals may be more likely to acquire and espouse evolutionarily novel values and preferences (such as liberalism and atheism and, for men, sexual exclusivity) than less intelligent individuals, but that general intelligence may have no effect on the acquisition and espousal of evolutionarily familiar values (for children, marriage, family, and friends)." Kanazawa, "Why Liberals and Atheists Are More Intelligent," 33. Another study reviewed the relationship between intelligence and religious belief in 137 countries and found a significantly negative correlation; see Lynn, Harvey, and Nyborg, "Average Intelligence Predicts," 11–15. And a study comparing atheists and religious people found similar levels of well-being in all groups but a preference for logic, skepticism, and nonconformity among atheists; see Caldwell-Harris et al., "Exploring the Atheist Personality," 659–672.
33. Some of the New Atheist writers like Richard Dawkins and Sam Harris are exceptions.
34. Paul, "The Evolution of Popular Religiosity and Secularism."
35. Smith and Denton, Soul Searching, 234.
36. Proponents and critics of religion both like to use the available research to argue for their perspective. However, an extensive review of the literature suggests the evidence is much more mixed; see Bloom, "Religion, Morality, Evolution," 179–199.
37. Smith and Denton, Soul Searching, 223.
38. Treas, "How Cohorts, Education, and Ideology Shaped a New Sexual Revolution," 267–283; Whitman and Glastris, "Was It Good for Us?"

39. Annang et al., "Parental Attitudes about Teenage Pregnancy," 225–237; Bernstein, "Behind Fall in Pregnancy," A1, 36.

CONCLUSION

1. Pasquale, "Secular Group Affiliates"; Bullivant and Ruse, *Oxford Handbook of Atheism*.

2. The case for finding meaning and morality in a nontheist worldview has been eloquently made by several of the New Atheist philosophers. See, for example: Dawkins, *The God Delusion*; Dennett, *Breaking the Spell*; Harris, *The End of Faith*; Hitchens, *God Is Not Great*. For a shorter but still thought-provoking article on atheism as a source of substantive values, see Ehrenreich, "Everything I Like About Religion."

3. Zuckerman, *Faith No More*; Smith, "Becoming an Atheist"; Steven LeDrew, "Discovering Atheism.: Heterogeneity in Trajectories to Atheist Identity and Activism." See also Jesse Smith's reply, "Comment: Conceptualizing Atheist Identity," and LeDrew's rejoinder, "Reply: Toward a Critical Sociology of Atheism," all in the same issue of *Sociology of Religion*.

4. Smith, "Creating a Godless Community"; Cimino and Smith, "The New Atheism."

5. Weber et al., "Psychological Distress"; Hwang et al., "Extending Religion-Health Research."

6. Hwang et al., "Extending Religion-Health Research."

7. Putnam and Campbell, *American Grace*; Purpora, *Landscapes of the Soul*; Beithalami and Keysar, "The Secularization of the American Sunday."

8. Iyengar, *Art of Choosing*.

9. Schwartz, *Paradox of Choice*.

10. Wellman and Corcoran, "Religion and Regional Culture"; Garcia, "The Social Context"; Nugent, "The Religious Demography."

11. Cragun et al., "On the Receiving End"; Gervais, Shariff, and Norenzayan, "Do You Believe in Atheists?"

12. Armet, "Religious Socialization."

13. Manning, *God Gave Us the Right*.

14. Lee, "Secular or Nonreligious?"

15. Zuckerman and Hjlem, *Studying Religion and Society*.

BIBLIOGRAPHY

Adler, Jerry, and Pat Wingert. "A Matter of Faith." *Newsweek*, December 15, 1997, 48.

Altemeyer, Bob, and Bruce Hunsberger. *Amazing Conversions: Why Some Turn to Faith and Others Abandon Religion.* New York: Prometheus Books, 1997.

———. *Atheists: A Groundbreaking Study of America's Nonbelievers.* Amherst, NY: Prometheus Books, 2006.

Alwin, Dwayne F. "Religion and Parental Childrearing Orientations: Evidence of a Catholic-Protestant Convergence." *American Journal of Sociology* 92, no. 2 (1986): 412–440.

Ammerman, Nancy. "Spiritual but Not Religious? Beyond Binary Choices in the Study of Religion." *Journal for the Scientific Study of Religion* 52, no. 2 (2013): 258–278.

———, ed. *Everyday Religion: Observing Modern Religious Lives.* New York: Oxford, 2007.

Annang, Lucy, Brad Lian, Faith Fletcher, and Dawn Jackson. "Parental Attitudes about Teenage Pregnancy: Impact on Sexual Risk Behaviour of African-American Youth." *Sex Education* 14, no. 2 (March 2014): 225–237.

Argue, Amy, David R. Johnson, and Lynn K. White. "Age and Religiosity: Evidence from a Three-wave Panel Analysis." *Journal for the Scientific Study of Religion* 38, no. 3 (1999): 423–435.

Armet, Stephen. "Religious Socialization and Identity Formation of Adolescents in High Tension Religions." *Review of Religious Research* 50, no. 3 (2009): 277–297.

Asay, Paul. "Who Is God? Even Kids Raised without Religion Need Spiritual Questions Answered." *Gazette*, Life Section, August 26, 2006, 1.

Ashley, Martin. "The Spiritual, the Cultural, and the Religious: What Can We Learn from a Study of Boy Choristers?" *International Journal of Children's Spirituality* 7, no. 3 (2002): 257–272.

Association of Religion Data Archive (ARDA), University Park, PA: Pennsylvania State University, http://www.thearda.com.

Bainbridge, William Sims. "Atheism." *Interdisciplinary Journal of Research on Religion* 1, no. 2 (2005): 1–24.

Baker, Joseph, and Buster Smith. "The Nones: Social Characteristics of the Religiously Unaffiliated." *Social Forces* 87.3 (2009): 252–263.

Balmer, Randall. *Mine Eyes Have Seen the Glory: A Journey into the Evangelical Subculture of America.* New York: Oxford University Press, 1989.

Banerjee, Neela. "Religion Joins Custody Cases, to Judges' Unease." *New York Times*, February 13, 2008, A1, A18.

Barber, Lucie W. "Are We Ready to Take Preschool Religious Education Seriously?" *Religious Education* 86, no. 1 (Winter 1991): 62–73.

Barrett, Justin L. "Born Believers." *New Scientist* 213, no. 2856 (March 17, 2012): 38–41.

Barton, David. "America's Most Biblical Hostile US President." *Wallbuilders*, December 20, 2013. http://www.wallbuilders.com/libissuesarticles.asp?id=106938.

Beithalami, Bejamin, and Ariela Keysar. "The Secularization of the American Sunday: Evidence from Time-Use Data." Presented at the *Society for the Scientific Study of Religion, Annual Conference*, Tampa, FL, November 2007.

Bellah, Robert, Richard Madsen, William M. Sullivan, Ann Swidler, and Steven Tipton. *Habits of the Heart: Individualism and Commitment in American Life*. Berkeley: University of California, 1985.

Bengtson, Vern L. "Beyond the Nuclear Family: The Increasing Importance of Multi-generational Bonds." *Journal of Marriage and the Family* 63 (2001): 1–16.

Bengtson, Vern L., Casey E. Copen, Norella M. Putney, and Merril Silverstein. "A Longitudinal Study of the Intergenerational Transmission of Religion." *International Sociology* 24, no. 3 (May 2009): 325–345.

Bengtson, Vern L., J. Timothy, and Robert E. L. Roberts. *How Families Still Matter: A Longitudinal Study of Youth in Two Generations*. New York: Cambridge University Press, 2002.

Berger, Peter. *The Sacred Canopy: Elements of a Sociological Theory of Religion*. New York: Doubleday, 1967.

Bernstein, Nina. "Behind Fall in Pregnancy, a New Teenage Culture of Restraint." *New York Times*, March 7, 2004, A1, A36.

Bloom, Paul. "Religion, Morality, Evolution." *Annual Review of Psychology* 63, no. 1 (2012): 179–199.

Bottoms, Bette L., Michael Nielsen, Rebecca Murray, and Henrietta Filipas. "Religion-Related Child Physical Abuse: Characteristics and Psychological Outcomes." *Journal of Aggression, Maltreatment and Trauma* 8, nos. 1–2 (2003): 87–114.

Bottoms, Bette L., Phillip R. Shaver, Gail S. Goodman, and Jianjian Qin. "In the Name of God: A Profile of Religion-Related Child Abuse." *Journal of Social Issues* 51, no. 2 (1995): 85–111.

Brinkerhoff, Merlin, and Marlene Mackie. "Casting off the Bonds of Organized Religion: A Religious Careers Approach to the Study of Apostasy." *Review of Religious Research* 34, no. 3 (1993): 235–257.

Bromley, David, ed. *Falling from the Faith: Causes and Consequences of Religious Apostasy*. Beverly Hills, CA: Sage, 1988.

———. "Linking Social Structure and the Exit Process in Religious Organizations: Defectors, Whistle-blowers, and Apostates." *Journal for the Scientific Study of Religion* 37, no. 1 (1998): 145–160.

Bullivant, Steven, and Michael Ruse, eds. *Oxford Handbook of Atheism*. New York: Oxford University Press, 2013.

Caldwell-Harris, Catherine L. "Understanding Atheism/Non-belief as an Expected Individual-Differences Variable." *Religion, Brain and Behavior* 2, no. 1 (2012): 4–22.

Caldwell-Harris, Catherine L., Angela L. Wilson, Elizabeth LoTempio, and Benjamin Beit-Hallahmi. "Exploring the Atheist Personality: Well-Being, Awe, and Magical Thinking in Atheists, Buddhists, and Christians." *Mental Health, Religion, and Culture* 14, no. 7 (September 2011): 659–672.

Campbell, David E. "Religious 'Threat' in Contemporary Presidential Elections." *Journal of Politics* 68, no. 1 (2006): 104–115.

Campbell, Joseph, ed. *The Portable Jung.* New York: Penguin, 1971.

Capps, Donald. "Religion and Child Abuse: Perfect Together." *Journal for the Scientific Study of Religion* 31, no. 1 (March 1992): 1–15.

Casper, Lynne M., and Suzanne M. Bianchi. *Continuity and Change in the American Family.* Thousand Oaks, CA: Sage, 2002.

Chaves, Mark, and Shawna Anderson. "Continuity and Change in American Religion, 1972–2008." In *Social Trends in American Life: Findings from the General Social Survey Since 1972,* edited by Peter V. Marsden, 212–239. Princeton, NJ: Princeton University Press, 2012.

Cimino, Richard, and Christopher Smith. "The New Atheism and the Formation of the Imagined Secularist Community." *Journal of Media and Religion* 10 (2011): 24–38.

———. "Secular Humanism and Atheism beyond Progressive Secularism." *Sociology of Religion* 68, no. 4 (2007): 407–424.

Cochran, John, and Ronald Akers. "Beyond Hellfire: An Exploration of the Variable Effects of Religiosity on Adolescent Marijuana and Alcohol Use." *Journal of Research in Crime and Delinquency* 26 (1989): 198–225.

Coleman, Barbara Carrick. "Appealing to the Unchurched: What Attracts New Members?" *Journal of Nonprofit and Public Sector Marketing* 10, no. 1 (2002): 77.

Coles, Robert. *The Moral Life of Children.* Boston, MA: Atlantic Monthly Press, 1986.

———. *The Spiritual Life of Children.* Boston, MA: Houghton Mifflin, 1990.

Cooper, Chase. "Confronting Religiously Motivated Psychological Maltreatment of Children: A Framework for Policy Reform." *Virginia Journal of Social Policy, and the Law* 20, no. 1 (Fall 2012): 1–42.

Copen, Casey, and Merril Silverstein. "Transmission of Religious Beliefs across Generations: Do Grandparents Matter?" *Journal of Comparative Family Studies* 28, no. 4 (2007): 497–510.

Corbin, Juliette, and Anselm Strauss. "Grounded Theory Research: Procedures, Canons, and Evaluative Criteria," *Qualitative Sociology* 13, no. 1 (1990): 3–21.

Council for Democratic and Secular Humanism. "Atheists Still Remain Black Sheep of Families." *Free Inquiry* 21, no. 4 (2001): 29.

Cragun, Ryan T., Barry Kosmin, Ariela Keysar, Joseph Hammer, and Michael Neilson. "On the Receiving End: Discrimination Towards the None-Religious in the United States." *Journal of Contemporary Religion* 27, no. 1 (2012): 105–127.

Crowley, Vivianne. *Jung: A Journey of Transformation: Exploring His Life and Experiencing His Ideas.* Wheaton, IL: Quest Books, 2000.

D'Andrea, Livia M., and Johann Sprenger. "Atheism and Non-Spirituality as Diversity Issues in Counseling." *Counseling and Values* 51 (2007): 149–158.

Davie, Grace. "Vicarious Religion: A Methodological Challenge." In Ammerman, *Everyday Religion*, 21–36.

Dawkins, Richard. *The God Delusion*. Boston, MA: Houghton Mifflin, 2006.

———. *Religion's Real Child Abuse*. The Richard Dawkins Foundation for Reason and Science, May 14, 2006. http://old.richarddawkins.net/articles/118-religion-39-s-real-child-abuse.

Dennett, Daniel. *Breaking the Spell: Religion as a Natural Phenomenon*. New York: Penguin Books, 2006.

Dickinson, G. Lowes, Armin W. Geertz, and Guðmundur Ingi Markússon, "Religion Is Natural, Atheism Is Not: On Why Everybody Is Both Right and Wrong." *Religion* 40, no. 3 (July 2010): 152–165.

Dudley, Roger L., and Margaret G. Dudley. "Transmission of Religious Values from Parents to Adolescents." *Review of Religious Research* 28, no. 1 (1986): 3–14.

Dudley, Roger L., and Randall L. Wisbey. "The Relationship of Parenting Styles to Commitment to the Church among Young Adults." *Religious Education* 95, no. 1 (Winter 2000): 39–43.

Dunbar, Robin, and Louise Barret, eds. *The Oxford Handbook of Evolutionary Psychology*. New York: Oxford University Press, 2007.

Ecklund, Elaine Howard, and Kristen Schultz Lee. "Atheists and Agnostics Negotiate Religion and Family." *Journal for the Scientific Study of Religion* 50, no. 4 (2011): 728–743.

Edgell, Penny, Joseph Gertais, and Douglas Hartman. "Atheists as Other: Moral Boundaries and Cultural Membership in American Society." *American Sociological Review* 71, no. 2 (2006): 211–234.

Ehrenreich, Barbara. "Everything I Like about Religion I Learned from an Atheist." *Humanist* 59, no. 6 (November/December 1999): 17.

Einstein, Mara. "The Evolution of Religious Branding." *Social Compass* 58, no. 3 (September 2011): 331–338.

Ellison, Christopher, John Bartkowsky, and Michelle Segal. "Conservative Protestantism and the Parental Use of Corporal Punishment." *Social Forces* 74, no. 3 (1996): 1003–1028.

Ellison, Christopher, and Darren Sherkat. "Conservative Protestantism and Support for Corporal Punishment." *American Sociological Review* 58, no. 1 (1993): 131–145.

Farkas, Steve, Jean Johnson, and Tony Foleno, with Ann Duffett and Patrick Foley. *For Goodness' Sake: Why So Many Want Religion to Play a Greater Role in American Society*. New York: Public Agenda, 2001.

Fay, Martha. *Do Children Need Religion? How Parents Today Are Talking about the Big Questions*. New York: Pantheon Books, 1993.

Finke, Roger, and Rodney Stark. *The Churching of America, 1776—2005: Winners and Losers in Our Religious Economy*. New Brunswick, NJ: Rutgers University Press, 2005.

Foltz, Richard. "The Religion of the Market: Reflections on a Decade of Discussion." *Worldviews* 11 (2007): 135–154.

Fuller, Robert. *Spiritual, but Not Religious: Understanding Unchurched America.* New York: Oxford University Press, 2001.

Gallagher, Sally K. "Children as Religious Resources: The Role of Children in the Social Re-Formation of Class, Culture, and Religious Identity." *Journal for the Scientific Study of Religion* 46, no. 2 (2007): 169–183.

Gallup, Inc. *The Unchurched American.* Princeton, NJ: Princeton Religion Research Center, 1978.

———. The Unchurched American—10 Years Later. Princeton, NJ: Princeton Religion Research Center, 1988.

Garcia, Alfredo. "The Social Context of Organized Nonbelief: County-Level Predictors of Nonbeliever Organizations in the United States. Presented at *Non-religion and Secularity Research Network, Third international Conference*, Claremont, CA, November 2014.

Gauthier, François, Tuomo Martikainen, and Linda Woodhead. "Religion in Consumer Society." *Social Compass* 58, no. 3 (2011): 291–301.

Geertz, Clifford. "Religion as a Cultural System." In *The Interpretation of Cultures: Selected Essays*, 87–125. New York: Basic Books, 1973.

Gervais, Will M., Azim F. Shariff, and Ara Norenzayan. "Do You Believe in Atheists? Distrust Is Central to Anti-Atheist Prejudice." *Journal of Psychology and Social Psychology* 101, no. 6 (2011): 1189–1206.

Glenn, Norval D. "The Trend in 'No Religion Respondents' in US National Surveys, Late 1950s to Early 1980s." *Public Opinion Quarterly* 51, no. 3 (1987): 293–314.

Goldstein, Niles Elliot, ed. *Spiritual Manifestos: Redesigning Worship To Reach The Unchurched.* Woodstock, VT: Skylight Paths Publishing, 2000.

Greeley, Andrew M., and Michael Hout. "Musical Chairs: Patterns of Denominational Change in the Unites States, 1947–1986." *Sociology and Social Research* 72 (1988): 75–86.

Greven, Philip. *Spare the Child: The Religious Roots of Punishment and the Psychological Impact of Physical Abuse.* New York: Knopf, 1991.

Grossman, Cathy Lynn. "Camps Sign Up Freethinkers." *USA Today*, July 27, 2006. http://usatoday30.usatoday.com/life/2006-07-26-camp_x.htm.

Gunnoe, Marjorie Lindner, and Kristin A. Moore. "Predictors of Religiosity among Youth Aged 17–22: A Longitudinal Study of the National Survey of Children." *Journal for the Scientific Study of Religion* 41, no. 4 (2002): 613–622.

Guthrie, Stewart. *Faces in the Clouds: A New Theory of Religion.* New York: Oxford University Press, 1993.

Hammond, Philip E. *Religion and Personal Autonomy: The Third Disestablishment in America.* Columbia: University of South Carolina, 1992.

Hanh, Thich Nhat. *Planting Seeds: Practicing Mindfulness with Children.* Berkeley, CA: Parallax Press, 2011.

Harper, Marcel. "The Stereotyping of Non-Religious People by Religious Students." *Journal for the Scientific Study of Religion* 46, no. 4 (2007): 539–552.

Harris, Sam. *The End of Faith: Religion, Terror, and the Future of Reason.* New York: W. W. Norton, 2004.

Heller, David. *Talking to Your Child about God*. New York: Bantam, 1990.

Herberg, Will. *Protestant, Catholic, Jew: An Essay in American Religious Sociology*, New York: Doubleday, 1955.

Herzbrun, Michael. "Loss of Faith: A Qualitative Analysis of Jewish Nonbelievers." *Counseling and Values* 43, no. 2 (1999): 129.

Hitchens, Christopher. *God Is Not Great: How Religion Poisons Everything*. Toronto: Emblem, 2007.

Hoge, Dean R., William Dinges, Mary Johnson, and Juan L. Gonzales Jr. *Young Adult Catholics: Religion in the Culture of Choice*. Notre Dame, IN: University of Notre Dame Press, 2001.

Hoge, Dean R., Benton Johnson, and Donald A. Luidens. *Vanishing Boundaries: The Religion of Mainline Protestant Baby Boomers*. Louisville, KY: Westminster/John Knox Press, 1994.

Hood, Ralph, Peter C. Hill, and Bernard Spilka. *The Psychology of Religion: An Empirical Approach*. New York: Guilford, 2009.

Horwath, Jan, Janet Lees, and Peter Sidebotham, "The Influence of Religion on Adolescent Family Life in England: An Explanatory Study of the View of Young People and Parents." *Social Compass* 59.2 (2012): 257–275.

Hout, Michael, and Claude Fisher. "Why More Americans Have No Religious Preference: Politics and Generations." *American Sociological Review* 67, no.2 (2002): 165–190.

Hsu, Caroline. "Rallying the Humanists." *US News and World Report*, August 8, 2005, 46.

Hunsberger, Bruce. "Background Religious Denomination, Parental Emphasis, and the Religious Orientation of University Students." *Journal for the Scientific Study of Religion* 15, no. 3 (1976): 251–255.

Hunsberger, Bruce, and Larry Brown. "Religious Socialization, Apostasy, and the Impact of Family Background." *Journal for the Scientific Study of Religion* 23, no. 3 (1984): 239–251.

Hunter, George. *Megachurch Methods: Church for the Unchurched*. Nashville, TN: Abingdon Press, 1997.

Hunter, James D. *Culture Wars: The Struggle to Control the Family, Art, Education, Law, and Politics in America*. New York: Basic Books 1992.

Hwang, Karen, Joseph H. Hammer, and Ryan T. Cragun. "Extending Religion-Health Research to Secular Minorities: Issues and Concerns." *Journal of Religion and Health* 50, no.3 (2011): 608–622.

Hyde, Kenneth E. 1990. *Religion in Childhood and Adolescence: A Comprehensive Review of the Research*. Birmingham, AL: Religious Education Press, 1990.

Ingersoll-Dayton, Berit, Neal Krause, and David Morgan. "Religious Trajectories and Transitions over the Life Course." *International Journal of Aging and Human Development* 55, no. 1 (2002): 51–70.

Iyengar, Sheena. *The Art of Choosing*. New York: Twelve/Hachette Book Group, 2010.

Jamieson, Alan. *Church Leavers: Faith Journeys Five Years On*. London: SPCK Publishing, 2006.

———. *A Churchless Faith*. London: SPCK Publishing, 2002.

Jenks, Richard. "Perception of Two Deviant and Two Non-Deviant Groups." *Journal of Social Psychology* 126, no.6 (1986): 783–791.

Johnson, Byron. "The Good News about Evangelicalism: It Isn't Shrinking and the Young Are Not Becoming Liberals." *First Things: A Monthly Journal of Religion and Public Life*, no. 210 (February 2011): 12–14.

Johnson, D. Paul. "From Religious Markets to Religious Communities: Contrasting Implications for Applied Research." *Review of Religious Research* 44.4 (2003): 325–340.

Johnson, Martin A., and Phil Mullins. "Moral Communities: Religious and Secular." *Journal of Community Psychology* 18, no. 2 (1990): 153–166.

Jones, Robert P., Daniel Cox, and Juhem Navarro-Rivera. *The 2012 American Values Survey: How Catholics and the Religiously Unaffiliated Will Shape the 2012 Election and Beyond*. Washington, DC: Public Religion Research Institute, 2012.

Jones, Tayari. "Among the Believers." *New York Times*, July 10, 2005, 13.

Kanazawa, Satoshi. "Why Liberals and Atheists Are More Intelligent." *Social Psychology Quarterly* 73, no. 1 (2010): 33–57.

Karim, Jamilla. *American Muslim Women*. New York: New York University Press, 2008.

Kelley, Dean. *Why Conservative Churches Are Growing: A Study in Sociology of Religion*. New York: Harper and Row, 1972.

Kochhar Humanist Education Center. *Establishing Humanist Education Programs for Children*. Washington, DC: American Humanist Association, 2011.

Kosmin, Barry, and Ariela Keysar. *American Nones: The Profile of the No Religion Population*. Hartford, CT: Institute for the Study of Secularity in Society, 2008.

———. *American Religious Identification Survey 2008*. Hartford, CT: Institute for the Study of Secularity in Society, 2008.

———. *Religion in a Free Market: Religious and Non-Religious Americans*. New York: Paramount Publishing, 2006.

Kosmin, Barry, Egon Meyer, and Ariela Keysar. *The American Religious Identification Survey 2001*. Graduate Center of the City University of New York, 2001.

Kirkwood, Peter. "The Decline of Christianity in Australia and America." *Eureka Street* 19, no. 11 (June 19, 2009): 24–25.

Krause, Neal, Christopher Ellison, Benjamin Shaw, John Marcum, and Jason Boardman. "Church-based Social Support and Religious Coping." *Journal for the Scientific Study of Religion* 40, no.4 (2001): 637–657.

Lalli, Nica. "Am I Raising Atheist Children?" *USA Today*, March 17, 2008, 11a.

Lasch, Christopher. *Culture of Narcissism: American Life in an Age of Diminishing Expectations*. New York: W. W. Norton, 1991.

Lazerwitz, Bernard, and Ephraim Tabory. "National Religious Context and Familiar Religiosity within a Jewish Framework." *Review of Religious Research* 44, no. 1 (2002): 22–37.

LeDrew, Steven. "Discovering Atheism: Heterogeneity in Trajectories to Atheist Identity and Activism." *Sociology of Religion* 74, no. 4 (2013): 431–453.

———. "Reply: Toward a Critical Sociology of Atheism: Identity, Politics, Ideology." *Sociology of Religion* 74, no. 4 (2013): 464–470.

Lee, Lois. "Secular or Nonreligious? Investigating and Interpreting Generic 'Not Religious' Categories and Populations." *Religion* 44, no. 3 (2014), 466–482.

Lee-St. John, Jeninne. "Sunday School for Atheists." *Time*, December 3, 2007, 99.

Lim, Chaeyoon, Carol Ann MacGregor, and Robert Putnam. "Secular and Liminal: Discovering Heterogeneity among Religious Nones." *Journal for the Scientific Study of Religion* 49, no. 4 (2010): 596–618.

Loeckenhoff, Corinna, Gail Ironson, Conall O'Cleirigh, and Paul T. Costa Jr. "Five-Factor Model Personality Traits, Spirituality/Religiousness, and Mental Health among People Living with HIV." *Journal of Personality*, no. 77 (2009): 1411–1436.

Lorber, Judith. *Gender and the Social Construction of Illness*. Thousand Oaks, CA: Sage, 1997.

Loy, David. "The Religion of the Market." *Journal of the American Academy of Religion* 65, no. 2 (Summer 2007): 275–290.

Luchau, Peter. "Atheism and Secularity: The Scandinavian Paradox." In Zuckerman, *Atheism and Secularity*, Vol. 2, 177–196.

Luckman, Thomas. *The Invisible Religion: The Problem of Religion in Modern Society*. New York: Macmillan, 1974.

Luo, Michael. "God '08: Whose, and How Much, will Voters Accept?" *New York Times Week in Review*, July 22, 2007, 4.

Lury, Celia. *Consumer Culture*. 2nd ed. New Jersey: Rutgers University Press, 2011.

Lynn, Richard, John Harvey, and Helmuth Nyborg. "Average Intelligence Predicts Atheism Rates Across 137 Nations." *Intelligence* 37, no. 1 (January 2009): 11–15.

Manning, Christel. *God Gave Us the Right: Conservative Catholic, Evangelical Protestant, and Orthodox Jewish Women Grapple with Feminism*. New Brunswick, NJ: Rutgers University Press, 1999.

Marler, Penny Long, and Kirk Hadaway. "'Being Religious' or 'Being Spiritual' in America: A Zero Sum Proposition?" *Journal for the Scientific Study of Religion* 41, no. 2 (2002): 289–300.

Marler, Penny Long, and David Roozen. "From Church Tradition to Consumer Choice: The Gallup Surveys of the Unchurched American." In *Church and Denominational Growth*, 253–277. Nashville, TN: Abingdon Press, 1992.

Maslow, Abraham H. *Motivation and Personality*. New York: Harper and Row, 1970.

———. "A Theory of Human Motivation." *Psychological Review* 50, no. 4 (1943): 370–396.

———. *Toward a Psychology of Being*. Princeton, NJ: D. Van Nostrand Company, 1962.

Mauss, Armand. "Dimensions of Religious Defection." *Review of Religious Research* 10, no. 3 (1969): 128–135.

McGowan, Dale, ed. *Parenting Beyond Belief: On Raising Ethical, Caring Kids without Religion*. New York: Amacom, 2007.

McGuire, Meredith. *Lived Religion: Faith and Practice in Everyday Life*. New York: Oxford University Press, 2008.

———. *Religion: The Social Context*. Belmont, CA: Wadsworth, 1997.

McKinley, James. "Texas Conservatives Win Curriculum Change." *New York Times*, Education, March 12, 2010. http://www.nytimes.com/2010/03/13/education/13texas. html.

McKinnon, A. M. "Ideology and the Market Metaphor in Rational Choice Theory of Religion: A Rhetorical Critique of 'Religious Economies.'" *Critical Sociology (Sage, Ltd.)*, 39, no. 4 (2013): 529–543.

Miller, Alan S., and Takashi Nakamura. "On the Stability of Church Attendance Patterns During a Time of Demographic Change." *Journal for the Scientific Study of Religion* 35, no. 3 (1996): 275–284.

Mitchell, Ute. "Rational Sunday School." *Humanist* 69, no. 3 (May/June 2009): 26–29.

Moore, R. Laurence. *Religious Outsiders and the Making of Americans*. New York: Oxford University Press, 1986.

Morgan, Jonathan. "Untangling False Assumptions Regarding Atheism and Health." *Zygon: Journal of Religion and Science* 48, no. 1 (March 2013): 9–19.

Music, Mark, and John Wilson. "Religious Switching for Marriage Reasons." *Sociology of Religion* 56, no. 3 (1995): 257–270.

Myers, Scott M. "An Interactive Model of Religiosity Inheritance: The Importance of Family Context. *American Sociological Review* 67 (1996): 858–866.

Nelsen, Hart M., and Alice Kroliczak. "Parental Use of the Threat 'God Will Punish': Replication and Extension." *Journal for Scientific Study of Religion* 23, no. 3 (1984): 267–277.

Nugent, Walter. "The Religious Demography of an Oasis Culture." In *Religion and Public Life in the Mountain West*, ed. by Jan Shipps and Mark Silk. Lanham, MD: Alta Mira, 2004.

Pals, Daniel. *Eight Theories of Religion*. New York: Oxford University Press, 2006.

Pasquale, Frank L. "A Portrait of Secular Group Affiliates." In Zuckerman, *Atheism and Secularity*, vol. 1, 43–87.

Paul, Gregory S. "The Evolution of Popular Religiosity and Secularism: How First-World Statistics Reveal Why Religion Exists, Why It Has Been Popular, and Why the Most Successful Democracies Are the Most Secular." In Zuckerman, *Atheism and Secularity*, vol. 1, 149–208.

Pearson, Patricia. "Mommy, Is Santa Jesus's Uncle?" *Maclean's*, December 22, 2003, 20–25.

Peter, Karl, Edward Boldt, Ian Whitaker, and Lance Roberts. "The Dynamics of Religious Defection among Hutterites." *Journal for the Scientific Study of Religion* 21, no. 4 (1982): 327–338.

Petts, Richard J., and Chris Knoester. "Parents' Religious Heterogamy and Children's Wellbeing." *Journal for the Scientific Study of Religion* 46, no. 3 (2007): 373–389.

Pew Forum on Religion and Public Life. *Faith in Flux*. Washington, DC: Pew Research Center, 2009

———. *Global Religious Landscape Survey*. Washington, DC: Pew Research Center, 2012.

———. *Growth of the Non-Religious*. Washington, DC: Pew Research Center, 2013.

———. *How the Faithful Voted: 2012 Preliminary Analysis*. http://www.pewforum. org/2012/11/07/how-the-faithful-voted-2012-preliminary-exit-poll-analysis/.

———. *Nones on the Rise*. Washington, DC: Pew Research Center, 2012.

———. *US Religious Landscape Survey 2008*. Washington, DC: Pew Research Center, 2008.

Phillips, Bruce. "Assimilation, Transformation, and the Long Range Impact of Inter-marriage." *Contemporary Jewry* 25, no. 1 (October 2005): 50–84.

Purpora, Douglas. *Landscapes of the Soul. The Loss of Moral Meaning in American Life*. New York: Oxford University Press, 2001.

Putnam, Robert. *Bowling Alone: The Collapse and Revival of American Community*. New York: Simon and Schuster, 2000.

Putnam, Robert, and David Campbell. *American Grace: How Religion Divides and Unites Us*. New York: Simon and Schuster, 2010.

Regnerus, Mark. "Shaping Schooling Success: Religious Socialization and Educational Outcomes in Urban Public Schools." *Journal for the Scientific Study of Religion* 39, no.3 (2000): 363–370.

Ridgely, Susan. "Children and Religion." *Religion Compass* 6, no. 4 (2012): 236–248.

Roof, Wade Clark. *Commitment and Community: Religious Plausibility in a Liberal Protestant Church*. New York: Elsevier, 1978.

———. *A Generation of Seekers: The Spiritual Journeys of the Baby Boom Generation*. San Francisco: HarperCollins, 1993.

———. *Spiritual Marketplace: Babyboomers and the Remaking of American Religion*. Princeton, NJ: Princeton University Press, 1999.

Roof, Wade Clark, and Lynn Gesch. "Boomers and the Culture of Choice." In *Work, Family, and Religion in Contemporary Society*, edited by Nancy Ammerman and Wade Clark Roof, 61–80. New York and London: Routledge, 1995.

Roper Center, *How Groups Voted in 2012*. http://www.ropercenter.uconn.edu/polls/ us-elections/how-groups-voted/.

Sahl, Allison Heard, and Christie Batson. "Race and Religion in the Bible Belt: Parental Attitudes toward Interfaith Relationships." *Sociological Spectrum* 31, no. 4 (2011): 444–465.

Sargeant, Kimon Howland. *Seeker Churches: Promoting Traditional Religion in a Non-traditional Way*. New Brunswick, NJ: Rutgers University Press, 2000.

Saroglou, Vassilis. "Religiousness as a Cultural Adaptation of Basic Traits: A Five-Factor Model Perspective." *Personality and Social Psychology Review* 14, no. 1 (2010): 108–125.

Schwartz, Barry. *The Paradox of Choice: Why More Is Less*. New York: Harper Peren-nial, 2004.

Sherkat, Darren E. "Religious Intermarriage in the United States: Trends, Patterns, and Predictors." *Social Science Research* 33, no. 4 (2004): 606–625.

Silk, Mark. "Religion and Region in American Public Life." *Journal for the Scientific Study of Religion* 44, no. 3 (2005): 265–270.

Silk, Mark, and Andrew Walsh. *One Nation, Divisible: How Regional Religious Differences Shape American Politics.* Lanham, MD: Rowman and Littlefield, 2008.

Simonič, Barbara, Tina Mandelj, and Rachel Novsak. "Religious-Related Abuse in the Family." *Journal of Family Violence* 28, no. 4 (May 2013): 339–349.

Singer, Peter. "Ethics and Intuitions." *Journal of Ethics* 9, nos. 3–4 (2005): 331–352.

Smith, Christian. *American Evangelicalism: Embattled and Thriving.* Chicago: University of Chicago Press, 1998.

Smith, Christian, with Melinda Denton. *Soul Searching: The Religious and Spiritual Lives of American Teenagers.* New York: Oxford University Press, 2005.

Smith, Jesse M. "Becoming an Atheist in America: Constructing Identity and Meaning from the Rejection of Theism." *Sociology of Religion* 22, no. 2 (2011): 215–237.

———. "Creating a Godless Community: The Collective Identity Work of Contemporary American Atheists." *Journal for the Scientific Study of Religion* 52, no. 1 (2013): 80–99.

———. "Comment: Conceptualizing Atheist Identity: Expanding Questions, Constructing Models, and Moving Forward." *Sociology of Religion* 74, no. 4 (2013): 454 -463.

Starhawk (Miriam Somos), Diane Baker, and Anne Hill. *Circle Round: Raising Children in Goddess Traditions.* New York: Bantam, 1998.

Stark, Rodney, and Roger Finke. *Acts of Faith: Explaining the Human Side of Religion.* Berkeley: University of California Press, 2000.

Stark, Rodney, Eva Hamburg, and Alan Miller. "Exploring Spirituality and Unchurched Religions in America, Sweden, and Japan." *Journal of Contemporary Religion* 20, no.1 (2005): 3–23.

Stark, Rodney, and William Sims Bainbridge. "Towards a Theory of Religion: Religious Commitment." *Journal for the Scientific Study of Religion* 19, no. 2 (1980): 114–128.

Starks, Brian. "Exploring Religious Self-Identification among US Catholics: Traditionals, Moderates, and Liberals." *Sociology of Religion* 74, no. 3 (2013): 314–342.

Stetzer, Edward, Richie Stanley, and Jason Hayes. *Lost and Found: The Younger Unchurched and the Churches That Reach Them.* Nashville: B and H Publishing, 2009.

Stolzenberg, Ross M., Mary Blair-Loy, and Linda J. Waite. "Religious Participation in Early Adulthood: Age and Family Life Cycle Effects on Church Membership." *American Sociological Review* 60, no.1 (1995): 84–103.

Strauber, Jocelyn E. "A Deal Is a Deal: Ante-nuptial Agreements Regarding the Religious Upbringing of Children Should Be Enforceable." *Duke Law Journal* 47, no. 5 (March 1998): 971–1012.

Strauss, Anselm, and Juliet Corbin. *Basics of Qualitative Research.* Thousand Oaks, CA: Sage, 2007.

Strobel, Lee, and Douglas D. Webster. "Should Churches Market Themselves to Baby Boomers and Younger Generations?" *CQ Researcher,* November 25, 1994, 1049.

Stump, Roger. "Regional Variations in the Determinants of Religious Participation." *Review of Religious Research* 27 (1986): 208–225.

Swidler, Ann. "Culture in Action: Symbols and Strategies." *American Sociological Review* 51, no. 2 (1986): 273–286.

Thornton, Arland, and Donald Camburn. "Religious Participation and Adolescent Sexual Behavior and Attitudes." *Journal of Marriage and the Family* 51, no. 3 (1989): 641–653.

Tierney, Dana. "Coveting Luke's Faith." *New York Times Magazine*, January 1, 2004, 66.

Treas, Judith. "How Cohorts, Education, and Ideology Shaped a New Sexual Revolution on American Attitudes Toward Nonmarital Sex, 1972–1998." *Sociological Perspectives* 45, no. 3 (Fall 2002): 267–283.

Twitchell, James. *Lead Us into Temptation: The Triumph of American Materialism.* Columbia University, 1999.

Uchtman, Vern. "Camp Quest 96." *Free Inquiry* 17, no. 1 (Winter 1996/97): 27.

Volokh, Eugene. "Parent-Child Speech and Child Custody Speed Restrictions." *New York University Law Review* 81 (2006): 631–733.

Walsh, Andrew, and Mark Silk, eds. *Religion and Public Life in New England: Steady habits Changing Slowly.* Lanham, MD: Alta Mira 2004.

Watson, Jaqueline. "Can Children and Young People Learn from Atheism for Spiritual Development? A Response to the National Framework for Religious Education." *British Journal of Religious Education* 30, no. 1 (2008): 49–58.

Weaver, Andrew J. Judith A. Samford, Virginia J. Morgan, David B. Larson, Harold G. Koenig, and Kevin J. Flannelly. "A Systemic Review of Research on Religion in Six Primary Marriage and Family Journals: 1995–1999." *American Journal of Family Therapy* 30, no. 4 (2002): 293–309.

Weber, Samuel, Kenneth Pargament, Mark Kunik, James Lomax, and Melinda Stanley. "Psychological Distress among Religious Nonbelievers: A Systematic Review." *Journal of Religion and Health* 51, no. 1 (March 2012): 72–86.

Welch, Kevin. "Community Development and Metropolitan Religious Commitment: A Test of Two Competing Models." *Journal for the Scientific Study of Religion* 22, no. 2 (1983): 167–181.

Welch, Michael R. "The Unchurched: Black Religious Non-Affiliates." *Journal for the Scientific Study of Religion* 17, no. 3 (1978): 289–294.

Wellman, James K., and Katie E. Corcoran. "Religion and Regional Culture: Embedding Religious Commitment Within Place." *Sociology of Religion* 74, no. 4 (2013): 496–520.

Whitman, David, and Paul Glastris. "Was It Good for Us?" *US News and World Report*, May 19, 1997, 56.

Wilkinson, Peter J., and Peter G. Coleman. "Strong Beliefs and Coping in Old Age: A Case-Based Comparison of Atheism and Religious Faith." *Ageing and Society* 30, no. 2 (February 2010): 337–361.

Wilson, Charles Reagan, and Mark Silk, eds. *Religion and Public Life in the South: In the Evangelical Mode.* Thousand Oaks, CA: Alta Mira, 2005.

Wilson, John, and Darren E. Sherkat. "Returning to the Fold." *Journal for the Scientific Study of Religion* 33, no. 2 (1994): 148–161.

Woodward, Kenneth.1990. "A Time to Seek: With Babes in Arms and Doubts in Mind, a Generation Looks to Religion." *Newsweek*, December 17, 1990, 50–56.

Wright, Stuart A. "Post-Involvement Attitudes of Voluntary Defectors from Controversial New Religious Movements." *Journal for the Scientific Study of Religion* 23, no. 2 (1984): 172–182.

Wulff, David M. *Psychology of Religion: Classic and Contemporary Views*. New York: John Wiley and Sons, 1991.

Wuthnow, Robert. *After Heaven: Spirituality in America Since the 1950s*. Berkeley: University of California Press, 1998.

Zuckerman, Phil. "Atheism: Contemporary Numbers and Patterns." In *The Cambridge Companion to Atheism*, ed. By Michael Martin, 47–65. New York: Cambridge University Press, 2007.

———, ed. *Atheism and Secularity*. Vols. 1 and 2. New York: Praeger, 2010.

———. "Atheism, Secularity, and Well-Being: How the Findings of Social Science Counter Negative Stereotypes and Assumptions." *Sociology Compass* 3, no.6 (2009): 949–971.

———. *Faith No More: Why People Reject Religion*. New York: Oxford University Press, 2012.

———. *Society without God*. New York: New York University Press, 2008.

Zuckerman, Phil, and Titus Hjelm. *Studying Religion and Society*. New York: Routledge, 2012.

INDEX

References to tables are indicated by "t" following page numbers.

"achieved identity," 58, 183

advertising, 147–48, 156

affiliation: definition of, 16; distinguished from preference, 57; indifference of affiliated individuals, 24; labels, use of, 15–18, 35, 47, 184; as normative, 188. *See also* Unchurched Believers

After Heaven (Wuthnow), 151

agent-based reasoning, 168–69

age of Nones, 21, 22, 49, 50–54

agnostics, 3, 14, 34, 43, 44, 82

AHA. *See* American Humanist Association

American Atheists, 32

American Council of Churches, 18

American Ethical Union, 117

American Humanist Association (AHA), 32, 83–84, 114–17, 193

American Religious Identification Survey (ARIS), 3, 16, 19–20, 197, 206n7, 206n23, 211n14

American Society of Muslims, 92

American Values Survey, 207n9, 209n5, 209n11

Ammerman, Nancy, 31

Anglo-American children compared to Asian-American children, 153–54

apostates, 15, 206n4, 208n14

ARDA. *See* Association of Religion Data Archives

ARIS. *See* American Religious Identification Survey

arranged marriages, 159–60

"ascribed identity," 58, 145, 183

Asian Americans, 22, 29, 91, 154

association, power of, 155–57

Association of Religion Data Archives (ARDA), 16, 19–21, 206n8

atheists: Britain's state-sponsored religious education program including, 211n2; decision of parent to continue as, 73–74; definition of, 32; explanation of parent to child, 70; gender of, 209n19; indifference and, 43, 44; intermarriage with religious partner, 55; lacking familial ties (no children), 55; negative bias of society toward, 23, 33, 74, 169, 176, 189; Nones as, 3, 14, 27, 28; organizations for, regional factor in creation of, 100; Philosophical Secularism and, 41, 42, 43; rejection of religion and, 144; religious education of children of, 48, 132; research needed on, 176, 183, 189; self-providing ethics and values to children, 122; spirituality and, 31; well-being and, 217n32; worldviews of, 24. *See also* New Atheism

attributing agency to phenomena, 168–69

baby boom generation, 17, 18, 54, 74, 136, 145, 160

Bainbridge, William Sims, 205n7

Balmer, Randal, 213n39

bar/bat mitzvahs. *See* rites of passage

234 | INDEX

Barrett, Justin, 168
Bellah, Robert, 41, 76, 144–45, 151, 152
"belonging without believing," 47, 208n23
Bengtson, Vern L., 210n40
Berger, Peter, 96, 213n37
Bethel Baptist (Jacksonville), 93
Bethke, Jefferson, 28–29, 30, 47
billboards, religious, 4–5
Black churches, 97–98
books for children on religion, 122–23
boring, religion considered to be: by
    children, 73, 87, 128, 135, 192; by None
    parents, 28, 131, 192
Bottoms, Betty, 174
Bowling Alone (Putnam), 150–51
Boy Scouts, 117
brainwashing, 82–83, 141–42, 165
Brinkerhoff, Merlin, 208n14
Britain, 117, 211n2
Bromley, David, 206n4
Bruce, Steve, 215n18
Buddhism, 39, 40, 41, 60, 87, 91, 116, 123
Bush, George W., 98, 99

Caldwell-Harris, Catherine, 168, 169
California, 90, 91
Camp Quest (residential summer camp),
    117
Carter, Jimmy, 99
"The Catechesis of the Good Shepard"
    (education program), 192
catechism. *See* Confraternity of Christian
    Doctrine (CCD)
Catholicism: influence on mainstream
    culture, 97–98; institutional power
    of, 93; as majority religion in New
    England cities, 85–86; outsourcing
    by Nones of Catholic background,
    132; post-Vatican II, 146; Protestant-
    Catholic tension in New England's
    past history, 95; religious education
    (CCD), 110, 130, 186, 210n41; religious
    holidays, 111; sexual abuse scandal and,

53, 93, 108, 165, 173; switching religion
    due to intermarriage, 209n12; upbring-
    ing of Nones as, 12, 22, 37, 39, 64, 108,
    127, 161
CCD. *See* Confraternity of Christian
    Doctrine
child abuse, 173–74, 216n21, 216n23
child care: grandparents providing, 63;
    religious institutions providing, 56
childhood religious socialization, 53
children: asking about religion, 1, 104–7,
    185, 195–96; bored by or no inter-
    est in religion, 73, 87, 128, 135, 192;
    brainwashing of, 82–83, 141–42, 165;
    desire of parents to have children "fit
    in," 81–85; effect of having, 7, 54–60,
    106, 107–14, 162–63, 185–86; imitation
    of adults, 69, 71–72, 185; integration
    in religious congregations, 211n43;
    interaction with, effect on parents'
    religious identity, 68–75; in intermar-
    riage of None and religious spouse,
    60–63; worrying as a parent, 164–65.
    See also children raised without
    religion; choice; family; Nones/None
    parents; transmitting worldview/reli-
    gion to children
children raised without religion, 162–79;
    child abuse, religious-related, 173–74,
    216n21, 216n23; construct validity of
    research, 175; extended family mem-
    bers and, 65–66; "naturally spiritual"
    hypothesis and, 77, 165, 166–70, 211n7;
    None parents who reclaim religion
    and, 178; as predictor of adult religious
    affiliation, 53, 106, 136, 141; premarital
    sex and, 179; research needed on, 183,
    186; research showing benefits of reli-
    gion, 170–73; research showing risks
    of religion, 173–78; sampling issues
    of research, 175–76. *See also* choice;
    transmitting worldview/religion to
    children

choice, 8, 138–61; American roots of choice narrative, 144–49; bias of parent as factor, 141–42; cultural impact of choice narrative, 149–53; framing of, 155–57; illusion of, 154–58; importance to None parents, 165, 184–85; learning tied to perception of choices, 153–54; maximizers vs. satisficers, 159–61, 185, 215n33; maximizing children's choices, 8, 102, 138–43, 184; outsourcing religious training for children and, 142–43; personal impact of, 153–54; restricting children's choices, 141, 157–58, 162–63, 185; tyranny of, 158–61; use of choice narrative, 139–40

Christians: America as nation of, 77, 152; children's books, 122–23; compared to other religions, 24; Conservative Christianity and US government, 99; conventional strategy of transmitting religion to children, 107t; cultural influence of, 90; cultural use of term, 16, 17, 184; None parents' disappointment over children becoming, 164; punishment of children, 173–74; self-providing strategy of transmitting religion to children, 107t; unchurched identifying as, 18, 47. See also Protestants; specific denominations

Christian Science, 97–98

Circle Round: Raising Children in Goddess Traditions (Starhawk), 122

civil rights movements, 145–46, 152

class status as factor, 6, 69, 91

Clinton, Hillary, 56

Coles, Robert, 167–68, 169

collectivist culture, 149

Colorado Springs, Colorado, 79–85, 87, 92, 93, 96, 99, 115, 211n6, 212n17

communion. See rites of passage

community aspects of religion, 56, 85, 104, 110, 113–14; finding an alternative community, 107t, 114–22, 136, 193–94

Confraternity of Christian Doctrine (CCD), 107t, 110, 130, 186, 210n41

conservative politics, 22, 28, 52–53, 98–99, 212n16

conservative Protestants. See Evangelical Christians

construct validity, 175

consumer culture, 146–48, 150

corporal punishment of children, 173

cultural heritage. See heritage/family tradition tied to religion

cultural impact of choice narrative, 149–53

cultural literacy requiring religious learning, 132–33

cultural outsiders. See outsiders

cultural revolution of 1960s, 17, 145, 214n4

Culture of Narcissism (Lasch), 150

Dawkins, Richard, 54, 208n17, 217n33

day care. See child care

death: explanation to child about, 70, 196; religiosity and, 51, 76–77

decision-making: maximizers and, 159–61, 185, 215n33; psychology of, 8, 185; satisficers and, 159, 161. See also choice

defectors, 15, 52, 206n4, 208n14

demographics of Nones, 3, 4, 6, 20, 21–25, 91

Dennett, Daniel, 33, 54

depression, 158, 159, 170

Durkheim, Emile, 168

Eastern religions, 30, 146. See also specific religion

Ecklund, Elaine Howard, 209n19

education. See public schools; religious education of children; transmitting worldview/religion to children

Eliade, Mircea, 24

emotional abuse of children, 174, 216n21, 216n23

The End of Faith (Harris), 54

ethical humanists, 43

Ethical Humanist Society of Great Chicago, 117
Ethical Humanist Society of Long Island, 117
ethics and morality: alternative community for transmitting, 121; biblical ethic of United States, 76; evolutionary psychology's view of religion and, 168; humanists and, 114; moral order provided by religion, 172; None parents seeks to impart, 163; secularism and, 33, 43; Unitarian Universalist Church and, 85, 115
ethnic heritage tied to religion, 55, 64, 91
Europe: "belonging without believing" in, 208n23; compared to American culture, 53; secularism in, 76, 215n18
Evangelical Christians: attitude toward Nones, 79, 212n17; becoming Philosophical Secularists, 42; becoming Spiritual Seekers, 39; children of Nones choosing to be, 164; good parenting of, 77; influence on mainstream culture, 52, 83, 98, 187; institutional power of, 93; literature on children's spirituality, 211n7; as Nones, 28–29, 38, 47; as outsiders, 95–96; recruiting Nones, 102; rise of, 146; upbringing of Nones as, 10–11, 61. See also conservative politics; fundamentalists
Evangelical megachurches, 56, 93, 213n39
evolutionary psychology, 168–69
exploration of different religions, 11, 47, 86. See also Spiritual Seekers
exposure effect, 155–57
expressive individualism, 145, 148–49
extended family. See family

Faces in the Clouds (Guthrie), 216n10
Faith No More (Zuckerman), 33
Falwell, Jerry, 98
family: encounter with extended family, 59, 63–68, 109–10; encounter with the child, 68–75; good parenting associated with church-going, 77; parenthood and identity, 185–86; symbolic accommodation of religious relatives, 66–68. See also children; heritage/family tradition tied to religion; transmitting worldview/religion to children
Finke, Roger, 205n7, 215n18
Fisher, Claude, 28
Focus on the Family, 80, 93
founding fathers, 144–45
Fox News, 211n6
framing, 155–57, 184
Franklin, Benjamin, 145
Frazer, James, 24
freedom of choice for children. See choice
freethinkers, 32, 36t, 41
Freethought, 34, 118, 182
Freudian thought, 166–67, 215–16n3
Fuller, Robert, 18, 30, 31, 39
fundamentalists: child abuse and, 174; children of, 164; as high-tension religions, 187–88; influence on mainstream culture, 97–98; Nones as, 14; as outsiders, 98, 187; radio talk shows, 90. See also Evangelical Christians

Gallagher, Sally K., 211n43
Gallup polls, 3, 15, 16, 18, 19–20, 214n1
gay rights, 52, 99, 115, 117, 145, 155
gender factor, 20, 21, 33, 55, 209n19
General Social Surveys, 20, 217n32
genuineness, 127–28
God, children asking questions about, 70–71
Gould, Stephen Jay, 43
grandparents. See family
Greek Orthodox upbringing of Nones, 40
Greene, David, 51–52
Guthrie, Stewart, 216n10

Habits of the Heart (Bellah), 144–45, 151
Hammond, Phil, 214n4

Harris, Sam, 33, 54, 208n17, 217n33
heritage/family tradition tied to religion, 47, 55, 64, 91, 112, 130–31, 144, 184
hierarchy of needs, 167
high-tension religions, 187–88
Hinduism, 14, 24, 41
Hitchens, Christopher, 54
Hjelm, Titus, 190
Hoge, Dean R., 206n14
holidays. *See* religious holidays
Hout, Michael, 28
Humanist Children's Programs, 117
humanistic psychology, 30, 166–68
humanists, 32, 34, 41, 43, 182. *See also* American Humanist Association (AHA)
Humanist Society of New Mexico, 117
Humanists of Greater Portland, Oregon, 117
Hwang, Karen, 175, 183
hypocrisy, 2, 65–66, 127, 191

Iannacone, Larry, 215n18
identity rights movements, 145
illusion of choice, 154–58
Indifferentism, 208n19
Indifferents: author's husband as, 190; children of Nones choosing to be, 163; definition of, 34–35, 208n19; grandparents' influence in reclaiming religion for sake of children, 64, 67–68; no animus toward religion, 44, 46, 48; None parents as, 14, 36t, 43–46, 116; as nonproviders (doing nothing to transmit religion), 134; outsourcing by, 132; religiously affiliated as, 132; as "true" Nones, 24, 183, 188; as type of secularists, 47
individualism, 144–46; vs. collectivism, 149–50; criticism of, 150; empowerment of, 153, 185; religious inclinations and, 169
individuation, 167

Institute for the Study of Secularism in Society and Culture (Trinity College), 19
institutional power, 92–93, 172
integrity, 127, 179
intelligence correlated with religious belief, 176, 217n32
intermarriage, 211–12n15; having children and religious complications, 59, 60–63; increase in, 57, 210n38; mixed-worldview marriages, 60–62, 68, 190; of None with religious partner, 54, 55, 185; Protestants vs. Catholics switching due to, 209n12
Irish Americans as Nones, 23
Islam. *See* Muslims
Islamic Society of North America, 92
Israel, secular Jews becoming religious in, 212n21
Iyengar, Sheena, 144, 149–50, 153, 154, 158, 159

Jacksonville, Florida, 79–84, 87, 93, 96, 99, 115, 212n17
Johnson, Benton, 206n14
Judaism: academic and media employment of Jews, 92; becoming local majority religion, 90–91; children's books, 123; community services offered by synagogues, 56; conventional strategy of transmitting religion to children, 107t; giving children Jewish identity, 55, 67, 68, 72, 131; influence on mainstream culture, 97–98; Jewish humanists, 32, 34, 48; Jewish upbringing of Nones, 13, 22, 37, 40, 64, 108, 123–24, 131, 161; outsourcing by Nones of Jewish background, 132; religious holidays, 111; secular Jews in Israel, 212n21; self-providing strategy of transmitting religion to children, 107t; of Spiritual Seeker, 41; statistics on US population identifying as, 211n15
Jung, Carl, 166–67

Kahneman, Daniel, 155
Kelley, Dean, 213n38
Keysar, Ariela, 19, 206n7, 211n12
Koran-burning event, 54
Kosmin, Barry, 19, 206n7, 211n12
Kroliczak, Alice, 217n26

labels, use of, 15–18, 35, 47, 146, 184
Lasch, Christopher, 150, 152
Latinos as Nones, 23
learning: learned competencies provided
    by religious involvement, 172; tied to
    perception of choices, 153–54
Lee, Kristen Schultz, 209n19
Lee, Lois, 188
liberals vs. conservatives, as Nones, 22, 53
life cycle theory, 56–57, 62, 73, 74
life force or energy, belief in, 39, 40,
    195–96
liminal Nones, 35
"lived religion," 46
local cultural context, 7, 88–96; clothing
    and, 88, 89; religious diversity and, 91–
    92; symbols and language of, 89
Loy, David, 148
Luidens, Donald A., 206n14
Lury, Celia, 146, 214n10

Mackie, Marlene, 208n14
Manning, Christel, personal journey of,
    1–2, 8–9, 50, 69, 71, 101, 104, 152, 165,
    189–96
marriage: arranged marriage vs. marriage
    of choice, 159–60; effect on Nones, 7,
    54–57, 185–86. See also intermarriage
married vs. unmarried, 22, 54, 56–57
Maslow, Abraham, 167, 169
Mauss, Armand, 208n14
maximizers, 159–61, 185, 215n33
McGowen, Dale, 122
megachurches. See Evangelical mega-
    churches
mesmerism, 30

methodology of research, 4, 35, 197–203;
    advantages of, 189; demographic
    information, 4, 201; interpreting data,
    79, 201–2, 208n20; interviews, 4–5,
    198–200; limits of, 189; neutrality vs.
    personalization of, 190, 203; observa-
    tional data, 4, 200–201; organizational
    data reports vs. surveys of individuals,
    17; qualitative data, 4, 35, 189, 197–98;
    role of researcher, 203; survey data, 197
millennial generation, 52, 54
minority status. See outsiders
Mohammed, Warith Deen, 77–78, 92
Moore, R. Laurence, 96–99, 102
Moral Majority, 98
morals. See ethics and morality
Mormons (LDS Church), 12, 77–78, 88, 97,
    143, 211n15
mortality and religiosity, 51, 52, 76–77
multiculturalism in America, 52
Music, Mark, 209n12
Muslims: becoming local majority
    religion, 91; institutional power of,
    92; intolerance and, 23, 54, 77–78, 88;
    solitary practice of, 14; Spiritual Seek-
    ers incorporating Islamic beliefs, 60;
    statistics on US population identifying
    as, 211n15
mysticism, 41, 60

narcissism, 150, 152
National Longitudinal Study of Adoles-
    cent Health, 217n32
National Prayer Breakfast, 78
National Study of Youth and Religion,
    170, 175
Native American religion, 30
naturalness hypothesis, 77, 165, 166–70,
    211n7
Nelsen, Hart M., 217n26
New Age, 30, 146
New Atheism, 33, 43, 54, 208n17, 217n33,
    218n2

New England, 85–87, 90, 93, 94–95, 101

New Haven, Connecticut, 2

new market theory of religion, 205n7

New Thought, 30

New York: minority religion as majority religion in certain locales, 90–91; religious diversity in, 91

nonconformity, 157

Nones/None parents: advice books for raising children, 122–23; assumptions/misconceptions about, 5, 23; catchall category in surveys, 15–16; common bonds among, 47–49, 76, 99–100, 184; definition of, 6, 14–20, 46–49; demographics of, 3, 4, 6, 20, 21–25, 91; diversity of, 14, 24–25, 106, 175, 181–85; examples of, 10–14; finding alternative community, 107t, 114–22; focus of study on, 35; increasing number of, 2, 17, 20, 46, 50, 53; major categories of, 27–34, 182; minority status of, 7, 10, 23; as misnomer, 47; negative image of, 23, 53, 76, 78; political leanings of, 22; pragmatism of, 112; raised in religious homes, 4, 14, 22, 32, 38, 51, 63; regional distribution of, 4, 13, 20, 21–22, 78–79, 186–87; research comparing religious adults with, 176, 183; social status of, 6, 91; sources of information about, 3, 181, 186, 197–202; undercounted in the South, 212n32; who they are, 3, 10–11; young people as, 50–54. See also children raised without religion; choice; family; marriage; reclaiming religion; transmitting worldview/religion to children; typology of Nones

nonprovider strategy (doing nothing to transmit religion to children), 107t, 133–37, 139, 194

nonreligious persons. See Nones/None parents

Obama, Barack, 22, 53, 54, 78, 209n58

organizational data reports, 16–17

outsiders, 7, 77, 79–102, 186–88; advice books for raising children, 122–23; alternative community as support for, 121–22, 187; class status as factor, 91; fighting back vs. fitting in, 81–85; fundamentalists as, 98, 187; institutional power and, 92–93; literature on, 187; major religions as shaping American culture, 90; minority religion becoming local majority religion, 90–91; narratives of, 79–81; None parents not feeling pressure as, 101; Nones choosing outsider status for themselves, 96–102; "passing," 81, 100; places that make Nones into, 79–80, 88–96, 187; pressure to join a church, 80, 101, 212n21, 212n32; race as factor, 91; religious diversity in regions, effect of, 91–92; religious privatization and, 94–96; similarity of Nones to other religious minorities, 88; types of, 14–15

outsourcing transmission of worldview/religion, 107t, 130–33, 142, 162, 186, 191–92

overstatement of religious commitment, 17, 46. See also heritage/family tradition tied to religion; labels, use of

Pacific Northwest, 91, 93

The Paradox of Choice (Schwartz), 155

parenthood. See children; children raised without religion; choice; family; Nones/None parents; transmitting worldview/religion to children

Parenting beyond Belief (McGowen), 122

Pasquale, Frank, 31–32

"passing," 81, 100

peak-end rule of memory of experience, 155

personal identification with religion, 16, 19, 102, 185–86

personal impact of choice, 153–54

personality, 177, 217n30

Pew surveys, 15, 22, 23; Growth of the Non-Religious survey, 212n17; Religious Landscape Survey, 3, 16, 19–20, 197, 210n38, 211n12

Philosophical Secularists: alternative strategy of transmitting religion to children, 107t; author becoming, 190, 196; choice of religion by children raised by, 49, 141, 143, 163; distinguished from Indifferents, 44; finding an alternative community, 114; grandparents' influence in reclaiming religion for sake of children, 64–65; intermarriage of, 61; offering substantive alternative worldviews, 100, 182–83; as outsiders, 47, 80; privacy of religion and, 87; risks and benefits of raising children without religion, 163–64, 178; self-providing strategy of transmitting religion to children, 107t; terminology needed to describe worldview of, 189; types of, 36t, 41–43

place of residence: high None zones, 7, 78; local cultural context as factor, 7, 88–96; low None zones, 7, 78; regional distribution of Nones, 4, 13, 20, 21–22, 78–79, 186–87. See also outsiders

Planting Seeds: Practicing Mindfulness with Children (Thich Nhat Hanh), 122

"plausibility structure," 213n37

pluralism, 39, 47, 52, 68, 91, 120, 140–41, 205n7. See also Spiritual Seekers

politics of religion. See conservative politics

polygamy, 97

pragmatism, 112

premarital sex, 179

prenuptial agreements on religion of children, 60

privacy of religion, 85–88

privatization of religion, 29, 30, 94–96, 101, 187, 205n7

Protestants (mainline): Catholic-Protestant tension in New England's past history, 95; community services offered by churches, 56; majority in United States, 77; switching religion due to intermarriage, 209n12; upbringing of Nones as, 11, 37–38, 42, 44–46, 116, 123–24, 134

psychological distress, 176, 217n30

public animus to atheism, 23

public culture. See local cultural context

public schools: homeschooling as alternative to, 84; parochial schools as alternative to, 87, 111, 131; as part of local culture, 89; religious proselytizing in, 82–83, 92

Puritans, 144

Putnam, Robert, 150–51

Quakers, 135

"question theology" theory, 51, 52

race as factor, 22, 91, 205n2

rational choice theorists, 215n18

rationalists, 32

"rational skeptics," 19

Reagan, Ronald, 98

reclaiming religion: benefits to children from, 172–73; Nones' tendency toward, 102; for religious education of children, 141; upon marriage or having children, 7, 54–57, 106, 107–14, 162–63, 185–86

red and blue states, 22

regional distribution of Nones, 4, 13, 20, 21–22, 78–79, 186–87. See also outsiders

rejection of organized religion: atheists and, 144; benefits of religion for children and, 173; common bond of Nones, 76, 100; reasons for, 209n5; by young people, 50–54. See also defectors

religion: consumer culture and, 147–48; definitions of, 15–16, 29, 46, 188, 207n1; high-tension religions, 187–88; institutional power of, 92–93, 172; intelligence correlated with, 176, 217n32;

majority of Americans affiliated with, 10, 23, 165; major religions as shaping American culture, 77, 90, 214n4; minority religion becoming local majority religion, 90–91; new and better ways to study, 8, 188–89; origins of, 168, 216n10; positive outcomes in children and, 8, 165, 170–85; as private matter, 85–88; spirituality equated with, 166; switching within a faith tradition, 147, 214n12. See also choice; heritage/family tradition tied to religion; religious education of children; transmitting worldview/religion to children; worldviews; specific denominations

Religion by Region series (eds. Silk and Walsh), 212n19

religiosity: combined with patriotism in United States, 77; definition of, 207nn1–2; indicators of, 27–28, 29, 183–84, 188; mortality and, 51, 52, 76–77; of United States, 5, 7, 16, 17–18, 33, 75

religious education of children: alternative organizations offering, 116–17, 193–94; children rejecting, 164; conventional, 104–5, 107t; outsourcing by Nones who remain uncommitted, 107t, 130–33, 142, 162, 186, 191–92; by parental worldview, 107t; reaffiliating with religion, 110. See also transmitting worldview/religion to children

religious holidays, 111, 113, 118–20, 123, 124–25, 129, 133–34, 135

Religious Outsiders and the Making of Americans (Moore), 96–99

religious privatization. See privatization of religion

religious proselytizing, 82–83, 86

Religious Right, 98–99

religious terrorism, 54

research methodology. See methodology of research

return to religion. See reclaiming religion

risk-taking, 177

rites of passage, 55, 77, 101, 110, 113, 168

rituals: conventional religious education and, 110; created by Nones, 125–26; home life and, 106; identity and, 104; participation as measure of religiosity, 207n2; rejection of religion and, 32, 41; returning to religion and, 110, 112–13. See also religious holidays; rites of passage

role model factor, 53, 72, 127–28, 172

Romney, Mitt, 78

Roof, Wade Clark, 18, 136, 145, 160

Rumi, 39

Sacred Heart University grant funding, 4

Sagan, Carl, 43

salience of worldview, 46

sampling issues of research, 175–76

satisficers, 159, 161

Scandinavia, 176, 208n23

Schwartz, Barry, 155, 158–59, 161, 215n33

science: secularism and, 32, 48; tension with religion, 51, 148

scriptural sanctioning of corporal punishment, 173

secular humanists, 32, 84

secularists: American view of, 76, 215n18; definition of, 30, 46, 188; gender gap and, 209n19; income levels and gender equality associated with, 33; indicators of, 28; Indifferent included as, 47; new and better ways to study, 8, 188–89; in New Haven, 2; Nones and, 5, 20, 24, 34, 207n9; organizations for, regional factor in creation of, 100; philosophical, 41–43; religious vs. secular Nones, 6, 27–30; research comparing religious adults with, 176; Scandinavians' personal happiness and, 176; study of, 19; varieties of, 31–34; worldview including, 6. See also atheists; humanists; Philosophical Secularists; skeptics secularization theory, 205n7

seeker churches, 210n25

seekers, 14, 15, 18–19, 31, 55, 79, 86–88,101, 115, 118, 120, 123, 130, 135, 163. *See also* Spiritual Seekers

seeker spirituality, 31, 36, 39–41, 145

self-actualization, 167, 169

self-identity, formation of, 58

self-provider strategy for transmitting religion to children, 107t, 122–30, 193

self-realization, 167

self-reliance and secularism, 33–34

self-transcendence, 167

Sheilaism, 41, 151

Silk, Mark, 90, 91, 93–95, 212n19, 212n32

Simonič, Barbara, 216n21

single. *See* married vs. unmarried

skeptics, 32, 41, 43

Smith, Christian, 170–72, 174–79

Smith, Joseph, 97

social and organizational ties from religious involvement, 172. *See also* community aspects of religion

social evolutionary theory, 24

social justice, 115

solitary practice of religion, 14, 16

Soul Searching: The Religious and Spiritual Lives of American Teenagers (Smith), 170–72, 177

sources of information, 186

sources of information, shortcomings of, 3, 186, 197–202

Southern Bible Belt, 78, 90, 93, 212n32

"spiritual but not religious," 15, 30, 38, 39, 40

spirituality: atheists and, 31; children deemed to be naturally spiritual, 77, 165, 166–70, 211n7; definitions of, 189; equated with religion, 166; Maslow's and Coles's use of term, 169; in personal experience, 145; personal spirituality crafted from various sources, 30. *See also* typology of Nones; worldviews

Spiritual Seekers: alternative strategy of transmitting religion to children, 107t; author as, 1, 190, 193; childhood phase as, 87; definition of, 15; diversity of worldview and, 30, 47; finding an alternative community, 114, 116; fuzziness of term "spiritual," 31; grandparents' influence in reclaiming religion for sake of children, 64–65; intermarriage of, 60–62; as legitimate worldview, 100; as major category of unaffiliated persons, 18, 34; as outsiders, 79–80, 81; reclaiming religion for sake of children, 55, 72–73, 178; self-providing ethics and values to children, 123–24; self-providing strategy of transmitting religion to children, 107t; types of, 14, 30–31, 36t, 39–41, 163, 178; Unitarian Universalist Church and, 84–85

Starhawk, 117, 122

Stark, Rodney, 28, 29, 46, 205n7, 207n9, 215n18

St. Peter's festival (Cape Ann), 90, 112

Sufi, 40

suspicion of organized religion, 14

Swedenborgianism, 30

symbols: in local cultural context, 89; of religion, 111, 129

teenagers: premarital sex, 179; as religious dropouts, 7, 18, 50; Smith's study of religious vs. nonreligious, 170–72, 174–79

theism, 32, 39, 40

Thich Nhat Hanh, 122

time, effect of, 7, 50–75. *See also* family; life cycle theory; marriage

tolerance, 52, 77, 92, 115, 120–21

transcendentalism, 30

transcendental meditation, 123–24

transmitting worldview/religion to children, 104–37, 186; alternative strategy, 107t, 114–22, 136, 193–94; belonging to community and, 113–14; conventional strategy, 107t, 108; fluidity in approaches, 136–37; going back to church, 107–14; home religious activities, 110–11; least popular strategy as nonprovider, 135; nonprovider strategy, 107t, 133–37, 139; outsourcing strategy, 107t, 130–33, 142, 162, 186, 191–92; religious education of children, 3, 13, 110; self-provider strategy, 107t, 122–30; strategies for, 106–7, 107t, 136

Twitchell, James, 147–48, 214n10

Tylor, Edward B., 24, 168

typology of Nones, 26–49, 182, 207n19; Indifferent, 36t, 43–46; None parents' worldviews, 35–36, 36t; Philosophical Secularists, 36t, 41–43; religious vs. secular Nones, 27–30; secularism, varieties of, 31–34; Spiritual Seekers, 30–31, 36t, 39–41; Unchurched Believers, 36–38, 36t; variations among sample surveyed, 26–27

unaffiliated persons: labels, use of, 15–18, 35, 47, 184; use of term in book, 21. See also atheists; Indifference; Nones/None parents; Philosophical Secularists; Spiritual Seekers; Unchurched Believers

Unchurched Believers: compared to Nones, 20; conventional strategy of transmitting religion to children, 108–9; definitions of, 15, 18, 30; freedom of choice for children, 140; Gallup polls to identify, 18; grandparents' influence in reclaiming religion for sake of children, 64; None parents as, 36–38, 36t, 162, 164; Nones as, 3, 28, 30, 34, 207n9; as nonproviders (doing nothing to transmit religion), 135; as outsiders, 80; outsourcing religious training for children, 130, 142, 162; reclaiming religion for sake of children, 55, 108, 178; as satisficers, 161; self-providing to children, 123; types of, 36–38, 36t, 48, 206n14; use of term in book, 21

Unitarian humanists, 32

Unitarian Universalist Association (UUA), 32, 115–17

Unitarian Universalist Church: child choosing to leave, 135, 142; extended family's view of, 67; offering alternative education programs, 83, 118, 132, 135, 139, 193–94; viewed as viable alternative by Nones, 61, 68, 72, 84–85, 133

United States: Anglo-American children compared to Asian-American children, 153–54; biblical ethic of, 76; community role of organized religion in, 56; negative view of Nones in, 76; personal choice in, 144–45, 153–54; religious intermarriage rates in, 57; religiousness of, 5, 7, 16, 17–18, 33, 75; three mainstream religions in, 77, 214n4

urban vs. rural distribution of Nones, 206n17

utilitarian individualism, 145, 148

values. See ethics and morality

voting trends, 212n16

Walsh, Andrew, 212n19

Weber, Samuel, 176

Whitman, Walt, 145

Why Conservative Churches Are Growing (Kelley), 213n38

"Why I Hate Religion, but Love Jesus" (Bethke's video), 28–29

Wiccans/witchcraft, 30, 40, 116

Willow Creek Community Church (South Barrington), 210n25, 213n39

Wilson, John, 209n12

women's rights, 115, 145. See also gender factor

worldviews: alternative worldview education model, 157, 193; of atheists, 24; choice of, 138, 214n1; commitment to, 5–6; comparison of religion with, 5–6; comprehensive worldview education curriculum of UUA, 117; construction of worldview identity by minority, 102; criticism of, 8; definition of, 5; fluidity in, 35, 136–37, 185; mixed-worldview marriages, 60–62, 68; of Nones, 20, 47–49, 188; Philosophical Secularists offering substantive alternative worldviews, 100, 182–83; place and, 7; salience of, 46; secular philosophy and, 43; secular worldview, 6, 33, 58; seeker spirituality and, 31; variety of None worldviews, 24, 36t, 47–49. *See also* transmitting worldview/religion to children; typology of Nones; *specific religions and types of Nones*

worrying as a parent, 164–65
Wuthnow, Robert, 145, 151, 152

Young, Brigham, 97
Young Life, 80, 83, 102
young people. *See* age of Nones; millennial generation; teenagers

Zuckerman, Phil, 33–34, 190, 208n14

Christel Manning is Professor of Religious Studies at Sacred Heart University in Fairfield, Connecticut, where she has taught since 1995. She is the author of *God Gave Us the Right*, a book about feminism and conservative religion, and co-editor of *Sex and Religion*. A graduate of Tufts University, she holds a PhD from the University of California, Santa Barbara. She lives with her husband and daughter in New Haven, Connecticut.